An AUSA Book

U.S. Army Field Manual 100–5
Blueprint for the AirLand Battle

DEPARTMENT OF THE ARMY

**Published with the
Institute of Land Warfare
Association of the U.S. Army**

BRASSEY'S (US), INC.
A Division of Maxwell Macmillan, Inc.
Washington • New York • London • Oxford
Beijing • Frankfurt • São Paulo • Sydney • Tokyo • Toronto

First Brassey's edition 1991

Publisher's Note
Brassey's has commercially published the *U.S. Army Field Manual 100–5* to
extend the audience reached through publication by the U.S. Army. We are
pleased to contribute by ensuring a wider audience, through Brassey's
worldwide system, to the U.S. Army's unclassified central blueprint for the
AirLand battle.

Brassey's (US), Inc.

Editorial Offices
Brassey's (US), Inc.
8000 Westpark Drive
First Floor
McLean, Virginia 22102

Order Department
Brassey's Book Orders
Macmillan Publishing Co.
100 Front Street, Box 500
Riverside, New Jersey 08075

Brassey's (US), Inc., books are available at special discounts for bulk
purchases for sales promotions, premiums, fund-raising, or educational use
through the Special Sales Director, Macmillan Publishing Company,
866 Third Avenue, New York, New York 10022.

Library of Congress Cataloging-in-Publication Data

United States. Dept. of the Army
    Blueprint for the AirLand Battle / Department of the Army. — 1st
Brassey's ed.
        p.   cm. — (U. S. Army field manual : 100–5)   (An AUSA book)
Originally published: Washington, D.C. : Dept. of the Army. 1986
"Published with the Institute of Land Warfare Association of the
U. S. Army."
    Includes bibliographical references (p.   ) and index.
    ISBN 0–08–041071–5 (softcover)
        1. United States. Army—Handbooks, manuals, etc.   2. Military
doctrine—United States—Handbooks, manuals, etc.   3. Tactics—
Handbooks, manuals, etc.   I. Title.   II. Series: United States.
Dept. of the Army. Field manual : no. 100–5.   III. Series: AUSA
Institute of Land Warfare book
UA24.A7   1991
355.4'0973—dc20   91–32696
                                                                      CIP

Printed in the United States of America

Field Manual
No.100-5

*FM 100-5
Headquarters
Department of the Army
Washington, DC, 5 May 1986

OPERATIONS

Preface

FM 100-5, *Operations*, is the Army's keystone warfighting manual. It explains how Army forces plan and conduct campaigns, major operations, battles, and engagements in conjunction with other services and allied forces. It furnishes the authoritative foundation for subordinate doctrine, force design, materiel acquisition, professional education, and individual and unit training. It applies to Army forces worldwide, but must be adapted to the specific strategic and operational requirements of each theater. While emphasizing conventional military operations, it recognizes that Army forces must be capable of operating effectively in any battlefield environment, including low intensity conflict and on the nuclear and chemical battlefield. Employment of nuclear and chemical weapons by US forces is governed by US national policy.

FM 100-5 is compatible with and will serve as the US implementing document for NATO land forces tactical doctrine (Allied Tactical Publication 35A), but is both more theoretical and more general so as to meet US needs in other theaters. US troops operating in the framework of FM 100-5 will execute NATO's forward defense plans in compliance with ATP 35A.

As the Army's principal tool of professional self-education in the science and art of war, FM 100-5 presents a stable body of operational and tactical principles rooted in actual military experience and capable of providing a long-term foundation for the development of more transitory tactics, techniques, and procedures. It provides operational guidance for use by commanders and trainers at all echelons and forms the foundation for Army service school curricula. FM 100-5 emphasizes flexibility and speed, mission type orders, initiative among commanders at all levels, and the spirit of the offense.

This edition reaffirms the Army's doctrinal thrust introduced in 1982. It reflects the lessons learned since that time from combat operations, teachings, exercises, wargames, and comments

*This publication supersedes FM 100-5, 20 August 1982.

from the Army in the field. Central aspects of AirLand Battle doctrine—its recognition of the importance of the operational level of warfare, its focus on the seizure and retention of the initiative, and its insistence on the requirement for multi-service cooperation—remain unaltered. The basic tenets of AirLand Battle doctrine—initiative, agility, depth, and synchronization—are reemphasized.

Users of this publication are encouraged to recommend changes which will improve the clarity and utility of this manual. Changes and comments should be forwarded to the Commandant, US Army CGSC, ATTN: ATZL-SWD, Fort Leavenworth, Kansas 66027-6900, using DA Form 2028 (Recommended Changes to Publications and Blank Forms).

Unless otherwise stated, whenever the masculine or feminine gender is used, both men and women are included.

Table of Contents

An AUSA Book

The Association of the United States Army, or AUSA, was founded in 1950 as a not-for-profit organization dedicated to education concerning the role of the U.S. Army, to providing material for military professional development, and to the promotion of proper recognition and appreciation of the profession of arms. Its constituencies include those who serve in the Army today, including Army National Guard, Army Reserve, and Army civilians, and the retirees and veterans who have served in the past, and all their families. A large number of public-minded citizens and business leaders are also an important constituency. The Association seeks to educate the public, elected and appointed officials, and leaders of defense industry on crucial issues involving the adequacy of our national defense, particularly those issues affecting land warfare.

In 1988 AUSA established within its existing organization a new entity known as the Institute of Land Warfare. Its purpose is to extend the educational work of AUSA by sponsoring scholarly publications, to include books, monographs, and essays on key defense issues, as well as workshops and symposia. Among the volumes chosen for designation as "An AUSA Institute of Land Warfare Book" are both new texts and reprints of titles of enduring value that are no longer in print. Topics include history, policy issues, strategy, and tactics. Publication as an AUSA Book does not indicate that the Association of the United States Army and the publisher agree with everything in the book, but does suggest that the AUSA and the publisher believe this book will stimulate the thinking of AUSA members and others concerned about important issues.

PART ONE
THE ARMY AND HOW IT FIGHTS

CHAPTER 1
Challenges for the US Army

The overriding mission of US forces is to deter war. The US Army supports that mission by providing combat ready units to the unified and specified commands which are charged with executing the military policies of the United States and waging war should deterrence fail.

All military operations pursue and are governed by political objectives. Today, the translation of success in battle to desired political outcomes is more complicated than ever before. At one extreme of the spectrum of conflict, the risk of nuclear war imposes unprecedented limitations on operational flexibility. At the other end, terrorist activities resist conventional military solutions. Between these extremes lies a wide range of possible conflicts which may escalate toward nuclear war and which will almost always involve counterterrorist operations.

Despite this complexity, the ability of Army units to fight in high-, mid-, and low intensity conflicts in concert with other services and with allies remains critical to the nation's survival. Success in battle may not alone assure the achievement of national security goals, but defeat will guarantee failure. This manual does not address the formulation of US strategies for deterrence or warfighting. It provides

Army leaders at all levels with doctrinal guidance for conducting campaigns and major operations and for fighting battles and engagements within the broader framework of military strategy.

IDENTIFYING THE CHALLENGES

Army forces must meet worldwide strategic challenges against the full range of threats from terrorism through low- and mid-intensity operations to high-intensity and nuclear operations. In areas of greatest strategic concern, they must be prepared to fight battles of unprecedented scope and intensity. The operations surrounding such battles will routinely involve cooperation with other services and allies and could be fought with or under the threat of nuclear or chemical weapons.

The skill and courage of leaders at all levels will be critical to success in operations across the spectrum of conflict. As in the past, the chaos of combat will place a premium on the initiative, spirit, cohesion, and mental and physical preparedness of soldiers and their units. While the importance of winning the first battle is not diminished, the ability to fight sustained campaigns is also vital to deterrence and to victory. Rigorous, realistic training for war must therefore go on continuously to assure Army units' readiness to fight short-notice wars, campaigns, and battles.

The Army must be ready to fight enemies whose capabilities vary widely. In high- or mid-intensity conflicts, these may be modern tank, motorized, and airborne forces like the Warsaw Pact armies or other similarly organized forces including Soviet surrogates. Less mechanized but otherwise well-equipped regular and irregular forces and terrorist groups can be expected to operate against Army forces in most parts of the world. In low intensity conflicts, light forces, insurgents, and terrorists may be the only military threat present.

The nature of modern battle and the broad geographical range of US interests make it imperative that Army units fight as part of a joint team with units of the US Air Force, the US Navy, the US Marine Corps, and representatives of appropriate civilian agencies. It is also critical that commanders prepare themselves to fight in coalition warfare alongside the forces of our nation's allies. As it has been throughout the twentieth century, teamwork in joint and combined operations will be an essential ingredient in any battles Army forces fight.

Operations in the foreseeable future will be fought in one of two basic environments. One environment may be an anticipated theater of war with an existing support structure of communications, air defense, logistic facilities, and ports. The other may be a relatively immature theater where Army leaders within a joint or combined context will have to choose between creating such a support base in the theater or fighting with only external support.

HIGH- AND MID-INTENSITY CONFLICT

The high- and mid-intensity battlefields are likely to be chaotic, intense, and highly destructive. They will probably extend across a wider space of air, land, and sea than previously experienced. The most important features of such conflicts are discussed separately in the following paragraphs. While each of these features can be understood separately, their *combined* effects constitute the actual setting of operations.

Nonlinear Operations. In high- or mid-intensity conflicts, Army forces must prepare to fight campaigns of considerable movement, not only to reduce vulnerability, but also to obtain positional advantage over the enemy. Rapid movement will be complemented by the use of advanced, highly lethal weapons throughout the battle area.

Even in conventional combat, operations will rarely maintain a linear character. The speed with which today's forces can concentrate and the high volumes of supporting fires they can bring to bear will make the intermingling of opposing forces nearly inevitable. Similarly, from the first hours of battle, deep reconnaissance, air mobility, long-range fires, and special operating forces (SOF) will blur the distinction between front and rear and will impose a requirement for all around defense and self-sufficiency on all units. Successful attack will require isolation of the battle area in great depth as well as the defeat of enemy forces in deeply echeloned defensive areas. Successful defense will require early detection of attacking forces, prompt massing of fires, interdiction of follow-on forces, and the containment and defeat of large formations by fire and maneuver. Throughout the battle area, attack and defense will often take place simultaneously as each combatant attempts to mass, economize locally, and maneuver against his opponent.

Fluidity will also characterize operations in the rear of forward deployed committed forces. Guerrillas, SOF, and terrorists will seek to avoid set-piece battles and to strike at scattered points of vulnerability. Defending forces will try to preempt such attacks with sweeps and raids throughout the battle area and will mass rapidly in response to guerrilla, SOF, or terrorist attacks wherever they occur.

Lethal Systems. Potential enemies of the United States can be expected to field large quantities of high quality weapons systems whose range and lethality equal or exceed our own. Potent ground and air systems, complemented by closely coordinated precision guided munitions, will be able to concentrate enormous combat power, especially at decisive points.

Sensors and Communications. Wide ranging surveillance, target acquisition sensors, and communications that provide information almost immediately will increase the range and scope of battle. Sensors offer the commander more than just timely information on deep enemy locations and activity. They also serve as the basis for attacking enemy follow-on forces with missiles (ASM and SSM), MLRS, tube artillery, fixed-wing aircraft, attack helicopters, SOF, and nonlethal means such as electronic combat and deception. Since these attacks can be of vital importance in battle, the sensors and communications means which make them possible are particularly valuable.

Nuclear Warfare. Even though the primary purpose of nuclear weapons is to deter their use by others, the threat of nuclear escalation pervades any military operation involving the armies of nuclear powers, imposing limitations on the scope and objectives even of conventional operations. US nuclear weapons may of course only be used following specific directives by the National Command Authorities (NCAs) after appropriate consultation with allies. Even were such authority granted, however, the employment of nuclear weapons would be guided more by political and strategic objectives than by the tactical effect a particular authorized employment might produce. Even so, any battlefield employment of nuclear weapons would certainly magnify the destructiveness of operations and could sharply alter their tempo. Beside the effects of physical damage, the psychological stress on soldiers would be severe. As a consequence, battles or even campaigns could last hours instead of days or weeks and could cripple both combatants.

Chemical Warfare. Chemical warfare has been practiced sporadically throughout this century, and US forces maintain a capability in this area primarily for deterrence. Chemical warfare presents many of the same complications as nuclear operations. However, because chemical weapons are more widespread and the inhibition against their use is lower for some nations, US forces are even more likely to face a chemical than a nuclear threat.

Biological Warfare. The US has renounced the use of biological weapons. However, this unilateral renunciation does not free our own forces from the threat of enemy biological warfare. Army forces must therefore continue to train to fight an enemy who could use biological weapons.

Command and Control. The more fluid the battlefield, the more important and difficult it will be to identify decisive points and to focus combat power there. Under such conditions, it is imperative that the overall commander's intent and concept of operations be understood throughout the force. Communications will be interrupted by enemy action at critical times and units will frequently have to fight while out of contact with higher headquarters and adjacent units. Subordinate leaders will be expected to act on their own initiative within the framework of the commander's intent.

Air Dimension. The airspace of a theater is as important a dimension of ground operations as the terrain itself. This airspace is used for various purposes including maneuver, delivery of fires, reconnaissance and surveillance, transportation, and command and control. The control and use of the air will always affect operations; the effectiveness of air operations in fact can decide the outcome of campaigns and battles. Commanders must consider the airspace to include the apportionment of air power in planning and supporting their operations. They must protect their own forces from observation, attack, and interdiction by the enemy and expect the enemy to contest use of the airspace.

Austere Support. Army forces must be prepared to fight their battles at the end of long, vulnerable lines of logistical support and must anticipate high consumption rates for all types of supplies. They may have to fight outnumbered against an enemy with significantly shorter supply lines. Logistical support may be austere in such situations and thereby markedly affect the design of campaigns and the planning and conduct of battles.

Urban Combat. Combat in built-up areas will be unavoidable in most theaters of war. Divisions and larger units will have to plan for attack and defense in urban areas and for fluid battles around them.

Obstacles. Mid- to high-intensity operations also will have to contend with substantial obstacles, some man made such as minefields and others natural such as rivers, mountains, and other hindering terrain. Such obstacles often favor the defense and permit economies of force but they also pose special challenges of force composition, task organization, maneuver, and timing.

Unconventional Warfare and Terrorism. In almost all conflicts, the Army will encounter terrorists, guerrillas, and saboteurs. Operating throughout the theater of war, they will threaten the security and continuity of our operations. They will usually be present even in high- and mid-intensity conflicts where their suppression will involve passive and active measures including the commitment of forces.

LOW INTENSITY CONFLICT

The growing incidence of war at the low end of the conflict spectrum demands Army action on the unique battlefields of low intensity conflict (LIC). This form of warfare falls below the level of high- and mid-intensity operations and will pit Army forces against irregular or unconventional forces, enemy special operations forces, and terrorists. LIC poses a threat to US interests at all times, not just in periods of active hostilities.

Fighting in the low end of the conflict spectrum requires special force composition and task organization, rapid deployment, and restraint in the execution of military operation. Army actions in LIC must be fully coordinated with national strategy and fused at the operational level into a coherent effort which will usually include economic and political actions as well as military activities.

In countering an insurgency, the Army may employ specially trained forces or training teams. This sort of activity, termed Foreign Internal Defense, may include the transfer of defense equipment, the training of foreign soldiers, advisory assistance, or even the commitment of combat forces. All military efforts in a counterinsurgency campaign will be made in concert with the initiatives of other US government agencies involved to ensure a synchronized national effort. The forces selected for Foreign Internal Defense will depend on the threat to be countered. Light and heavy forces, aviation units, logistical support, and a variety of training teams may be used for counterinsurgency efforts.

There are also peacetime contingency operations which require the employment of Army forces. These can include demonstrations of force, raids, or rescue missions, and larger operations undertaken to protect US interests, lives, and property. These contingency operations require intensive intelligence collection, thorough planning, and rapid deployment of light forces at the decisive time and place.

As in the past, the Army will also participate in peacekeeping operations which support diplomatic efforts to achieve, restore, or maintain peace in an area of armed conflict. Such operations may be unilaterally or internationally manned and directed. Whatever the case, they will be sensitive and will require a high degree of unit and individual discipline in the forces committed. Units of peacekeeping forces use force only in cases of self defense.

Independent and state-supported terrorists employ violence in attempting to influence the policies of governments. In a very real sense, terrorists pursue strategic objectives through LIC. Army doctrine calls for preventive action—antiterrorism—along with reactive measures—counterterrorism—to meet the terrorist threat to US forces, representatives, and agencies and to the security of American citizens and property.

Terrorism constitutes a threat which must be dealt with within the Army's daily operations and which will continue to be of concern in high- and mid-intensity conflicts. Awareness of the threat and recognition that the indicators of terrorist activity differ from those of the enemy on the conventional battlefield are essential to countering terrorism. Leaders at all levels must develop a broad view of this conflict which will guide them in securing their operations and in protecting their soldiers from terrorists as well as from conventional enemy military forces.

MEETING THE CHALLENGES

The US Army can meet these challenges. Superior performance in combat depends on three essential components. First and foremost, it depends on superb soldiers and leaders with character and determination who will win because they simply will not accept losing. Next, it depends on a sound, well-understood doctrine for fighting. Finally, it depends on weapons and supporting equipment sufficient for the task at hand. These three components must be unified harmoniously into effective fighting organizations. This is done through well-thought out organizational design and effective training programs.

LEADERSHIP AND SOLDIERS

Wars are fought and won by men, not by machines. The human dimension of war will be decisive in the campaigns and battles of the future just as it has been in the past.

The fluid, compartmented nature of war will place a premium on sound leadership, competent and courageous soldiers, and cohesive, well-trained units. The conditions of combat on the next battlefield will be unforgiving of errors and will demand great skill, imagination, and flexibility of leaders. As in the wars of the past, however, American soldiers will fight resolutely when they know and respect their leaders and believe that they are part of a good unit. How to develop effective leaders is addressed in FM 22-100 and FM 22-999.

DOCTRINE

An army's fundamental doctrine is the condensed expression of its approach to fighting campaigns, major operations, battles, and engagements. Tactics, techniques, procedures, organizations, support structure, equipment and training must all derive from it. It must be rooted in time-tested theories and principles, yet forward-looking and adaptable to changing technologies, threats, and missions. It must be definitive enough to guide operations, yet versatile enough to accommodate a wide variety of worldwide situations. Finally, to be useful, doctrine must be uniformly known and understood.

The doctrine presented in the following chapters seeks to develop the full potential of the Army. It takes into account the challenges outlined on the previous pages and is applicable to joint, combined, and tactical operations worldwide. The principles of AirLand Battle doctrine reflect past usages in the US Army and the tested ideas of past and modern theorists of war. The nine principles of war are fundamental to US Army doctrine. They are elaborated in FM 100-1 *The Army* and reprinted here in Appendix A, for convenient reference. Recent studies have also been used to gain insights into the likely nature of contemporary operations. While AirLand Battle doctrine focuses primarily on mid- to high-intensity warfare, the tenets of AirLand Battle apply equally to the military operations characteristic of low intensity war. Such operations of course pose a different challenge than those of high- and mid-intensity conflict. That challenge must be met with initiative in leaders, special preparation in training, and flexibility and restraint in operations. FM 100-20, *Low Intensity Conflict,* addresses this subject in detail.

TRAINING AND READINESS

Clausewitz stated the purpose of peacetime armies very clearly. He said: "The whole of military activity must relate directly or indirectly to the engagement. The end for which a soldier is recruited, clothed, armed, and trained, the whole object of his sleeping, eating, drinking, and marching *is simply that he should fight at the right place and the right time.*"

Forward deployed forces may have to fight on a few hours' notice. Other components of the force may have only days or weeks to make final preparations for war. Commanders must have effective plans for those important days or weeks and must train for the specific missions they anticipate. They must ensure that each officer, noncommissioned officer (NCO), and soldier is prepared for battle and is equipped to perform his job as part of the unit.

Training is the cornerstone of success. It is a full-time job for commanders in peacetime, and it continues in wartime combat zones as well. On the day of battle, soldiers and units will fight as well or as poorly as they were trained in preceding days.

Soldiers receive most of their training in their units. There they can best train as individuals and as members of teams under conditions that approximate battle.

Unit training aims at developing maximum effectiveness with combined and supporting arms in specific, mission-essential tasks. This means ensuring that standardized procedures and battle drills are used to gain the greatest possible coordination and speed. Once basic standards have been achieved, commanders should attempt to perform the same tasks under more difficult conditions. Unit training should simulate as closely as possible the battlefield's tempo, scope, and uncertainty. Units and headquarters that will fight together in teams, task forces, or larger units should train together routinely. Such combined arms training is far more effective and realistic than the training of units in isolation from their routine attachments and support.

The complexities of combat make it increasingly important to concentrate on training programs for leaders and teams. Those who direct the employment of weapons and small units must be competent in their use. Commanders must also take time to train subordinate leaders and staff members, building their confidence and requiring them to exercise initiative. This is best done by training them to react to changes which require fast, independent decisions based on broad guidance and mission orders. Such practices enhance the morale, confidence, and effectiveness of small units and improve the performance of higher levels of command as well.

Unit readiness cannot be achieved without logistical readiness—the availability and proper functioning of materiel, resources, and systems to maintain and sustain operations on a fluid, destructive, and resource-hungry battlefield. Training support units is as important as training tactical units. Support units should also be rigorously trained under realistic conditions.

CHAPTER 2

Fundamentals of AirLand Battle Doctrine

T he US Army's basic fighting doctrine is called AirLand Battle. It reflects the structure of modern warfare, the dynamics of combat power, and the application of the classical principles of war to contemporary battlefield requirements. It is called AirLand Battle in recognition of the inherently three-dimensional nature of modern warfare. All ground actions above the level of the smallest engagements will be strongly affected by the supporting air operations of one or both combatants.

STRUCTURE OF MODERN WARFARE

War is a national undertaking which must be coordinated from the highest levels of policymaking to the basic levels of execution. Military strategy, operational art, and tactics are the broad divisions of activity in preparing for and conducting war. Successful strategy achieves national and alliance political aims at the lowest possible cost in lives and treasure. Operational art translates those aims into effective military operations and campaigns. Sound tactics win the battles and engagements which produce successful campaigns and operations. While the principles of war apply equally to strategy, operational art, and tactics, they apply differently to each level of war.

STRATEGY

Military strategy is the art and science of employing the armed forces of a nation or alliance to secure policy objectives by the application or threat of force. Military strategy sets the fundamental conditions of operations in war or to deter war. It establishes goals in theaters of war and theaters of operations. It assigns forces, provides assets, and imposes conditions on the use of force. While its formulation is beyond

CONTENTS

the scope of this manual, strategy derived from policy must be clearly understood to be the sole authoritative basis of all operations.

OPERATIONAL ART

Operational art is the employment of military forces to attain strategic goals in a theater of war or theater of operations through the design, organization, and conduct of campaigns and major operations. A campaign is a series of joint actions designed to attain a strategic objective in a theater of war. Simultaneous campaigns may take place when the theater of war contains more than one theater of operations. Sequential campaigns in a single theater occur when a large force changes or secures its original goal or when the conditions of the conflict change. An offensive campaign may follow a successful defensive campaign, for example, as it did in Korea in 1950. Or a new offensive campaign may have to be undertaken if strategic goals change or are not secured in the initial campaign. A major operation comprises the coordinated actions of large forces in a single phase of a campaign or in a critical battle. Major operations decide the course of campaigns.

Operational art thus involves fundamental decisions about when and where to fight and whether to accept or decline battle. Its essence is the identification of the enemy's operational center-of-gravity—his source of strength or balance—and the concentration of superior combat power against that point to achieve a decisive success (See Appendix B for a discussion of center of gravity). No particular echelon of command is solely or uniquely concerned with operational art, but theater commanders and their chief subordinates usually plan and direct campaigns. Army groups and armies normally design the major ground operations of a campaign. And corps and divisions normally execute those major ground operations. Operational art requires broad vision, the ability to anticipate, a careful understanding of the relationship of means to ends, and effective joint and combined cooperation. Reduced to its essentials, operational art requires the commander to answer three questions:

(1) What military condition must be produced in the theater of war or operations to achieve the strategic goal?

(2) What sequence of actions is most likely to produce that condition?

(3) How should the resources of the force be applied to accomplish that sequence of actions?

TACTICS

While operational art sets the objectives and pattern of military activities, tactics is the art by which corps and smaller unit commanders translate potential combat power into victorious battles and engagements. Engagements are small conflicts between opposed maneuver forces. Covering forces, guard forces, patrols, units in defense and units moving to contact fight engagements when they encounter the enemy. Engagements are normally conflicts of a few hours' duration fought between divisions and smaller forces. Such engagements may or may not bring on battle.

Battles consist of a series of related engagements. Battles last longer, involve larger forces, and often produce decisions that affect the subsequent course of the campaign. Battles occur when large forces—divisions, corps, and armies—commit themselves to fight for significant goals. They are often fought when the deliberate attack of one force meets determined resistance from the defender. Battles can also result from meeting engagements between forces contesting the initiative. These battles may result from the determination of opposed commanders to impose their will on their enemy. Battles can also arise without strong direction when large forces meet and neither withdraws. Such actions may not even be recognized as battles until they have gone on for some time.

Battles may be short and intense and fought in a relatively small area (as on the Golan Heights in 1973), or they may vary in intensity over a period of days and weeks and extend over a wide area (as in the battle of the Bulge). In either case the battles of committed divisions, corps, or armies will be surrounded by a larger area in which both combatants try to concentrate forces and support for the battle. Action in this surrounding area can strongly affect the outcome of the battle.

Battles may not take place at all if the enemy can be rapidly overwhelmed in a series of minor engagements and prevented from mounting a coherent defense. On the other hand, battles can also produce stalemates which favor neither side.

Battles or significant tactical gains made without battle determine the course of campaigns. Though battles often decided wars in the last century, recent experience suggests that battles between competent forces are more likely to decide phases of campaigns. They may be important enough to force an attacker to assume the defensive or allow the defender to take the operational offensive. Kursk, El Alamein, and the battle of the "Chinese Farm" in the Sinai are examples of such watershed battles. More commonly, tactical success by the attacker leads to a fluid operational interlude which lasts until the defender reestablishes a tenable resistance or the attacker overextends himself. Similarly, tactical success by the defender is more likely to defer a decision or reduce the attacker's advantage than permit an immediate shift to the offensive.

Sound tactics win battles and engagements by moving forces on the battlefield to gain positional advantage over the enemy; by applying fire support to facilitate and exploit that advantage; and by assuring the sustainment of friendly forces before, during, and after engagement with the enemy. Sound tactics employ all available combat, combat support, and combat service support where they will make the greatest contribution to victory.

DYNAMICS OF COMBAT POWER

The dynamics of combat power decide the outcome of campaigns, major operations, battles, and engagements. Combat power is the ability to fight. It measures the effect created by combining maneuver, firepower, protection, and leadership in combat actions against an enemy in war. Leaders combine maneuver, firepower, and protection capabilities available to them in countless combinations appropriate to the situation. They also attempt to interfere with the enemy leader's ability to generate the greatest effect against them by interfering with the enemy's ability to effectively maneuver, apply firepower, or provide protection. Therefore, while quantitative measures of available capability are important, the quality of available capabilities, the ability of the leader to bring them to bear, and the ability of the leader to avoid the enemy's efforts to degrade his own capabilities before or during battle may be equally or more important. This explains why the larger or stronger force does not always win.

In the course of campaigns, major operations, battles, and engagements, the balance of combat power may shift back and forth between opponents. This is especially likely when engaged forces are roughly equal in capabilities. When physical strengths are nearly equal, the moral qualities of skill, courage, character, perseverance, innovativeness, and strength of will of both soldiers and leaders are always decisive. There are also many cases in history where forces inferior in physical quantitative or qualitative measures but superior in moral qualities achieved success. In such cases, the skill of leaders in using the environment to advantage, applying sound tactical or operational methods, and providing purpose, direction, and motivation to their soldiers and subordinate leaders was always crucial.

At both the operational and tactical levels, the generation of combat power requires the conversion of the potential of forces, resources, and tactical opportunity into actual capability through violent and coordinated action concentrated at the decisive time and place. Superior combat power is generated through a commander's skillful combination of the elements of maneuver, firepower, protection, and leadership in a sound plan flexibly but forcefully executed.

MANEUVER

Maneuver is the movement of forces in relation to the enemy to secure or retain positional advantage. It is the dynamic element of combat—the means of concentrating forces at the critical point to achieve the surprise, psychological shock, physical momentum, and moral dominance which enable smaller forces to defeat larger ones. The effects of maneuver may also be achieved without movement by allowing the enemy himself to move into a disadvantageous position, as in an ambush or with stay-behind forces. In either case, maneuver will rarely be possible without firepower and protection. Operational maneuver requires protection from enemy air power. Tactical maneuver may require suppressive fires and covering terrain. Effective maneuver keeps the enemy off balance and thus also protects the force. It continually poses new problems for the enemy, renders his reactions ineffective, and eventually leads to his defeat.

Maneuver occurs at both the operational and the tactical levels. *Operational maneuver* seeks a decisive impact on the conduct of a campaign. It attempts to gain advantage of position before battle and to exploit tactical successes to achieve operational results. *Tactical maneuver* seeks to set the terms of combat in a battle or engagement. It is the means of gaining and sustaining the initiative, exploiting success, preserving freedom of action, and reducing the vulnerability of friendly forces. At both levels, effective maneuver is vital to achieving superior combat power.

At all levels, effective maneuver demands air and ground mobility, knowledge of the enemy and terrain, effective command and control, flexible operational practices, sound organization, and reliable logistical support. Successful tactical maneuver depends on skillful movement along indirect approaches supported by direct and indirect fires. It may also use deception and concealment to cause an enemy to move. It requires imaginative, bold, competent, independent commanders; discipline, coordination, and speed; well-trained troops; and logistically ready units. Effective operational maneuver requires the anticipation of friendly and enemy actions well beyond the current battle, the careful coordination of tactical and logistical activities, and the movement of large formations to great depths.

FIREPOWER

Firepower provides the destructive force essential to defeating the enemy's ability and will to fight. Firepower facilitates maneuver by suppressing the enemy's fires and disrupting the movement of his forces. Firepower exploits maneuver by neutralizing the enemy's tactical forces and destroying his ability and will to fight. Firepower may also be used independent of maneuver to destroy, delay, or disrupt uncommitted enemy forces. Current weapons and means of massing fires make firepower devastatingly effective against troops, materiel, and facilities in greater depth and accuracy and with more flexibility than ever before. Tactical leaders must understand the techniques of controlling and integrating fire, maneuver and protection, coordinating direct and indirect fires, utilizing air and naval fires, and substituting massed fires for massed troops. Commanders must understand the techniques of integrating Air Force, Naval, and Army firepower effectively in the conduct of campaigns and major operations.

Firepower supports friendly operational maneuver by damaging key enemy forces or facilities, creating delays in enemy movement, complicating the enemy's command and control, and degrading his artillery, air defense, and air support. At the operational level, firepower can also disrupt the *movement, fire support, command and control, and sustainment* of enemy forces.

Maximum effective firepower against the enemy requires that many functions be coordinated and performed well. Systems and procedures for allocating priorities must be effective. Targets must be efficiently located and identified. Gunnery must be rapid and accurate. Firing systems and supporting equipment must be mobile and moved to advantageous positions. There must be a steady supply of the proper munitions in adequate quantities. Hardware must be maintained and replaced as necessary. The various components of the firing system must be protected from enemy action. And most importantly, effective firepower depends on well-trained crews, observers, and fire direction personnel.

PROTECTION

Protection is the conservation of the fighting potential of a force so that it can be applied at the decisive time and place. Protection has two components. The first includes all actions that are taken to counter the enemy's firepower and maneuver by making soldiers, systems, and units difficult to locate, strike, and destroy. Among those actions are security, air defense, dispersal, cover, camouflage, deception, suppression of enemy weapons, and mobility. Tactical commanders provide security against surprise maneuver, maintain camouflage discipline, fortify fighting positions, conduct rapid movements, suppress enemy weapons, provide air defense, conceal positions, deceive the enemy, and take other measures to prevent unnecessary combat losses. Operational commanders take similar measures on a larger scale. They protect the force from operational level maneuver and concentrated enemy air support. Air superiority operations, theater wide air defense systems and protection of air bases are important activities associated with maximizing combat power at the operational level.

The second component of protection includes actions to keep soldiers healthy and to maintain their fighting morale. It also means guarding their equipment and supplies from loss or damage. Tactical commanders take care of their soldier's basic health needs and prevent unnecessary exposure to debilitating conditions. They consider the welfare and morale of soldiers and try to build cohesion and esprit in units. In addition they supervise preventive maintenance and expeditious repair, and practice supply economy. Operational commanders ensure systems are in place for adequate medical care, expeditious return of minor casualties to duty, and preventive medicine. They protect stocks of supplies and ensure their proper distribution. They provide effective systems for maintenance evacuation and rapid replacement or repair of hardware. At times, they husband and ration supplies or enforce strict controls and priorities to ensure strength at the decisive time and place.

LEADERSHIP

The most essential element of combat power is *competent* and *confident leadership*. Leadership provides purpose, direction, and motivation in combat. It is the leader who will determine the degree to which maneuver, firepower, and protection are maximized; who will ensure these elements are effectively balanced; and who will decide how to bring them to bear against the enemy. There are no ready formulas to govern this process. Only excellence in the art and science of war will enable the commander to generate and apply combat power successfully. Thus no peacetime duty is more important for leaders than studying their profession and preparing for war. The regular study of military history and biography is invaluable in this regard.

In the current conditions of combat, no challenge exceeds leadership in importance. The personal influence of large joint and combined force, field army, corps, and division commanders will have a major bearing on the outcomes of battles and campaigns. Leaders at lower levels will play equally important parts in winning the smaller engagements that make up battles.

The skill and personality of a strong commander represent a significant part of his unit's combat power. While leadership requirements differ with unit size and type, all leaders must be men of character; they must know and understand soldiers and the material tools of war. They must act with courage and conviction in the uncertainty and confusion of battle. The primary function of tactical leaders is to induce soldiers to do difficult things in dangerous, stressful circumstances. Successful combat

leaders have differed in style and technique but all have been accomplished, effective soldiers.

Leaders develop potential combat power in their units through preparation prior to battle. Preparation includes many matters of long-term concern to the Army—force design, equipment design, and procurement, to name only a few. The tactical unit commander has a more immediate perspective. To him, preparation means planning, logistical readiness, training, and motivation. These factors affect unit potential until the moment of engagement. Successful commanders have always continued training programs throughout campaigns on and near the battlefield. They recognized that every endeavor causes the unit to learn either good or bad habits. Continuous training under all conditions ensures that what is learned is positive and will contribute to success in battle. Commanders must demand excellence in execution under all conditions and must strive to make it habitual.

In the final analysis and once the force is engaged, superior combat power derives from the courage and competence of soldiers, the excellence of their training, the capability of their equipment, the soundness of their combined arms doctrine, and above all the quality of their leadership.

AIRLAND BATTLE DOCTRINE

AirLand Battle doctrine describes the Army's approach to generating and applying combat power at the operational and tactical levels. It is based on securing or retaining the initiative and exercising it aggressively to accomplish the mission. The object of all operations is to impose our will upon the enemy—to achieve our purposes. To do this we must throw the enemy off balance with a powerful blow from an unexpected direction, follow up rapidly to prevent his recovery and continue operations aggressively to achieve the higher commander's goals. The best results are obtained when powerful blows

are struck against critical units or areas whose loss will degrade the coherence of enemy operations in depth, and thus most rapidly and economically accomplish the mission. From the enemy's point of view, these operations must be rapid, unpredictable, violent, and disorienting. The pace must be fast enough to prevent him from taking effective counteractions.

Our operational planning must orient on decisive objectives. It must stress flexibility, the creation of opportunities to fight on favorable terms by capitalizing on enemy vulnerabilities, concentration against enemy centers of gravity, synchronized joint operations, and aggressive exploitation of tactical gains to achieve operational results. Our tactical planning must be precise enough to preserve synchronization throughout the battle. At the same time, it must be flexible enough to respond to changes or to capitalize on fleeting opportunities to damage the enemy. Success on the battlefield will depend on the Army's ability to fight in accordance with four basic tenets: *initiative, agility, depth,* and *synchronization.*

INITIATIVE

Initiative means setting or changing the terms of battle by action. It implies an offensive spirit in the conduct of all operations. Applied to the force as a whole, initiative requires a constant effort to force the enemy to conform to our operational purpose and tempo while retaining our own freedom of action. Applied to individual soldiers and leaders, it requires a willingness and ability to act independently within the framework of the higher commander's intent. In both senses, initiative requires audacity which may involve risk-taking and an atmosphere that supports it.

There are at least two kinds of risk in combat. One is the risk of losing men and equipment to attain the mission. The other is that a chosen course of action may not be successful, or even if successful, fail to achieve the desired effect. All leaders must take prudent risks of both types independently, based on their own judgment.

In the defense, initiative implies quickly turning the tables on the attacker. The defender must act rapidly to negate the attacker's initial advantage of choice of time and place of attack. Intelligence operations seek advance warning. Planning anticipates likely enemy courses of action so no time is lost in shaping the battle— setting the tempo and conditions of enemy operations—and in making adjustments. Once the attacker is committed to a particular course of action the defender must frustrate it, then preempt any adjustments.

This will cause the initiative to pass to the defender. Tactical successes in seizing the initiative are used as leverage to seize the initiative at the operational level.

In the attack, initiative implies never allowing the enemy to recover from the initial shock of the attack. This requires surprise in selecting the time and place of attack; concentration, speed, audacity, and violence in execution; the seeking of soft spots; flexible shifting of the main effort; and prompt transition to exploitation. The goal is the creation of a fluid situation in which the enemy steadily loses track of events and thus coherence. The defender is not given the time to identify and mass his forces or supporting fires against the attack because of the ambiguity of the situation presented to him and the rapidity with which it changes. Retaining the initiative over time requires thinking ahead, planning beyond the initial operation, and anticipating key events on the battlefield hours, days, and weeks ahead.

In the chaos of battle, it is essential to decentralize decision authority to the lowest practical level because overcentralization slows action and leads to inertia. At the same time, decentralization risks some loss of precision in execution. The commander must constantly balance these competing risks, recognizing that loss of precision is usually preferable to inaction. Decentralization demands subordinates who are willing and able to take risks and superiors who nurture that willingness and ability in their subordinates. If subordinates are to exercise initiative without endangering the overall success of the force, they must thoroughly understand the commander's intent and the situational assumptions on which it was based. In turn, the force commander must encourage subordinates to focus their operations on the overall mission, and give them the freedom and responsibility to develop opportunities which the force as a whole can exploit to accomplish the mission more effectively. Force commanders must then be able to shift their main effort quickly to take advantage of enemy vulnerabilities their subordinates discover or create.

AGILITY

Agility—the ability of friendly forces to act faster than the enemy—is the first prerequisite for seizing and holding the initiative. Such greater quickness permits the rapid concentration of friendly strength against enemy vulnerabilities. This must be done repeatedly so that by the time the enemy reacts to one action, another has already taken its place, disrupting his plans and leading to late, uncoordinated, and piecemeal enemy responses. It is this process of successive concentration against locally weaker or unprepared enemy forces which enables smaller forces to disorient, fragment, and eventually defeat much larger opposing formations.

To achieve this, both leaders and units must be agile. Friction—the accumulation of chance errors, unexpected difficulties, and the confusion of battle—will impede both sides. To overcome it, leaders must continuously "read the battlefield," decide quickly, and act without hesitation. They must be prepared to risk commitment without complete information, recognizing that waiting for such information will invariably forfeit the opportunity to act. Units likewise must be physically and psychologically capable of responding rapidly to changing requirements. Formations at every level must be capable of shifting the main effort with minimum delay and with the least possible necessity for reconfiguration and coordination.

In the end, agility is as much a mental as a physical quality. Our Army has traditionally taken pride in its soldiers' ability to "think on their feet" and to see and react rapidly to changing circumstances. Mental flexibility must be developed during the soldier's military education and maintained through individual and unit training.

DEPTH

Depth is the extension of operations in space, time, and resources. Through the use of depth, a commander obtains the necessary space to maneuver effectively; the necessary time to plan, arrange, and execute operations; and the necessary resources to win. Momentum in the attack and elasticity in defense derive from depth.

Momentum in the attack is achieved and maintained when resources and forces are concentrated to sustain operations over extended periods, adequate reconnaissance is provided beyond areas of immediate concern, committed enemy forces are adequately fixed, uncommitted enemy forces are interdicted or otherwise prevented from interfering, adequate air protection is provided, the enemy's command and control system is disrupted, adequate reserves and follow and support forces are provided, vulnerable rear area facilities are protected, logistic resources are moved forward, and combat forces project tactical operations deep into the enemy's vulnerable areas.

Elasticity in the defense is achieved and maintained when resources and forces are deployed in depth, adequate reconnaissance is provided beyond areas of immediate concern, reserves are positioned in depth with adequate maneuver room to strike critical blows at exposed enemy forces, uncommitted enemy forces are delayed or prevented from interfering with the defense of forward deployed or counterattacking forces, adequate air protection is provided, the enemy's command and control system is disrupted, vulnerable rear area facilities are protected, and defending forces aggressively concentrate combat power in critical areas.

In tactical actions, commanders fight the enemy throughout the depth of his dispositions with fires and with attacks on his flanks, rear, and support echelons. Such operations in depth degrade the enemy's freedom of action, reduce his flexibility and endurance, and upset his plans and coordination. Commanders retain reserves and adjust their main efforts to exploit tactical opportunities and carry the fight into the depths of the enemy's formations or defenses. At the same time, they guard their own freedom of action by protecting their rear areas and support forces.

In pursuit of operational objectives, large unit commanders observe enemy movements in depth and protect their own vulnerabilities throughout the theater. In conjunction with air and naval operations, they employ maneuver, fires, and special operations to attack enemy units, facilities, and communications throughout the theater and to force the enemy to fight battles on their terms. Following battle, theater operations in depth are used to extend the advantages gained by tactical success or to limit losses.

Exploitation of depth in operations demands imagination, boldness, foresight, and decisiveness in leaders. Commanders must see beyond the requirements of the moment, actively seek information on the area and the enemy in depth, and employ every asset available to extend their operations in time and space. They must also capitalize on natural and man made obstacles by using less mobile forces to exploit these obstacles, thereby freeing mobile forces to maneuver over more favorable terrain.

SYNCHRONIZATION

Synchronization is the arrangement of battlefield activities in time, space and purpose to produce maximum relative combat power at the decisive point. Synchronization is both a process and a result. Commanders synchronize activities; they thereby produce synchronized operations.

Synchronization includes but is not limited to the actual concentration of forces and fires at the point of decision. Some of the activities which must be synchronized in an operation—interdiction with maneuver, for example, or the shifting of reserves with the rearrangement of air defense—must occur before the decisive moment, and may take place at locations far distant from each other. While themselves separated in time and space, however, these activities are synchronized if their combined *consequences* are felt at the decisive time and place.

Thus in an attack, supporting fires are synchronized with maneuver if, as attacking forces break out of defilade, supporting fires are shifted from counterfire against enemy artillery to suppression of enemy direct fire systems. Or on a larger scale, main and supporting attacks are synchronized if the latter takes place at precisely the right time and place to divert enemy forces and fires from the main effort as it strikes the enemy. At the operational level, two major operations are synchronized if the first, by attracting the bulk of enemy forces, uncovers a key objective for decisive attack by the other.

So defined, synchronization may and usually will require explicit coordination among the various units and activities participating in any operation. By itself, however, such coordination is no guarantee of synchronization, unless the commander first visualizes the consequences to be produced and how activities must be sequenced to produce them. Synchronization thus takes place first in the mind of the commander and then in the actual planning and coordination of movements, fires, and supporting activities.

Synchronization need not depend on explicit coordination if all forces involved fully understand the intent of the commander, and if they have developed and rehearsed well-conceived standard responses to anticipated contingencies. In the chaos of battle, when communications fail and face-to-face coordination is impossible, such implicit coordination may make the difference between victory and defeat. The enemy for his part will do everything in

SYNCHRONIZATION

AIR
INTERDICTION

T_2 to T_3

CRITICAL
TIME AND
PLACE

FLOT

FLOT

T_3

T_3

X X X

ASSEMBLY
AREA

Legend
T = Time

T_1 to T_2

XX

X X X

his power to disrupt the synchronization of friendly operations. The less that synchronization depends on active communication, the less vulnerable it will be.

In the end, the product of effective synchronization is maximum economy of force, with every resource used where and when it will make the greatest contribution to success and nothing wasted or overlooked. To achieve this requires anticipation, mastery of time-space relationships, and a complete understanding of the ways in which friendly and enemy capabilities interact. Most of all, it requires unambiguous unity of purpose throughout the force.

CLOSE, DEEP, AND REAR OPERATIONS

Close, deep, and rear operations comprise a special and continuous synchronization requirement. For commanders at division and above, synchronization of close, deep, and rear operations will normally require deliberate planning and staff coordination, and such operations will frequently employ different assets. At brigade and below, close, deep, and rear activities are practically indistinguishable and will usually be conducted with the same assets. At every level, however, commanders must understand the relationship among these three arenas and their combined impact on the course of battle.

CLOSE OPERATIONS

Close operations at any echelon comprise the current activities of major committed combat elements, together with their immediate combat support and combat service support. At the operational level, close operations comprise the efforts of large tactical formations—corps and divisions—to win current battles. At the tactical level, close operations comprise the efforts of smaller tactical units to win current engagements.

At any echelon, close operations include the close, deep, and rear operations of subordinate elements. Thus the close operation of a corps includes the close, deep, and rear operations of its committed divisions or separate brigades.

Not all activities taking place in proximity to the line of contact are close operations. For example, some forward surveillance and target acquisition may be functionally related to deep operations. Similarly, some engineer activities in the forward area may be related to rear operations. Activities are part of close operations if they are designed to support the current fight.

Among the activities typically comprising close operations are—

- Maneuver (including deep maneuver).

- Close combat (including close air support).

- Indirect fire support (including counterfire).

- Combat support/combat service support of committed units.

- Command and control.

Close operations bear the ultimate burden of victory or defeat. The measure of success of deep and rear operations is their eventual impact on close operations.

DEEP OPERATIONS

Deep operations at any echelon comprise activities directed against enemy forces not in contact designed to influence the conditions in which future close operations will be conducted. At the operational level, deep operations include efforts to isolate current battles and to influence where, when, and against whom future battles will be fought. At the tactical level, deep operations are designed to shape the battlefield to assure advantage in subsequent engagements. At both levels, successful deep operations create the conditions for future victory.

Such operations are not new to warfare nor to the American Army. The concept of interdicting the enemy's supplies, follow-on forces, reserves, and communications to impede his ability to commit these at times and places of his choosing is a familiar feature of modern war. In our own recent history, World War II, Korea, and Vietnam furnish numerous examples of successful (and unsuccessful) efforts to isolate the battlefield, paralyze the enemy's support and command and control systems, and to prevent, delay, or disrupt the closure of uncommitted enemy formations. The principal difference in such operations today is the increasing availability of means to conduct them at the tactical as well as the operational level.

At both levels, the principal targets of deep operations are the freedom of action of the opposing commander and the coherence and tempo of his operations. As with close operations, not all activities focused forward of the line of contact are deep operations. Counterfire, for example, is intended primarily to support the current fight, even though the targets attacked in the counterfire effort may be located at great distances from the forward line of own troops (FLOT). Similarly, electronic warfare efforts to disrupt the enemy's control of engaged forces are part of close operations, even though the targeted emitters may be well to the enemy's rear.

Among the activities typically conducted as part of deep operations are—

• Deception.

• Deep surveillance and target acquisition.

• Interdiction (by ground or air fires, ground or aerial maneuver, special operating forces (SOF), or any combination of these).

• Command, control, and communications countermeasures.

• Command and control.

Because of the relative scarcity of resources with which to perform these activities, deep operations must be focused against those enemy capabilities which most directly threaten the success of projected friendly operations. These must be attacked decisively, with enough power to assure the desired impact. That will be the

more true when—as will frequently be the case—seizure and retention of the initiative depend on successful prosecution of deep operations.

REAR OPERATIONS

Rear operations at any echelon comprise activities rearward of elements in contact designed to assure freedom of maneuver and continuity of operations, including continuity of sustainment and command and control. Rear operations may have little immediate impact on close ground operations, but are critical to subsequent operations, whether in exploiting success or recouping failure. At the operational level, rear operations focus on preparing for the next phase of the campaign or major operation. At the tactical level, rear operations underwrite the tempo of combat, assuring the commander the agility to take advantage of any opportunity without hesitation or delay.

Four rearward activities in particular must be conducted as part of rear operations: assembly and movement of reserves, redeployment of fire support, maintenance and protection of sustainment effort, and maintenance of command and control. Reserves must be positioned to support their anticipated commitment and secured from observation and attack. Probable deployment routes must be free of obstruction, and the actual movement of reserves protected from enemy observation and interdiction. Fire support assets likewise must be redeployed to support future operations, and that redeployment protected from enemy detection and interference. Sustainment facilities and supplies must be secured against ground, air, and missile attack, and stocks to support projected operations accumulated without decreasing the support to currently engaged units. And command posts and communications networks must be deployed where they can continue the fight without a break in operating tempo.

In addition to these critical activities, others relevant to rear operations include—

- Establishment and maintenance of lines of communications (LOCs).

- Traffic regulation and control.

- Medical and field services.

- Refugee control and maintenance of civil order.

By themselves, none of these activities would normally have much impact on the current battle. However, because it is precisely these activities which will be the targets of the enemy's deep operations, their protection can easily begin to divert needed assets from the forward battle. To preclude this, units involved in rear operations must be equipped and trained to protect themselves against all but the most serious threats, using both passive and active measures. Soldiers and leaders at all levels must be alert to the rearward threat and psychologically prepared to deal with it. And force commanders and staffs must continually reevaluate the possibility of more serious threats to rear operations, and plan measures to meet them with minimum penalty to on-going close operations.

COMMAND AND CONTROL

Common to all operations—close, deep, and rear—is the necessity for superior command and control. The command and control system which supports the execution of AirLand Battle doctrine must facilitate freedom to operate, delegation of authority, and leadership from any critical point on the battlefield. Plans are the initial basis of action, but commanders must expect considerable variation from plans in the course of combat. Ideally, the initial plan for an operation will establish the commander's intent and concept of operations and the responsibilities of subordinate units. It will, however, leave the greatest possible operational and tactical freedom to subordinate leaders. The plan must therefore be flexible enough to permit variation by subordinates in pursuit of the commander's goals.

Whenever possible, subordinate leaders should receive their orders face-to-face from their commanders on the ground chosen for the operation. Commanders should restrict the operations of their subordinates as little as necessary. Mission orders that specify what must be done without prescribing how it must be done should be used in most cases. Control measures should secure cooperation between forces without imposing unnecessary restrictions on the freedom of junior leaders. The larger force should remain alert to and be prepared for exploitation of advantages developed by subordinate units through the course of any operation.

A command and control system seeking to promote such flexibility and freedom to operate independently must emphasize certain specific operational techniques and command practices. First, it must optimize the use of time by routine use of warning orders, situation updates, and anticipatory planning and positioning of forces.

The command and control system must also stress standardized training in operations and staff practices to assure mutual understanding between leaders and units. In turn, this requires both military education throughout the Army and its sister services and reinforcing training within units. War gaming, rehearsals, and realistic training promote initiative and flexibility by preparing units and their leaders for cooperation in the chaos of combat without time-consuming coordination.

Further, the command and control system must permit tactical leaders to position themselves wherever the situation calls for their personal presence without depriving them of the ability to respond to opportunities or changing circumstances with the whole force. If, for example, a division commander operating forward with a leading brigade decides to shift his main effort to capitalize on the unexpected success of a supporting attack, his command and control system must assure rapid execution of his order without sacrificing momentum or coordination. This requires solid staff work and strongly developed skills of tactical anticipation. Leaders throughout the force must be ready to change directions of movement, bases of fire, support arrangements, and task organizations without hesitation during operations. Succession of command when a leader is killed or disabled must be provided for in advance and accomplished without disruption of the operation.

This need for flexibility in command and control is greater for the committed maneuver unit commander than for anyone else. He cannot depend on constant direction, but must fight independently even when he cannot communicate outside his own zone or sector. He must know the intention of the commander two levels above him, understand the concept of operation of his immediate commander, and know the responsibilities of the units on his flanks and in support of his operations. If he understands these things, the committed commander can conduct his operation confidently, anticipate events, and act freely and boldly to accomplish his mission without further orders.

If an unanticipated situation arises, committed maneuver unit commanders should understand the purpose of the operation well enough to act decisively, confident that they are doing what their superior commander would order done were he present. The 9th Armored Division's seizure of the Remagen bridge epitomizes the freedom of action and initiative required in combat. In that instance, an infantry platoon leader who understood the goal of his division commander acted promptly and without orders to secure an advantage that altered the course of the Army's whole campaign.

The same principles apply at the operational level of war. Lead times are longer and forces are slower to move, but mission-orders, anticipation of requirements, and initiative are equally important. The inherently joint nature of campaign planning and direction makes mutual understanding and practiced cooperation all the more important in theater operations.

Staffing, equipment, and organizational concerns vary among levels of command. In every case, however, the only purpose of command and control is to implement the commander's will in pursuit of the unit's objective. The system must be reliable, secure, fast, and durable. It must collect, analyze, and present information rapidly. It must communicate orders, coordinate support, and provide direction to the force in spite of enemy interference, destruction of command posts, or loss and replacement of commanders. *The ultimate measure of command and control effectiveness is whether the force functions more effectively and more quickly than the enemy.*

AIRLAND BATTLE IMPERATIVES

The nine principles of war described in FM 100-1 (and reproduced in Appendix A) provide timeless general guidance for the conduct of war at strategic, operational, and tactical levels. They are the enduring bedrock of US Army doctrine.

The fundamental tenets of AirLand Battle doctrine describe the characteristics of successful operations. They are the basis for the development of all current US Army doctrine, tactics, and techniques. All training and leadership doctrines and all combat, combat support, and combat service support doctrine are derived directly from, and must support, these fundamental tenets.

While initiative, agility, depth, and synchronization characterize successful AirLand Battle operations, the imperatives listed below prescribe key operating requirements. These provide more specific guidance than the principles of war and the AirLand Battle tenets, and apply to all operations. They are historically valid and fundamentally necessary for success on the modern battlefield. The ten imperatives of AirLand Battle are—

- Ensure unity of effort.
- Anticipate events on the battlefield.
- Concentrate combat power against enemy vulnerabilities.
- Designate, sustain, and shift the main effort.
- Press the fight.
- Move fast, strike hard, and finish rapidly.
- Use terrain, weather, deception, and OPSEC.
- Conserve strength for decisive action.
- Combine arms and sister services to complement and reinforce.
- Understand the effects of battle on soldiers, units, and leaders.

ENSURE UNITY OF EFFORT

Commands must not only ensure unity of effort within their own organizations, but must also promote it with supporting and supported elements as well as with sister services and allies. The fundamental prerequisite for unity of effort within Army organizations is an effective system of command which relies upon leadership to provide purpose, direction, and motivation; emphasizes well-understood common doctrine, tactics, and techniques as well as sound unit standing operating procedures (SOPs); and takes effective measures to limit the effects of friction. Leaders set the example, communicate their intent clearly, build teamwork, promote sound values, accept responsibility, delegate authority, anticipate developments, take decisive actions, and accept risks. Command and control systems emphasize implicit coordination measures such as sound training in a common doctrine, standing operating procedures, methods, and techniques, and well-rehearsed battle drills. Missions are clear and concise. Plans are simple. Control mechanisms are easy to apply, understand, and communicate. Habitual relationships are used to maximize teamwork. A main effort is always clearly designated and ground plans are thoroughly coordinated with plans for air support. All actions throughout the force are performed so as to ensure the success of the main effort. Liaison among units must be automatic and effective.

ANTICIPATE EVENTS ON THE BATTLEFIELD

The commander must anticipate the enemy's actions and reactions and must be able to foresee how operations may develop. Predictions about the enemy and even our own troops can never be relied on with certainty, but it is nevertheless essential to anticipate what is possible and likely and prepare for those possibilities. Anticipating events and foreseeing the shape of possibilities hours, days, or weeks in the future are two of the most difficult skills to develop, yet among the most important. They require wisdom, experience, and understanding of the enemy's methods, capabilities, and inclinations, outstanding intelligence, and confidence in the knowledge of how one's own forces will perform. Anticipation and foresight are critical to turning inside the enemy's decision cycle and maintaining the initiative.

CONCENTRATE COMBAT POWER AGAINST ENEMY VULNERABILITIES

Concentrating combat power against enemy vulnerabilities is also fundamental to AirLand Battle operations. Commanders must seek out the enemy where he is most vulnerable to defeat. To know what his vulnerabilities are, commanders must study the enemy, know and take into account his strengths, find his inherent vulnerabilities, and know how to create new vulnerabilities which can be exploited to decisive effect. Having identified or created enemy vulnerabilities, the commander must have the mental and organizational flexibility to shift his main effort as necessary to gain the greatest possible advantage. Combat power must be concentrated to reach points of enemy vulnerability quickly without loss of synchronization.

DESIGNATE, SUSTAIN, AND SHIFT THE MAIN EFFORT

In operations characterized by initiative, agility, depth, and synchronization, it is imperative that commanders designate, sustain and shift the main effort as necessary during operations. The main effort is assigned to the element with the most important task to accomplish within the commander's concept. The commander concentrates his support to ensure quick success by this element. The commander identifies the main effort when he states his concept of the operation. This provides a focus of effort that each subordinate commander uses to link his actions to the actions of those around him. The main effort assures synchronization in the operation while leaving the greatest possible scope for initiative. During operations, the main effort is sustained with supporting forces and assets. If conditions change and success of the overall mission can be obtained more cheaply or quickly another way, the commander shifts his main effort to another force. Priorities of support also change to assure the success of the newly designated main effort.

PRESS THE FIGHT

Commanders must press the fight tenaciously and aggressively. Campaigns or battles are won by the force that is most successful in pressing its main effort to a conclusion. To sustain the momentum of early successes, leaders must deploy forces in adequate depth and arrange for timely and continuous combat support and combat service support at the outset of operations. Then, they must accept risks and

tenaciously press soldiers and systems to the limits of endurance for as long as necessary.

MOVE FAST, STRIKE HARD, AND FINISH RAPIDLY

Speed has always been important to combat operations, but it will be even more important on the next battlefield because of the increasing sophistication of sensors and the increasing lethality of conventional, nuclear, and chemical fires. To avoid detection, our force concentrations must be disguised. To avoid effective counterstrikes, they must be brief. Engagements must be violent to shock, paralyze, and overwhelm the enemy force quickly. They must be terminated rapidly to allow the force to disperse and avoid effective enemy counterstrikes.

USE TERRAIN, WEATHER, DECEPTION, AND OPSEC

Terrain and weather affect combat more significantly than any other physical factors. Battles are won or lost by the way in which combatants use the terrain to protect their own forces and to destroy those of the enemy. The ground and the airspace immediately above it have an immense influence on how the battle will be fought. They provide opportunities and impose limitations, giving a decisive edge to the commander who uses them best. The impact of weather on ground and air mobility and the effect both have on weapons will affect tactics and the timing and course of operations. One of the best investments of the commander's time before battle is an intensive, personal reconnaissance of the terrain. Similarly, effective deception and tight operations security can enhance combat power by confusing the enemy and reducing his foreknowledge of friendly actions.

CONSERVE STRENGTH FOR DECISIVE ACTION

Successful commanders conserve the strength of their forces to be stronger at the decisive time and place. Commanders must minimize the diversion of resources to nonessential tasks and retain a reserve for commitment when needed most. Commanders must also keep troops secure, protected, healthy, disciplined, and in a high state of morale. In addition they must keep equipment ready and stocks of supplies available for commitment when needed. Finally, units must be maintained in a high state of training. Dispersed and rapid movement, proper formations, covered and concealed fighting positions, aggressive patrolling, good operations security, protection of troops and equipment from adverse weather and disease, and good supply and maintenance discipline are all examples of measures which conserve a force's strength.

COMBINE ARMS AND SISTER SERVICES TO COMPLEMENT AND REINFORCE

The greatest combat power results when weapons and other hardware, combat and supporting arms, Army units, and other service elements of different capabilities are employed together to complement and reinforce each other. Arms and services *complement* each other by posing a dilemma for the enemy. As he evades the effects of one weapon, arm, or service, he exposes himself to attack by another. At the level of weapons systems, one good example of complementary combined arms employment would be the use of guns and missiles in the air defense of a key installation. Another would be using mines, mortars, or grenade launchers to cover the dead space of a machine gun's field of fire. A tactical example of complementary combined arms would be combining infantry and armor in task forces or combining infantry-heavy and armor-heavy task forces in brigades. Another example of tactical level complementary combined arms employment between the services is when Air Force Aircraft attack tanks in defilade and out of reach of direct ground fires and attack helicopters while artillery and direct fires suppress enemy air defenses. At the

operational level, an example would be Air Force Air Superiority operations and ground maneuver, or employing light infantry formations in highly mountainous regions to free armor and mechanized forces for use in less restricted areas.

Arms and services *reinforce* each other when one increases the effectiveness of another or several combine to achieve mass. Some examples at the technical level would be engineers helping to develop an infantry strong point which greatly enhances the combat power of the infantry, the scout helicopter spotting targets for the attack helicopter, artillery suppression of enemy fires during an assault, or the massing of all antitank fires against an armored threat. Tactically, reinforcement might involve concentrating all types of maneuver forces or fires to create mass. It might also involve heliborne lift of light infantry. Operationally, it could mean using Naval amphibious shipping or Air Force tactical airlift to deliver soldiers to the battlefield, intelligence support to Army units from Air Force, Naval, or national sources, Air Force interdiction to support maneuver on the ground, or US Army units protecting air bases from ground attack.

Ideally, both effects are combined in one action as when mines, artillery, and tanks combine to defeat an attack. All three reinforce to damage the enemy simultaneously to some degree. The mines and artillery fire slow the enemy and complement the tank fire which can obtain more hits against the stalled enemy.

UNDERSTAND THE EFFECT OF BATTLE ON SOLDIERS, UNITS, AND LEADERS

Commanders and their staffs must understand the effects of battle on soldiers, units, and leaders because war is fundamentally a contest of wills, fought by men not machines. Ardant DuPiq, a 19th century soldier and student of men in battle, reminded us that "you can reach into the well of courage only so many times before the well runs dry." Even before that Marshall De Saxe, writing in the 18th century, pointed out that "A soldier's courage must be reborn daily," and went on to say that the most important task of leaders was to understand this, to care for and prepare soldiers before battle, and to use tactics during battle which take this into account.

Commanders must understand that in battle, men and units are more likely to fail catastrophically than gradually. Commanders and staffs must be alert to small indicators of fatigue, fear, indiscipline, and reduced morale, and take measures to deal with these *before* their cumulative effects drive a unit to the threshold of collapse. Staffs and commanders at higher levels must take into account the impact of prolonged combat on subordinate units. Military organizations can fight at peak efficiency for only so long. Prolonged demands of combat cause efficiency to drop even when physical losses are not great. Well trained, physically fit soldiers in cohesive units retain the qualities of tenacity and aggressiveness longer than those which are not.

Good leadership makes the vital difference in the staying power and effectiveness of units. Although all units experience peaks and valleys in combat effectiveness, well-trained, cohesive units under good leadership sustain far higher average effectiveness. Staffs and commanders need to take this variance in performance into account in their planning by matching units to missions, rotating units through difficult tasks to permit recuperation to the extent possible, and by basing their expectations of a unit's performance on a full knowledge of its current capabilities.

Because modern combat requires greater dispersal of units, the quality and effectiveness of junior leaders has a proportionately greater impact. Prior to combat, senior leaders must place great emphasis on junior leader development. During combat, commanders must monitor and take measures to sustain the effectiveness of leaders to the extent possible.

AirLand Battle doctrine is evolutionary. While the conditions of warfare change with time and circumstance, the fundamental dynamics of violent conflict remain unaltered. The essential qualities of skill, tenacity, boldness, and courage which have always marked successful armies and commanders will continue to determine the victor in battle in the future, as they have in the past.

AirLand Battle doctrine exploits those qualities, together with the technological prowess, self-reliance and offensive spirit which characterize the American soldier. It requires combined arms and joint forces to extend the battlefield and thus hold at risk all enemy forces, harnessing advanced technologies to provide synchronized reconnaissance, real-time intelligence fusion, target attack, and maneuver. While respecting the increased complexity and lethality of modern weapons, however, AirLand Battle doctrine also recognizes that such weapons are no better than the skill with which they are brought to bear on the enemy. Properly understood and instilled through effective training, the principles of operation prescribed by AirLand Battle doctrine will produce the skill to match the US Army's will to win.

CHAPTER 3

Operational and Tactical Planning and Execution

AirLand Battle doctrine recognizes that modern warfare is likely to be fluid and nonlinear. Therefore it takes an enlarged view of the battlefield, stressing unified air, ground, and sea operations throughout the theater. It recognizes that the theater of operations in a campaign extends from ports and support areas far to the rear of the line of contact to similarly distant sources of enemy support. Likewise the tactical battlefield with its unified close, deep, and rear operations includes every area and enemy unit that can affect the outcome of the immediate fight and the future operations of a force. AirLand Battle doctrine distinguishes the operational level of war—the design and conduct of campaigns and major operations—from the tactical level which deals with battles and engagements. It asserts that whether attacking or defending, success depends on securing the initiative as early as possible and exercising it aggressively. It requires that every weapon, asset, and combat multiplier be used to gain that initiative, to throw the enemy off balance with a powerful blow from an unexpected direction, and to follow up rapidly to prevent his recovery. At both the operational and tactical levels, initiative, agility, depth, and synchronization are the essence of AirLand Battle doctrine. This chapter discusses the planning and conduct of campaigns, major operations, battles, and engagements.

PLANNING AND CONDUCTING CAMPAIGNS AND MAJOR OPERATIONS

The principal task of theater commanders and their subordinate commanders is to concentrate superior strength against enemy vulnerabilities at the decisive time and place to achieve strategic and policy aims. The overall joint or allied commander in each theater of operations plans and executes campaigns and major operations that optimize the use of all available combat, combat

CONTENTS

support, and combat service support forces. Ground, air, and naval operations are synchronized to support each other and to fulfill the requirements of the overall joint commander's campaign plan. Army and Air Force component commanders will normally be subordinated to him. There may also be Navy and Marine component commanders. Moreover these forces may be multinational.

Operational level commanders try to set favorable terms for battle by synchronized ground, air, and sea maneuver and by striking the enemy throughout the theater of operations. Large scale ground maneuver will always require protection from enemy air forces and sometimes also from naval forces. Commanders will therefore conduct reconnaissance, interdiction, air defense, and special operations almost continuously. Air interdiction, air and ground reconnaissance, raids, psychological warfare actions, and unconventional warfare operations must all be synchronized to support the overall campaign, and its supporting major operations on the ground, especially at critical junctures.

The Army Component Commander (ACC) may be the theater army commander, an army group commander, an army commander, or, in some cases, a corps commander. He and his chief subordinates must maintain synchronization over large areas. This will always involve close cooperation with air forces and will often require joint planning and operations with naval forces. In addition to maintaining effective cooperation with other armed forces of the US, the ACC and his staff will also have to cooperate with allied air, ground, or naval forces. In many cases, the forces of allied nations will be assigned to US corps and armies. The US corps must also be prepared to fight under command of allied commanders. In either instance, effective cooperation and operational synchronization will depend on good liaison and clear understanding of the capabilities and doctrine of the allied forces involved. Chapter 11 discusses joint and combined operations.

Ground operations require coordinated movement and effective concentration of large units—corps, field armies and army groups—against the enemy in spite of his efforts to interdict the friendly forces' movement. Traffic control, air defense, deception, and service support must all function harmoniously to support basic operational movements. Key forces and facilities—some of them deep in the rear area—must be protected during this movement.

Coordination of actions that support movement of large forces will take on special importance following major operations and battles. Large unit commanders will then attempt to exploit tactical gains or to withdraw and reorganize units. Air defense, air and ground transportation, reconnaissance and security, service support and traffic control will be the chief concerns as these large movements occur.

CAMPAIGN PLANNING

Operational planning begins with strategic guidance to a theater commander or with the commander's recognition of a mission in an active theater of operations. Operational commmanders and their staff officers use the estimate of the situation and planning process described in FM 101-5. They will normally be involved in joint and combined operations, however, and will therefore cooperate with commanders and staffs of other services and other nationalities as they plan at the operational level. In planning and conducting joint operations, they will use prescribed joint operations planning and execution systems.

Operational planning concentrates on the design of campaigns and major operations. At theater level, campaign planning entails converting broad strategic guidance into a campaign plan for a joint/combined force. Operational planning within each theater of operations focuses on execution of the campaign plan and on the staging, conduct, and exploitation of major operations.

Each joint or combined commander responsible for a theater of operations makes a campaign plan to implement the joint or combined strategic guidance and to give direction to his subordinate component commands. Ground operations planning must be coordinated with air and naval operations plans to assure mutual support.

Campaign plans set long-term goals—strategic aims such as control of a geographical area, reestablishment of political boundaries, or the defeat of an enemy force in the theater of operations. These must be accomplished in phases in most cases. Accordingly, the campaign plan normally provides both a general concept of operations for the entire campaign and a specific plan for the campaign's first phase.

Initially, the commander must specify how the enemy is to be defeated. The method chosen must, of course, be attainable with the means at hand. It should also aim for the fastest possible solution at the lowest possible cost in lives and materiel.

Above all else, the method selected must be effective. A protracted campaign rarely serves strategic purposes well and usually increases the force's exposure to damage or defeat. An effective campaign plan orients on what Clausewitz called the enemy's "centers of gravity," his sources of physical strength or psychological balance. If such a center of gravity is attacked (or occasionally merely threatened), the enemy's position becomes untenable.

There are a number of general ways to defeat a large enemy force in a theater. Each has historical precedents and can be used either singly or in combination. These begin with physical destruction of the enemy force, the most costly albeit direct way of winning. They extend to less direct methods such as reducing the enemy's strength by defeating or otherwise depriving him of his allies; separating his armies in the field to confront him with piecemeal defeat; preventing his deployment; destroying his logistic support; occupying decisive terrain to force him to fight under unfavorable conditions; or carrying the war into his homeland.

Strategic guidance will constrain operational methods by ruling out some otherwise attractive alternatives. Withholding of nuclear weapons, prohibiting the unopposed surrender of territory or cities, exempting the territory of certain nations from operations, and limiting the use of aerial bombing are examples of the curbs that strategy may impose on operations.

Strategic aims and guidance, reasonable assumptions about enemy intentions and capabilities, available resources, and the geography of theater, together form the starting point of campaign planning. Staff estimates are thus broader in campaign planning than in tactical operations.

Units with operational responsibilities perform intelligence operations and analyses for the campaign, its major operations, as well as its battles. These actions take a larger view of the theater and of the enemy. They are oriented on larger enemy units, to include air and naval formations, and units with specialized operational capabilities. They cover the entire theater of operations, its airspace as well as contiguous waters.

As in tactical level analysis, numbers, types, mobility, morale, and equipment of enemy forces are considered. Additionally, operational level commanders take into account the enemy's doctrine and patterns of large unit operations, the personalities and idiosyncrasies of his senior commanders, and his air and naval capabilities. Campaign planners also review the influences of alliances on enemy courses of actions, the differences in quality and capabilities of troops of different nationalities, the attitudes of the civilian population in areas controlled by the enemy, and the enemy's dependence on external support and particular facilities. Finally, they advise the commander on the enemy's capacity for and vulnerability to nuclear or chemical weapons, unconventional warfare, and psychological operations.

Most important, because of the scope and duration of campaigns and major operations, and the consequently broad range of enemy options, operational intelligence must attempt to probe the mind of the enemy commander. It must see the theater through his eyes, visualize which courses of action are open to him, and estimate which he is most likely to adopt.

Operational considerations of terrain also differ. Most theaters of operations are separated from others by considerable distances or major physical features such as mountain ranges, large rivers, or even oceans. Terrain within a theater possesses an inherent geological structure which aids operational analysis. River valleys or basins, plateaus, river deltas, peninsulas, mountain or highland regions, plains, and islands all have operational significance. And facilities important to movement, air support, and combat service support—ports, highways, rail lines, and sources of food, fuel, and water—will affect the operations of both combatants.

Large unit commanders and their staffs must be able to visualize the theater of operations in the rough terms of localities. The intelligence estimate must set those localities in their proper relationship to permit the commander to direct operations far beyond his field of view and to plan well into the future.

In preparing the campaign intelligence estimate, staff officers make use of the reconnaissance and surveillance assets of all services, allies, and national agencies. They also use all available human sources from agents to guerrillas and long-range reconnaissance units and the meteorological and geographical references on the area.

Factors affecting friendly capabilities and courses of action include the relative strength, composition, dispositions, and general readiness of ground, air, and naval forces. Campaign planners normally have to take allied strengths into account as well. The arms and equipment of these forces are considered as well as their special capabilities and limitations. Quality of staffs,

logistics support, ease of interoperability, and personalities and abilities of individual allied commanders all merit consideration. Capabilities for long distance movement, interoperability of ground, air, and naval forces, and allied forces' freedom to operate outside their own national territories should also be reviewed.

Once he has determined the enemy's center of gravity and analyzed the major factors which affect the campaign, the commander in a theater of operations selects a course of action. He elaborates this in his concept of operation for the campaign. Ideally, the concept embodies an indirect approach that preserves the strength of the force for decisive battles. While articulating the long-range goal of the force, it should also lay out the conduct of the first phase of the campaign in some detail. In almost all cases, deception will be vital to operational success. The commander must attempt to mislead the enemy concerning when, where, and how he will concentrate for battle and what his ultimate aims are. Ground operations must be fully synchronized with air and sea operations; air interdiction should complement ground maneuver in both the short and long terms.

The plan for the first phase of the campaign states the commander's intent, distributes forces to major subordinate units, disposes the force for operations, and coordinates air and naval support of ground maneuver. The general object of the plan is to set the terms for the next battle to the greatest advantage of the friendly force.

Good campaign plans also provide options for the operation underway and for the period following the coming battle. "Branches" to the plan—options for changing dispositions, orientation, or direction of movement and accepting or declining battle—preserve the commander's freedom of action. Such provisions for flexibility anticipate the enemy's likely actions and give the commander a means of dealing with them quickly. Expressed as contingency plans, such branches from the plan can be of decisive importance since they shorten the friendly decision cycle and may allow the large unit commander to act faster than his opponent.

Actions after battle or *sequels* are also an important means of anticipating the course of action and accelerating the decision cycle. Sequels to a future battle are based on possible outcomes—victory, defeat, or stalemate. They establish general dispositions, objectives, and missions for subordinate units after the battle. They then can be amended as necessary and ordered into effect.

Such plans are crucial to operational success because they determine how tactical success will be exploited or the operational consequences of tactical setbacks minimized. Transition to exploitation, counteroffensive, withdrawal, retreat, or reorientation of the main effort should be addressed as possible sequels to the planned battle. All of these actions depend on timely execution. They can only be carried out effectively if they have been planned in advance. In most cases, they will require the retention of an operational reserve.

MAJOR OPERATIONS PLANNING

Much of what has been said about campaign planning applies to the planning of major operations within the campaign. Major operations are planned well in advance. Major operations planning may begin before war or as "branches" and "sequels" to a campaign plan which identify missions, forces, and resources. Operational commanders must also anticipate shifts in the direction of operations. In December of 1944, Patton was able to wheel much of Third US Army 90 degrees in less than 72 hours to respond to the crisis which resulted in the Battle of the Bulge because his staff had conducted the necessary preliminary planning even before Third Army received the mission to do so.

Major operations are the coordinated elements of phases of a campaign. The success or failure of a major operation will have a decisive impact on the conduct of a particular phase of a campaign. For example, two successive major operations were conducted during the breakout phase of the WWII campaign which began with the landing of allied forces in Normandy and ended with link-up with Russian forces on the Elbe River. "Operation Goodwood," launched by British forces under Montgomery, attracted the bulk of German reserves to the northern part of the Normandy beachhead. US forces under Bradley then launched "Operation Cobra" in the south, resulting in a successful breakout. The landings at Inchon by X Corps and the supporting breakout of the balance of Eighth Army from Pusan in the Korean war are another example of complementary major operations.

While major operations are usually joint operations, they may also occasionally be independent operations. Even then, however, joint planning will be required. Normally, one major ground operation will receive priority and constitute the main effort. This decision at the level of campaign planning will affect various aspects of air and naval planning by outlining priorities and effects desired to complement large scale ground action. In general, operational planning commits forces and support to corps and armies for an extended period. Commanders of corps and armies receive long-range objectives and great freedom in design of their own operations. Operational plans also provide for close integration of psychological operations, unconventional warfare, and civil-military operations in support of the campaign.

CONDUCTING CAMPAIGNS AND MAJOR OPERATIONS

At the operational level of war, large unit commanders mass or maneuver tactical formations to bring the enemy to battle under the best terms possible. Attacks in depth with air-delivered weapons, missiles, and airmobile troops isolate portions of the enemy's force for attack or break up the continuity of his operation.

The operational situation may be static and positional or it may be fought in the fluid circumstances of open warfare in which large units move rather freely. The defender commonly tries to stabilize operations until he can assume the offensive himself. The attacker tries to promote the conditions of open warfare in which enemy forces can be separated and defeated piecemeal and large operational gains can be made.

In small theaters or where force densities are high, static conditions are likely to arise. When the campaign is fought over a large area or between relatively small forces, open warfare may predominate. In most cases, the two conditions are likely to alternate with periods of stability following large operational gains. The mobility of modern armies, however, makes open warfare possible even in small theaters of operations.

In static situations, operational commanders attempt to seize the initiative by defeating enemy attacks or rupturing enemy defenses. Only by producing a fluid situation can they make large gains and gain the advantages of maneuver on a large scale.

In open warfare, large unit commanders conduct aggressive reconnaissance and employ advance security forces to preserve their freedom of action. In trying to mass decisive strength at the decisive point, commanders maintain contact with the enemy and adjust their movements to conceal their intentions and to bring their forces to bear against an enemy vulnerability.

This requires the coordinated movement of large forces to preserve mutual support, sufficient air defense, adequate service support, and ready access to operational reserves. Original plans for concentration may demand modification as the enemy situation changes or becomes clear. Therefore, tactical formations must be able to modify directions of movement or orientation of defenses during operations.

During battle, the larger operation continues. Tactical formations may have to be moved in response to the operational situation or the battle itself may have to be shaped to meet operational objectives. The greatest concern of the large unit commander during battle will be to defeat the enemy's operational reserves and commit his own at the decisive time and place. Friendly operational reserves—corps or divisions held in reserve by the large unit commander—are used to exploit the results of battle by penetrating enemy defenses completely. In defense, such reserves execute the commander's counterstroke to defeat the attack or initiate the counteroffensive. In case of a reverse, the operational reserve can limit the enemy's success or cover the force's withdrawal.

A vital consideration for operational commanders during a campaign is sensing *culminating points*. Culminating points are reached when the balance of strength shifts from the attacking force to its opponent. This happens when an attacker has pushed as far as he can without losing his advantage over the defender. Overextension, lengthening lines of support, and the cumulative effects of battle losses and rear area protection efforts can sap the attacker's strength and compel him to assume the defense if he has been unable to defeat the defender. (See Appendix B for a more detailed discussion of culminating points).

In the attack, operational commanders design their campaigns to defeat the enemy prior to reaching their culminating point. Defending commanders try to avoid a decision until the attacker has to assume the defense himself. The attacker must sense his own culminating point and avoid overextension. Since all offensive operations end in defensive dispositions, this phase of the campaign should be foreseen and planned.

PLANNING AND CONDUCTING TACTICAL OPERATIONS

Tactical operations are the conduct of battles and engagements within the context of campaigns and major operations. They are the domain of corps and smaller units. They are supported by higher echelons of command who set the terms of battle and provide support for it. Brigades and smaller units may fight engagements—smaller, separate actions—either as part of a battle or as separate actions. Tactical success is measured by the success or failure to achieve aims set by higher commanders.

Battles are large engagements involving brigades and larger forces. They may be localized, brief and intense or they may involve numerous engagements over a large area that take days to resolve. In any case, their effects are felt over a large area, and actions outside of the area of direct, sustained combat can greatly influence their outcome.

The conduct of battles differs from that of campaigns and major operations in some important respects. Speed of response, ability to change direction, and sensitivity to short-term events are among these differences. Conduct of both depends on initiative, agility, depth, and synchronization, however, and, in both, leaders should observe the imperatives of modern combat.

In conducting battles and engagements, commanders must act vigorously and boldly. They must follow the course of the fight throughout the contested area to seize opportunities for decisive action. They must also be willing to take risks in order to inflict heavy losses on the enemy and to retain the initiative.

Corps and divisions conduct mutually supporting operations simultaneously in three areas—close, deep, and rear. All tactical operations require overall unity of effort throughout the battle, using every available element of combat power. Tactical operations must consider the effects of enemy air power, of nuclear and chemical weapons, and of electronic warfare operations. Most importantly, tactical operations are influenced by the nonquantifiable elements of combat power: courageous, well-trained soldiers, and skillful, effective leaders.

To ensure success, tacticians concentrate on—

- Anticipating the enemy.
- Indirect approaches.
- Deception and effective OPSEC.
- Speed and violence.
- Flexibility and reliance on the initiative of junior leaders.
- Rapid decision-making.
- Clearly defined objectives and operational concepts.
- A clearly designated main effort.
- Actions throughout the depth of the battle area.
- Joint operations with our sister services.

TACTICAL PLANNING

Tactical planning centers on preparation for battles and engagements. Like operational planning, tactical planning begins with the assignment of a mission or with the commander's recognition of a requirement. It continues until the mission is complete. The planning process is described in detail in FM 101-5. In essence it requires full definition of the mission, collection of all pertinent information, development and analysis of options, and, finally, a decision which forms the basis for a plan or order. This process is a continuous cycle. Planning is as thorough as time allows. The key to successful planning is anticipation of future events and being prepared for contingencies.

After the mission has been analyzed, the most important task of a staff is collecting information. This normally amounts to updating existing estimates and analyzing the facts in the light of the unit's new mission.

All primary staff officers have responsibilities for collecting information and making estimates before and during operations. Not only do they collect information, they also supervise operations to bring strength, readiness, training, and supply stocks to the highest levels possible prior to the operation. The aim of all these activities is to provide the commander with the greatest strength possible and a clear understanding of the situation. Planning for combat service support is discussed in Chapter 4.

Preparing the intelligence estimate differs from other planning. It concentrates on physical phenomena—terrain and weather—which cannot be significantly modified. It also demands the acquisition of information about the enemy that the opposing commander tries to withhold and misrepresent.

In tactical planning, the *scheme of maneuver* is the central expression of the commander's concept for close operations. The scheme of maneuver—

* Outlines the movements of the force.
* Identifies objectives or areas to be retained.
* Assigns reponsibilities for zones, sectors, or areas.
* Prescribes formations or dispositions when necessary.
* Identifies maneuver options which may develop during an operation.

The commander's scheme of maneuver usually determines the subsequent allocation of forces and governs the design of supporting plans or annexes. Fires, barriers, air defense priorities, electronic warfare (EW), deception efforts, combat support, and combat service support (CSS) arrangements are normally guided by and coordinated with the scheme of maneuver.

Whenever possible, commanders design their tactical plans to avoid the enemy's strength and strike at his weaknesses. Maneuver units can inflict the greatest damage on the enemy by avoiding head-on encounters with his deployed forces. Instead they should operate on his flanks and rear, where direct fire is most effective, psychological shock is the greatest, and the enemy is least prepared to fight. Maneuver in defensive counterattacks is particularly important and must be planned in detail. By coordinating attacks on the enemy in depth with attacks on his forward units, the commander—

* Preserves or secures the initiative.
* Upsets the enemy's plan.
* Disrupts his coordination.
* Destroys his most sensitive forces—reserves, artillery, command and control, and logistic support.

The tactical plan should gain surprise. It should use indirect approaches and flank positions which do not attract immediate attention. Subordinate commanders should have the greatest possible freedom to maneuver.

The tactical plan should include supplementary control measures such as routes, axes, objectives, and battle positions for implementation on order. Such measures provide the necessary flexibility for responding to changes in the situation. Their use gives the commander a substantial advantage by allowing him to implement changes quickly.

The plan should also designate axes of advance and routes for the commitment or movement of reserves or for the forward or rearward passage of one unit through another. It should also identify air axes for the maneuver of attack helicopter and air cavalry units or for the helicopter movement of air assault units and other forces.

Movement of supporting units is also critical to the success of the tactical plan. Commanders must assure the uninterrupted support of field artillery, air defense, air support, engineer, military intelligence, and logistic units. To do so, they must plan multiple routes throughout the area of operations and closely control their use. Military police must be prepared to facilitate these movements, to prevent congestion, and to respond to changes in the maneuver plan.

When planning operations, the commanders must take into account the effects of nuclear and chemical weapons. Commanders must avoid creating lucrative targets as they maneuver. They should also avoid positions which can be isolated by the obstacles that nuclear weapons create. Commanders must constantly seek to minimize the overall risk by dispersing their commands into small units that are not worthwhile targets. Yet they must concentrate sufficient combat power to accomplish the mission.

This dilemma is dynamic. The degree of risk changes as the distance between opposing forces changes. Initially, maneuver forces will disperse to avoid presenting lucrative targets. As the distance from the enemy decreases, maneuver units will concentrate over multiple routes at the decisive time and place, then disperse again after defeating the enemy.

The tactical plan must also consider the airspace over a unit's area of responsibility. Air and ground movements in support of the commander's scheme of maneuver must be coordinated with the Air Force, Army aviation, air defense units, and ground maneuver units.

Effective tactical planning is the best way to assure synchronization in execution. Usually, the more effective the plan, the less synchronization will be hostage to active command and control once operations begin.

Once committed to combat, however, commanders must be prepared to modify their actions to fit the situation. This requires balance and judgment. The commander should not abandon his plan too readily, thus forfeiting the coordination it represents. Under the pressures of combat—uncertainty, unexpected events, and great

violence—the commander must rely on his initial estimate and resist the temptation to change his plan at the first difficulty.

At the same time, even the most farsighted plan will have to be adjusted to accommodate changes at some point. The commander must be able to recognize that critical point. He must also be well-informed about the situation to make this judgment and have the means to react to opportunities or threats without losing synchronization.

CONDUCTING TACTICAL OPERATIONS

Air-land battle tactical offensives are rapid, violent operations that seek enemy soft spots, rapidly shift the main effort, and exploit successes promptly. The attacker creates a fluid situation, maintains the initiative, and destroys the coherence of the enemy defense. Using supporting and reserve units flexibly, the attack continues for as long as it takes to achieve objectives.

Air-land battle tactical defenses combine static and dynamic elements. Fires, obstacles, and static elements of the defense stop or contain enemy movement. Delays and counterattacks slow and defeat segments of the attacking force. Deep and rear operations extend tactical opportunities and preserve freedom of action. These actions allow the defender to break the attacker's momentum, to present him with the unexpected, to defeat his combined arms cooperation, and to gain the initiative and win.

Tactical commanders will fight the enemy in an *area of operations*, a specific zone or sector assigned to them. But they must also identify and monitor enemy activities outside their areas of operation which could affect their future operations. This larger *area of interest* will vary in size and shape from operation to operation. It should include all enemy activities which might affect the friendly force throughout the duration of the operation in question, and may therefore extend forward, to the flanks, and to the rear of the area of operations. Commanders plan actions against enemy forces behind and beyond their forward line of own troops (FLOT) as part of tactical operations. Both deep and rear operations may require the reconnaissance and strike support of higher echelons of command and, frequently, of their supporting aerial forces.

At the tactical level, the commander structures close operations with maneuver, fires, and obstacles to concentrate superior combat power on the enemy's flanks and rear. Whether attacking or defending, the tactical commander fights a unified battle against the enemy's committed forces and his forces in depth and preserves his own freedom of action in the rear area.

CLOSE OPERATIONS

Close operations involve the fight between the committed forces and the readily available tactical reserves of both combatants. Its principal elements are the coordinated plans for maneuver and fire support. These elements, however, rely on the integrated suppport of all other arms and services.

PLANNING AREAS

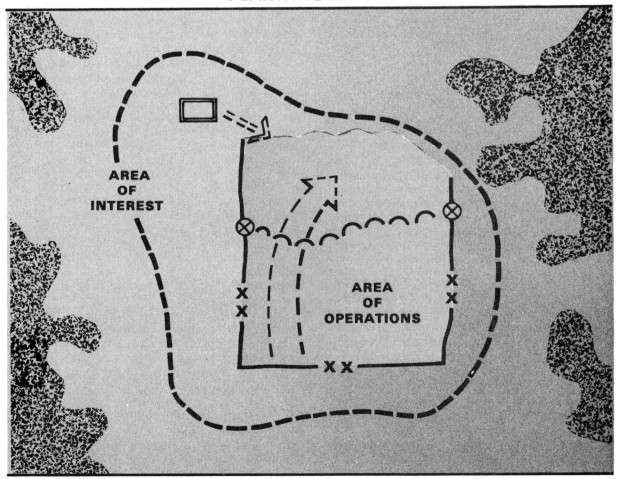

At the tactical level, corps and smaller units maneuver to attack the enemy's flanks, rear, or supporting formations. By doing so, they sustain the initiative, exploit success, and reduce their own vulnerability. Normally supported by direct and indirect fires, tactical commanders maneuver to obtain a local position of advantage. Often part of the maneuvering force of battalion size or smaller provides fire to support movements of other parts. Once it comes into contact with the enemy, such a maneuvering force advances using fire and movement. In using fire and movement, one element of an engaged force adds its suppressive direct fires to the supporting indirect fires of mortars, artillery, naval guns, or close air support. This firepower makes movement by another element possible. A force may close with the enemy by alternating its elements between fire and movement.

In tactical operations, the commander assigns the main effort to one of his subordinate elements. He supports the main effort with every asset available and strives to throw the enemy off balance by striking at enemy vulnerabilities which he creates as the enemy uncovers. If the main effort does not succeed or if in the course of the fight an unanticipated enemy vulnerability develops, tactical commanders from corps to company level must rapidly be able to shift the orientation of the main effort or shift the main effort to another unit.

To remain flexible, the tactical commander needs to retain a reserve and operate from appropriate formations. He should also provide for likely contingencies by identifying supporting attacks, exploitation axes, counterattack plans, and defensive positions in depth or on flanks as "on-order" tasks. Such supplementary actions should be shown on tactical overlays, supported with planned fires, and, when possible, with obstacles. In smaller units, battle drills provide this flexibility. In brigades, divisions, and corps, though, supplementary control measures and contingency plans make it possible.

DEEP OPERATIONS

The commander supports his basic scheme of maneuver with deep operations against specific enemy forces in depth that threaten his success. In either attack or defense, well-timed deep operations against enemy forces not yet in contact are necessary for success. Successful deep operations limit the enemy's freedom of action, alter the tempo of operations in favor of the friendly force, and isolate the close fight on advantageous terms. Deep operations are an integral part of the overall plan; they selectively attack vulnerable enemy forces and facilities as a synchronized part of the unified tactical effort. Divisional brigades and smaller tactical units do not normally conduct separate deep operations. But their tactical planning and operations must anticipate the arrival of enemy follow-on forces, prevent surprise through normal security measures forward, and deceive the enemy as to the best time and place to commit those follow-on forces.

At each appropriate level of command, deep operations must be based on a careful analysis of enemy capabilities to interfere with current and planned operations. Only those enemy forces that threaten the conduct of friendly operations are relevant. Of those which are relevant, priority should be given to those targets vulnerable to interdiction which are most critical to the enemy's operations. A thorough IPB and timely intelligence from organic and supporting sources help to identify targets whose loss or damage will most diminish the enemy's ability to concentrate forces, to control operations, or to support the battle at critical times.

To conduct deep operations successfully, the fire support coordinator, the G3, and the G2 must pay close and continuous attention to the unit's area of interest. The size of the area of interest will vary with the mission, terrain, and mobility of the enemy. Areas of interest include territory adjacent to and beyond a unit's area of operations. They extend to any area from which enemy forces may be capable of affecting a particular friendly forces' operation. Commanders develop areas of interest to support their specific operations. A division commander, for example, should anticipate the enemy's ability to influence his operation and his divisions' own requirements for future operations in order to define his area of interest.

Named areas of interest (NAI), covering routes or avenues of approach, directions of enemy movement, and specific enemy units are the critical points in an area of interest. They focus the intelligence collection effort and the fires of a unit during the battle. Corps or divisions may restrict the fires of adjacent, supporting, or subordinate units by a variety of control measures. Close coordination between levels of command is necessary to assure that deep operations plans support the overall concept of operations and neither duplicate nor impede each other.

The corps area of interest overlaps those of its divisions just as the division's area of interest and deep actions overlay those of its brigades. Each level of command conducts deep operations simultaneously. In many instances, enemy units will concern both superior and subordinate commanders. For example, both corps and divisions may follow the second echelon divisions of an enemy army.

Commanders may prohibit the engagement of particular forces or physical targets in a subordinate's area of operation if it is to their advantage to allow the unimpeded movement of the enemy in certain areas or to prevent the destruction of a facility. In some cases, corps or division commanders may limit their subordinates' responsibilities to close actions and reserve all actions in depth for themselves. Ordinarily, however, all appropriate levels of command will fight in depth.

Corps and larger units have access to service and national intelligence collection means which directly support the planning and conduct of deep operations. Divisions,

separate brigades, and regiments must depend more heavily on intelligence obtained by higher levels of command for their operations in depth.

Commanders attack critical targets in depth with organic and supporting weapons. Long-range weapons will be relatively scarce. Consequently, they should be used against targets whose loss or disruption will yield the greatest benefit to current and anticipated close operations. The primary strike assets for deep attack are aerial, artillery, and missile weapons. However, conventional and unconventional ground and air maneuver units can also interdict enemy movement and neutralize key facilities in depth. Tactical electronic warfare systems can be used in lieu of fire support to attack enemy command and control of follow-on forces. If their use were authorized, nuclear weapons would be particularly effective in engaging follow-on formations or forces in depth because of their inherent power and because of reduced risk to friendly troops. Deception also plays a part in delaying, disrupting, and diverting an enemy and in frustrating his plans for committing follow-on forces.

Target development is an intelligence activity that supports the commander's efforts to identify, locate, and strike high value targets—key enemy forces, facilities, or assets—as part of his deep operations plan. In order to assess target value, candidate targets must be evaluated using tactically meaningful criteria. High value targets are those which are—

- *Relevant* to the overall operation planned or in progress, in that they can affect the force's ability to accomplish the mission.

- *Most threatening* to accomplishment of the mission. Since not all relevant targets can be dealt with, they must be prioritized.

- *Most damaging* to the coherence of enemy operations. Among relevant and threatening targets, these are the targets of choice.

Intelligence officers develop basic target information, then employ intelligence, surveillance, and target-acquisition assets to locate targets accurately enough for attack. Following such attacks, intelligence officers assess their effects and monitor the target to assure that the commander's intention has been accomplished.

Only in rare cases will commanders be able to destroy enemy forces in depth. However, they will often be able to delay, disrupt, or divert selected enemy forces by destroying portions of those forces, by interrupting their support, or by creating obstacles in depth. To obtain the desired tactical result, these efforts must be synchronized with the overall operation.

In the offense, deep operations initially isolate, immobilize, and weaken defenders in depth. As the attack continues, actions against deep targets sustain momentum by preventing the reorganization of coherent defenses, by blocking the movement of enemy reserves, and by preventing the escape of defending units. In the defense, the commander uses deep actions to prevent the enemy from concentrating overwhelming combat power at the time and place of his choice. The major objectives may be to separate and disrupt attacking echelons, to protect the defender's maneuver, or to degrade the enemy's fire support, command and control, communications, combat support, and combat service support.

Deep operations open opportunities for decisive action by reducing the enemy's closure rate or coordination. They create periods of friendly *local* superiority in which to win battles or engagements. If the enemy is prevented from reinforcing his committed forces at a critical time, he may be defeated in detail.

REAR OPERATIONS

Operations in the rear area contribute to the unified battle plan by preserving the commander's freedom of action and assuring uninterrupted support of the battle. They are, in effect, the defense against the enemy's deep operations.

The commander's concept for rear operations stresses security of all rear area activities and facilities. The demands of the overall battle determine the priorities for the rear operations. Routes needed by reserves and the reserves themselves, airbases and fire support, and combat support and combat service support units whose assistance to the main effort is vital should receive the highest priority for protection in the rear area. Certain key facilities or features such as traffic choke points, tunnels and bridges, ammunition and fuel storage points, and dams may also require special protection. Air defense and security against ground attack are equally important; both must be carefully planned. Most crucial will be the establishment of a reliable system for gauging and monitoring the true situation in the rear.

To concentrate protective efforts on key units, features, and facilities, the commander will have to accept risks elsewhere. Rear area installations that do not contribute immediate or continuous support to tactical operations should be expected to defend themselves against all but the greatest threats during the critical period of the battle.

Rearward security will require the commander to balance a variety of competing risks. For example, clustering of support activities reduces their vulnerability to ground attack, but can increase their vulnerability to air, missile, or nuclear/chemical attack. Likewise, locating key facilities away from high-speed routes minimizes their vulnerability to enemy ground penetrations, but may also reduce their accessibility to units requiring support. And dispersal of critical stocks—fuel, ammunition, and spares—reduces the risks of loss, but also reduces the ease and speed of distribution. The commander must therefore continually reassess the enemy threat to his rear, and adjust his rear operations as that threat and his own tactical situation change.

Because of the threats of air strikes, air assault, guerrilla action, the interference of infiltrators, or penetrating enemy forces, all units in the rear area should have plans to defend themselves and to move if necessary. Scatterable mines, fires, and tree blow-down will impede the movement of reserves, artillery units, and engineers unless key routes are scouted periodically. Alternate routes should be planned for units whose movement is vital to the commander's plan.

The placement of reserves, air defense artillery (ADA) units, engineers, cavalry, military police (MP), field artillery, and command posts all require special attention. All may have key roles in the battle to retain freedom of action in the rear area.

Army aviation units as the most mobile forces available may have to be used to counter rear area threats—particularly air landings and penetrations of high speed forward detachments. However, commitment of aviation units, artillery forces, or the reserve forces to the rear battle will almost invariably come at the expense of the main effort. The intent of enemy deep operations may be precisely to divert attention and effort away from the point of decision at a crucial time. Accordingly, as much as possible, other forces, especially MPs, should be used in preference to forces committed to or projected for use in the close fight.

Dangerous approaches to the rear and potential landing zones can be obstructed prior to battle. They can also be observed and guarded by small forces during battle or avoided when the rear area is organized. See FM 90-14 for details.

MAJOR FUNCTIONAL AREAS

To be effective, the operations of all units must be coordinated combined arms actions. Assets available to support operations vary with the level of command, the type of force, and the supporting forces available. In most cases, however, commanders at both operational and tactical levels must coordinate the following functions:

- Maneuver.
- Conventional, nuclear, and chemical fires.
- Intelligence.
- Tactical air operations.
- Joint suppression of enemy air defense.
- Engineer support.
- Air defense.
- Communications.
- Airspace coordination.
- Deception.
- Electronic warfare.
- Reconstitution.
- Psychological operations.
- Amphibious operations.
- Special operating forces.
- Civil-military operations.
- Logistic (see Chapter 4).

The combat and combat support arms of the Army, joined by tactical air forces, routinely cooperate in combined arms operations. Commanders must understand the basic capabilities of each arm as well as the complementary and reinforcing effects of combined arms to apply AirLand Battle doctrine.

This section describes the major functional activities which must be synchronized in time, space, and aim. It also describes the general capabilities of the combat and combat support arms. Full discussion of each is found in the appropriate branch manual. Specific treatments of combined arms action at each level of command can be found in field manuals for tactical units. Combat service support functions apart from reconstitution are described in the next chapter. The characteristics of CSS units and more details about support of operations are treated in FM 100-10.

MANEUVER

Maneuver and firepower are inseparable and complementary elements of combat. Although one might dominate a phase of the battle, the coordinated use of both characterizes all operations. Their joint use makes the destruction of larger enemy forces feasible and enhances the protection of a friendly force. When nuclear weapons are available for use, maneuver may mainly exploit the effects of fire.

Maneuver units may be task-organized for a particular mission to improve their combined arms capabilities. Battalions and companies normally perform a single function in their parent unit's plan whatever their organization. They defend, attack, or delay in cooperation with other battalions and companies. These units support their maneuver with their own mortars and also receive fire support from field artillery units as well as the support of engineers, chemical units, electronic warfare units, and Army aviation in some cases.

Divisions and brigades combine the efforts of their own units with the support they receive from higher echelons of command in their tactical operations. They fight combined arms battles and engagements employing every tactical means available. Different kinds of maneuver battalions, field artillery, aviation, engineers, ADA, tactical air support and sometimes naval fire support are integrated in support of brigade and division actions. Thus, organic and supporting combat, combat support, and combat service support units all combine to make vital complementary and supplementary contributions to these operations.

Corps combine arms in a similar fashion. They employ different types of divisions, separate brigades, and cavalry regiments in complementary ways. They arrange combat support and combat service support and integrate the support of other services to accomplish their missions.

Basic types of maneuver units are discussed in the following paragraphs:

Light Infantry. Light infantry can operate effectively in most terrain and weather. Light infantry may be the dominant arm in low intensity conflicts, particularly given their rapid strategic deployability. In such cases, they can take the initiative from light regular forces and insurgents by fighting them on equal terms. Heavier or more mobile units can support light infantry in large battles or engagements. In operations where armored forces predominate, light infantry units can—

- Capitalize on natural obstacles such as wetlands, forests, and mountains and occupy strongpoints in close terrain as pivots for operational and tactical level maneuver.

- Make initial penetrations in difficult terrain for exploitations by armor and mechanized infantry.

- Attack over approaches that are not feasible for heavy forces.

- Capture or defend forested and built-up areas.

- Control restrictive routes for use by other forces.

- Follow and support exploiting heavy forces when augmented with transportation.

- Conduct rear area operations, capitalizing on air mobility.

In operations in which light forces predominate, airborne, airmobile, or other light infantry lead the combined arms attack, and all other arms support the infantry.

Mechanized Infantry. Mechanized infantry complements armor through its ability to seize and hold ground. It provides overwatching antitank fires and suppresses enemy infantry and antitank guided missile elements. Infantrymen can dismount—

- To patrol difficult terrain.

- To clear or to emplace obstacles and minefields.

- To infiltrate and attack enemy positions.

- To protect tanks in urban and wooded areas and in limited-visibility conditions.

Mechanized infantrymen have the same mobility as tankers but less firepower and protection. Armor and mechanized infantry must perform as a team to defeat enemy armored forces. When equipped with infantry fighting vehicles, the mechanized infantry can accompany tanks in mounted assault, although care must be taken in determining when and where infantry must dismount to accomplish their mission. In the attack, such infantrymen can act as fixing forces. In the defense, they act as pivot points for maneuvering tank-heavy forces.

Motorized Infantry. Motorized infantry is more rapidly deployable than mechanized infantry, but more capable than light infantry of meeting and defeating heavy forces in open terrain. Motorized infantry derives its combat power from rapid ground mobility, heavy firepower, and superior command and control. It lacks the armor protection to survive against heavy forces in conditions where the terrain precludes rapid maneuver and affords little cover and concealment.

In conditions favoring its employment, motorized infantry can—

- Attack and destroy enemy forces in open terrain.

- Envelop or infiltrate weakly held enemy positions and attack vital assets in their rear.

- Exploit penetrations of stronger positions by heavier forces.

- Pursue and destroy retreating enemy forces.

- React rapidly to locate and destroy enemy forces operating in friendly rear areas.

- Dismount and fight as light infantry if necessary.

Armor. In mounted warfare, the tank is the primary offensive weapon. Its firepower, protection from enemy fire, and speed create the shock effect necessary to disrupt the enemy's operations and to defeat him. Tanks can destroy enemy armored vehicles, infantry, and antitank guided missile units. Tanks can break through suppressed defenses, exploit the success of an attack by striking deep into the enemy's rear areas, and pursue defeated enemy forces. Armored units can also blunt enemy attacks and launch counterattacks as part of a defense.

Armored units have several significant limitations. They are vulnerable in close terrain, such as forests and cities, and in limited-visibility conditions. They cannot cross most rivers and swamps without bridging, and they require substantial logistical support. Armor units are also slow to deploy strategically because their weight and amount of equipment require deployment by sea.

Cavalry. The basic tasks of cavalry units are reconnaissance and security. The ability of armored cavalry units to find the enemy, to develop the situation, and to provide the commander with reaction time and security also make them ideal for economy-of-force missions. Cavalry forces can delay an attacking enemy as well as assist in a withdrawal. When they are equipped or reinforced with tanks, cavalry units are also capable of attacking and defending, although these are not their normal missions.

Aviation. Three types of Army aviation units participate in combined arms operations: attack helicopters, air cavalry, and combat support aviation. Speed of movement, freedom from the effects of ground obstacles, and sensitivity to weather conditions characterize all aviation operations.

In today's Army, while aviation is relegated largely to support of ground maneuver, it increasingly offers opportunities for actual maneuver by air. Thus, attack helicopter units provide highly maneuverable antiarmor firepower. They use natural cover and speed to compensate for their vulnerabilities. They are ideally suited for situations in which rapid reaction time is important or terrain restricts ground forces. Attack helicopters are best suited for attacking moving enemy armor formations. Attack helicopter units—

- Overwatch ground maneuver forces with antitank fires.

- Attack the flanks and rear of attacking or withdrawing enemy formations.

- Counterattack enemy penetrations alone or in support of ground maneuver units.

- Conduct raids in enemy-held territory.

- Dominate key terrain by fire in support of ground maneuver forces.

- Engage enemy helicopters and close support aircraft.

Working alone or in conjunction with tactical aircraft, attack helicopters can defeat enemy armored formations. To be most effective, however, such missions require other combined arms elements to suppress enemy air defense.

Air cavalry units perform the same missions of reconnaissance and security as ground cavalry and are organic to all cavalry units. Because of their greater mobility, air cavalry troops can reconnoiter and maintain surveillance over a much larger area in a shorter period of time than ground troops can. During security operations, air cavalry reconnoiters, screens forward and to the flanks of moving ground forces, and acts as a rapid reaction force.

Combat support aviation gives dismounted infantry and ground antitank units an air assault capability, enabling them to move rapidly to the enemy's flanks or rear or by repositioning them rapidly in the defense. Combat support aviation can quickly move towed field artillery units and other lighter elements of the combined arms team as the commander dictates. It can also provide critical combat service support to

forward areas in the defense and to attacking formations when ground lines of communication have been interdicted or overloaded.

CONVENTIONAL, NUCLEAR, AND CHEMICAL FIRES

Fire support includes mortars, field artillery, naval gunfire, army aviation, and air-delivered weapons. The long range and great flexibility of the fire support system make it possible to shift the focus and concentration of fire support rapidly over wide ranges. The commander can use it to support his scheme of maneuver, to mass firepower rapidly without shifting maneuver forces, and to delay, to disrupt, or to destroy enemy forces in depth. Commanders use the fire support system to destroy, neutralize, or suppress surface targets including enemy weapons, formations or facilities, and fires from the enemy's rear. They also employ it to suppress enemy air defense and, upon approval by National Command Authorities, to execute nuclear packages as indicated by higher headquarters. In a large-scale nuclear conflict, fire support could become the principal means of destroying enemy forces. The scheme of maneuver would then be designed specifically to exploit the effects of the fire support.

Field Artillery. The principal fire support element in fire and maneuver is the field artillery. It not only provides conventional, nuclear, or chemical fires with cannon, rocket, and missile systems; but it also integrates all means of fire support available to the commander. Field artillery is capable of suppressing enemy direct fire forces, attacking enemy artillery and mortars, and delivering scatterable mines to isolate and to interdict enemy forces or to protect friendly operations. It contributes to deep operations by delaying or disrupting enemy forces in depth and by suppressing enemy air defense systems to facilitate Army and Air Force air operations. The artillery can also screen operations with smoke or illuminate the battlefield. Normally as mobile as the maneuver force it supports, field artillery can provide continuous fire in support of the commander's scheme of maneuver.

The commander exercises overall direction of the fire support system. Its weapons—mortars, guns, howitzers, rockets, guided missiles, and applicable tactical aircraft—are coordinated through a network of fire support teams, liaison parties, fire direction centers, and fire support elements. The commander uses this network to mass fires against area targets or to direct fires against point targets.

Fire support must be integrated with the unit's scheme of maneuver and its surveillance and target-acquisition efforts. The fire support system must be flexible enough to supply conventional fires without interruption as the tactical situation changes.

Commanders at all levels are responsible for integrating fire support into their plans. Corps and division commanders who command their own artillery employ their artillery commanders as fire support coordinators. Supporting artillery units provide commanders below division level with fire support officers. At all levels, fire support elements are capable of coordinating all the fire support necessary to the commander's plans. Air Force and Navy liaison teams at all levels down to battalion assist in coordinating fires provided by their respective services.

In integrating fire support into operations, the most important considerations are adequacy, flexibility, and continuity. In offensive operations, the main attack gets priority fire support while long-range systems strike defenses in depth, enemy reserves, or targets such as command posts, bridges, and defiles. In the defense, a broader balance of fire support is necessary, but the main effort is still allocated stronger fire support. Priority of support should change automatically when the commander shifts his main effort.

When maneuver forces have missions such as raids, deep attacks, or covering force operations, which take them beyond supporting distance of the main body, commanders must make special provision for their fire support. This may be provided by direct support field artillery battalions, dedicated batteries, or mortar support, depending on the size of the force and its mission.

Commanders must also make special provisions for foreseeable contingencies or phases of a maneuver operation. These may include—

- Time-on-target attacks of ambush areas in coordination with direct fires and a particular obstacle.

- Obscuration of open areas with smoke to facilitate ground maneuver.

- Suppression of enemy air defense (SEAD) fires in conjunction with attack helicopter, close air support, or joint air attack team operations.

- Final protective fires around a defensive position.

- Interdiction of a specific follow-on unit to complete an attack in progress.

Commanders also ensure flexibility by—

- Holding some of their artillery in general support.

- Giving artillery units on-order missions which orient them on likely contingencies.

- Reserving some of the distributed CAS missions for the force commander's use.

Commanders ensure continuous support by designating routes for artillery units and by planning air movement of weapons and ammunition. When rapid offensive progress occurs or defensive counterstrokes are planned beyond the FLOT, commanders must ensure that artillery units are in position to support the maneuver.

The large number of targets acquired during combat requires that commanders establish priorities. They can express these priorities in allocating assets, in positioning fire support units, in constraining ammunition expenditure, or in focusing the attack on specified types of targets.

The commander will also control fires by using standard control measures. Specific details of fire support planning and coordination are in FM 6-20.

Fire support of offensive maneuver using Army aviation assets poses unique planning and control problems. Because of the tempo of such operations, special provision must be made to assure artillery coverage of air assault targets. Typically, close air support and attack helicopters will have to furnish initial fire support until surface artillery is able to move into range. Even then, artillery coverage is apt to be limited, and control measures must allow for the effective integration of ground and air fires.

Nuclear Weapons. Nuclear fires may be delivered by aircraft, missiles, or cannon. A decision to use nuclear weapons would be based on strategic considerations at the highest policy levels. The authority to use nuclear weapons will be conveyed from the National Command Authority (NCA) through the operational chain of command. Even after authority is granted for employment of nuclear weapons, employment will be guided by strategic purposes more than by tactical effect. Accordingly, nuclear fire planning is subject to unique considerations.

First, far more than conventional fire planning, nuclear fire planning will require a high level of anticipation. Typically, nuclear packages grouping a specified number of weapons having specified delivery system/yield characteristics will be preplanned for use against specified target categories. Such packages are designed to achieve varying military effects, and thereby furnish NCAs and theater commanders with a range of options through which to accomplish desired strategic results.

Because of this high degree of preplanning, effective weapons employment will require continuous refinement of package targeting before and after release of weapons. Release will be predicated on a high confidence that the effects achieved will be precisely those intended—no more, no less. Commanders of delivery units must ensure

that all supporting activities—target acquisition, special ammunition distribution, nuclear control personnel and equipment, and operational security—are maintained continuously in a high state of readiness to execute on relatively short notice. This must be accomplished with minimum degradation of conventional fire support and without an abrupt and detectable shift in operating pattern.

Finally, nuclear planning must of course reflect the constraints and directives of higher authority to include procedures for warning friendly units, restrictions on collateral damage, and responsibilities for post-strike analysis. Special care must be taken not to create obstacles to friendly maneuver through the use of nuclear fire. Friendly aircraft of all services must be warned to avoid areas scheduled for nuclear strikes. The echelon which requests nuclear weapons should coordinate warning procedures to friendly forces through the theater Commander in Chief (CINC) or joint force commander (JFC).

In general, preferred targets might be—

- Enemy nuclear delivery systems.
- Key command and control elements.
- Support forces in the rear of committed elements.
- Follow-on or deep-echeloned forces.
- Reserves.

Divisions and corps will develop packages for possible use in their areas of operations based on the above criteria and their particular situations. Each echelon of command will review its subordinate echelons nuclear fire plans and will integrate them into its own plans. Plans at all echelons will be developed to permit *but not depend upon* nuclear weapons employment.

Chemical Weapons. US policy prohibits the first use of lethal or incapacitating chemical munitions. However, because the United States has reserved the right to retaliate if enemies use chemical weapons, Army units must be prepared to conduct offensive chemical operations. Such preparation acts as a deterrent to enemy use of chemicals. Only the NCA can grant authority to employ chemical munitions. When granted, such authority will also provide specific guidance governing their use. While the use of chemical weapons does not bear the enormous strategic risks associated with nuclear weapons, it can equally alter the course of operations in a theater significantly.

Commanders must be prepared to integrate chemical weapons into their fire plans on receipt of chemical release. Because the chemical expenditure rates necessary to produce a significant effect on a well-trained, well-equipped enemy are high, commanders must carefully consider how chemical weapons will affect their own operations and logistics.

Chemical agents are either persistent or nonpersistent. When properly employed in mass and without warning, chemical fires can—

- Cause high casualties among poorly trained or poorly equipped troops.

- Degrade the effectiveness of weapons, vehicles, and command posts by causing their operators to wear protective equipment.

- Restrict the use of weapons, supplies, and equipment by contamination.

- Disrupt rear area operations and troop movement.

- Enhance the effects of other fire support by slowing enemy movement.

- Reduce the speed, cohesion, and freedom of movement of enemy formations.

- Restrict or deny the use of key terrain.

- Force the enemy to undertake decontamination operations, thereby producing fresh targets for chemical or other fire support means.

INTELLIGENCE

Intelligence operations are the organized efforts of a commander to gather information on terrain, weather, and the enemy. Obtaining useful intelligence *prior to* the initiation of operations is a vital task. Assembling an accurate picture of the battlefield requires centralized direction, simultaneous action at all levels of command, and timely distribution of information throughout the command. Intelligence operations normally begin before a tactical operation and continue as the battle develops. Intelligence operations may employ any of the unit's resources—units in contact with the enemy, cavalry units, patrols, electronic warfare units, field artillery radars—and they routinely rely on higher levels of command for intelligence support. Local population and government agencies also add to the intelligence picture.

Commanders provide direction for the intelligence effort by articulating the priority intelligence requirements (PIR) and information requirements (IR) needed in the decision-making process. To ensure that intelligence provides the basis for timely tactical decisions, commanders must plan and control intelligence operations with the same level of interest and personal involvement that they devote to combat operations. In particular, they must assure that intelligence is distributed to meet their subordinates' needs.

The intelligence officer (G2 or S2) must inform the commander and all others concerned regarding the enemy situation and capabilities, terrain, and weather. He—

- Conducts continuous intelligence preparation of the battlefield (IPB).

- Directs intelligence-collection activities.

- Assesses their results.

- Refines the requirements for further collecting efforts.

- Develops targets.

- Provides OPSEC information to the G3.

The G2 or the S2 converts the commander's PIR and IR into specific missions for available collection resources. He directs the evaluation and interpretation of information collected from all sources, and he directs the timely dissemination of intelligence and combat information to the concerned units.

Tactical commanders focus their intelligence operations within both their areas of operation and their larger area of interest. The IPB should start well before combat operations begin. It is a continuous, integrated, and comprehensive analysis of the effects of enemy capabilities, terrain, and weather on operations. The IPB should extend throughout a unit's entire area of interest, focusing on specific units or NAI designated by the commander. It includes forward and rear areas as well as adjacent terrain. Using overlays, graphic displays, and templating techniques, the IPB process increases the accuracy and timeliness of the intelligence available to the commander.

TACTICAL AIR OPERATIONS

The first consideration in employing air forces is gaining and maintaining the freedom of action to conduct operations against the enemy. Control of the air environment gives commanders the freedom to conduct successful attacks which can neutralize or destroy an enemy's warfighting potential. This campaign for control is a continuous attempt to gain and maintain the capability to use the enemy's airspace to perform combat missions and to deny the enemy the use of friendly airspace. Control of the air environment enables land forces to carry out a plan of action without interference from an enemy's air forces. Without this control, tactical flexibility is lost.

Integrated strategic, operational, and tactical actions produce a cumulative effect on the enemy's ability to wage war. Successful strategic attacks directed against the heartland will normally produce direct effects on an enemy nation or alliance. Their impact on the military forces engaged in tactical action, however, may be delayed because of the inherent momentum of forces actively engaged in combat and those reserve forces ready to enter the action. Consequently, an air commander must exploit the devastating firepower of airpower to disrupt that momentum and place an enemy's land forces at risk. Air forces must attack not only those enemy forces in contact, but enemy forces held in reserve or rear echelons as well.

The strengths of the enemy in terms of forces, battle sustaining supplies, and combat reserves are most vulnerable to air attack when concentrated, but these targets may be relatively secure when dispersed in their battle areas. While the urgency of enemy actions may require direct attacks against forces in contact, air forces are normally more efficiently used to attack in depth those targets whose destruction, disruption, or delay will deny the enemy the time and space to employ forces effectively. The effect of these attacks is greatest when the enemy is engaged in a highly mobile, maneuver scheme of operation dependent on urgent resupply of combat reserves and consumables. A systematic and persistent plan of attack produces a connected series of actions and reactions that are closely coordinated between air and land commanders. Although battlefield situations may interrupt this plan of attack, air and land commanders must remain committed to their coordinated actions and must not allow the impact of airpower to be diverted away from the main objective.

The success of both offensive and defensive operations can depend greatly on massing airpower at decisive points. Effective actions to gain air superiority and to interdict an enemy can limit the flexibility of his forces, deny him reinforcements, and enhance opportunities for friendly commanders to seize the initiative through counteroffensive action. Close air support can enhance counteroffensive actions by creating opportunities to break through enemy lines, protecting the flanks of a penetration, or preventing the counter-maneuver of enemy surface forces. Defensive requirements to blunt an enemy offensive may also dictate the need for close air support. Close air support can protect the maneuver and withdrawal of land forces, protect rear area movements, or create avenues of escape.

Although adequate resources are required to defend friendly airspace, restricting such defense to aircraft on ground alert or orbiting on airborne alert, both increases the vulnerability of these aircraft and concedes air initiative to the enemy.

Enemy air can quickly mass attacks that can preoccupy the defense's attentions and actions, even to the extent of restricting friendly ground forces primarily to defensive actions. When air forces are primarily reactive, an air commander can reverse this disadvantage only by taking offensive actions which will compel an enemy to react rather than initiate. Offensive air action denies the enemy the flexibility to concentrate his air effort, and it gives to friendly forces the flexibility, initiative, and opportunity to control the timing and tempo of action.

Tactical air force missions which contribute most directly to land operations are counter air, air interdiction, close air support, special operations, airlift, and surveillance and reconnaissance.

The objective of *counter air operations* is to gain control of the air environment. Counter air operations protect friendly forces, ensure our freedom to use the aerospace environment to perform other air missions and tasks, and deny the use of that environment to the enemy. The ultimate goal of counter air is air supremacy. There are three types of complementary and mutual supportive operations which are conducted to establish and maintain air superiority. Offensive counter air (OCA) operations are conducted to seek out and neutralize or destroy enemy air forces at a time and place of our choosing. OCA achieves this by seizing the offensive at the initiation of hostilities, conducting operations in the enemy's airspace, and neutralizing or destroying the enemy's air forces and the infrastructure supporting his air operations.

Suppression of Enemy Air Defenses (SEAD) neutralizes, destroys, or temporarily degrades enemy air defensive systems in a specific area by physical/electronic attack. The goal of SEAD operations is to allow friendly forces to perform their other missions effectively without interference from enemy air defenses.

Defensive Counter Air (DCA) missions are conducted to detect, identify, intercept, and destroy enemy air forces that are attempting to attack friendly forces or penetrate friendly airspace, These missions defend friendly lines of communication, protect friendly bases, and support friendly land forces while denying the enemy the freedom to carry out offensive operations.

Air interdiction (AI) operations delay, disrupt, divert, or destroy an enemy's military potential before it can be brought to bear effectively against friendly forces. These combat operations are performed at such distances from friendly surface forces that detailed integration of specific actions with the fire and movement of friendly forces is normally not required. AI attacks are usually executed against enemy surface forces, movement networks (including lines of communication), command, control, and communications networks, and combat supplies. Interdiction of the enemy can delay the arrival or buildup of forces and supplies, disrupt the enemy's scheme of operation and control of forces, divert valuable enemy resources to other uses, and destroy forces and supplies.

AI attacks are normally executed by an air commander as part of a systematic and persistent effort. An air interdiction effort is developed to limit the enemy's mobility to maneuver forces, while forcing the enemy into high rates of consumption, and to create opportunities for friendly forces to exploit the disabilities produced by interdiction attacks. The weight, phasing, and most importantly, the timing of interdiction attacks can provide friendly forces the time or opportunity to seize the initiative and deny that same opportunity to an enemy.

Air interdiction attacks against targets which have a near term effect on the operations or scheme of maneuver of friendly forces, but are not in close proximity to friendly forces, are referred to as battlefield air interdiction (BAI). The primary difference between BAI and the remainder of the air interdiction effort is the near term effect and influence produced against the enemy in support of the land component commander's scheme of maneuver. BAI attacks require joint coordination at the component level during planning and may require coordination during execution. BAI is executed by the air component commander as an integral part of a total air interdiction effort.

Close air support missions support land operations by attacking hostile targets in close proximity to friendly surface forces. Close air support can support offensive, counteroffensive, and defensive surface force operations with preplanned or immediate attacks. All preplanned and immediate close air support missions require access to the battlefield, timely intelligence information, and accurate weapons delivery.

Close air support enhances land force operations by providing the capability to deliver a wide range of weapons and massed firepower at decisive points. Close air support can surprise the enemy, create opportunities for the maneuver or advance of friendly forces through shock action and concentrated attacks, protect the flanks of friendly forces, blunt enemy offensives, and protect the rear of land forces during retrograde operations.

Special operations influence the accomplishment of strategic, operational, or tactical objectives through the conduct of low visibility, covert, or clandestine military actions. Special operations are usually conducted in enemy controlled or politically sensitive territories and may complement general purpose force operations. Virtually all air forces have the potential for employment in special operations. To execute special operations, forces are normally organized and employed in small formations capable of both supporting actions and independent operations, with the purpose of providing timely and tailored responses throughout the spectrum of conflict. Special operating forces may conduct/support conventional operations, unconventional warfare, counterterrorist operations, collective security, psychological operations, certain rescue operations, and other mission areas such as interdiction or offensive counter air operations.

Airlift missions deploy, employ, and/or support conventional operations and unconventional warfare, and sustain military forces. Airlift is performed in peace and war. In combat, airlift projects power through airdrop, extraction, and airlanding of ground forces and supplies. Through mobility operations, the joint or combined force commander can manuever fighting forces to exploit an enemy's weaknesses. In combat support missions, airlift provides logistics support through the transportation of personnel and equipment. In peacetime, airlift provides the opportunity to enhance national objectives by providing military assistance and supporting civilian relief programs.

Airlift may be performed from a strategic or operational/tactical perspective. Strategic (intertheater) airlift transcends the boundary of any one theater and is executed under the central direction of higher authority. In contrast, operational/tactical (intratheater) airlift is performed within a theater of operations and supports theater objectives through the rapid and responsive movement of personnel and supplies.

Surveillance and reconnaissance missions collect information from airborne, orbital, and surface-based sensors. Air Force and Navy surveillance and reconnaissance efforts are a part of national intelligence gathering and systematic observation process. These operations provide a wide variety of information necessary to the development of national security policy, force postures, planning actions, force employment, and informed responses in times of crisis.

Surveillance operations collect information continuously from the air, land, and sea. Reconnaissance operations are directed toward specific targets. Through surveillance and reconnaissance, varied data can be collected such as meteorological, hydrographic, geographic, electronic, and communications characteristics, on any given area of the Earth's surface. The products of reconnaissance and surveillance operations have strategic, operational, and tactical applications in both peace and war. Strategic and operational/tactical surveillance and reconnaissance provide timely notification of hostile intent and actions as well as other information vital to the NCA and combat commanders. These operations are instrumental in identifying the composition and capability of hostile and potentially hostile forces. As a result, the total capability of foreign nations to conduct war can be assessed and our forces can be tailored to effectively counter the threat.

JOINT SUPPRESSION OF ENEMY AIR DEFENSES

Joint suppression of enemy air defenses (J-SEAD) increases the overall effectiveness of friendly air-land operations. The two types of J-SEAD are "campaign" and "localized."

The Theater Air Commander conducts the theaterwide J-SEAD operation against specific surface-to-air defense systems. The locations of most campaign targets will dictate this. However, Army surface-to-surface weapons will complement these efforts. More than one J-SEAD operation may be necessary during a campaign.

Localized J-SEAD operations attack specific targets or support airborne, airmobile, or other air operations. Battalions and larger Army units plan localized

J-SEAD operations to protect friendly aircraft and to maximize the effect of air support. Such operations normally involve jammers, suppressive fires, and passive measures such as camouflage or deception to degrade the effects of enemy air defenses. Localized J-SEAD operations can use field artillery, attack helicopters, direct fire weapons, and electronic warfare.

ENGINEER SUPPORT

The *engineer system* has three basic purposes: it preserves the freedom of maneuver of friendly forces; it obstructs the maneuver of the enemy in areas where fire and maneuver can be used to destroy him; and it enhances the survivability of friendly forces with protective construction. Engineer plans must be fully coordinated with the scheme of maneuver and fire support plans. They must allocate units and furnish a clear list of mission priorities. Engineer operations are time and labor intensive. They must begin as early as possible and be flexible enough to change as the battle develops.

Combat engineers contribute to the combined arms team by performing mobility, countermobility, and survivability missions. Mobility missions include breaching enemy minefields and obstacles, improving existing routes or building new ones, and providing bridge and raft support for crossing major water obstacles. Countermobility efforts limit the maneuver of enemy forces and enhance the effectiveness of US fires. Engineers improve the survivability of the friendly force by hardening command and control facilities and key logistic installations and by fortifying battle positions in the defense. In addition, combat engineers are organized, equipped, and trained to fight as infantry in tactical emergencies.

The engineer plan must be coordinated with the plans for maneuver and fires. At maneuver brigades and battalions, the S3 prepares the engineer plan. In divisions and corps, the engineer prepares the engineer plan under the direction of the G3. At all levels, engineer planning must consider the requirements not only for current operations, but for future operations as well. For instance, obstacles should be planned not only with current needs in mind but also with regard for the options they provide for future close operations.

Time, equipment, and materials may restrict the amount of engineer work accomplished before and during battle. Engineer plans must reflect these limitations realistically. They must provide the desired balance between survivability, mobility, and countermobility tasks and assign priorities. Normally, they should be concentrated in support of the main effort rather than being distributed evenly throughout the force.

In offensive operations, engineers normally concentrate their efforts in supporting maneuver by—

- Improving and maintaining routes.

- Laying bridges.

- Breaching and removing obstacles.

- Installing protective obstacles to the flanks of the attacking forces.

Some corps engineer units may be attached to or placed under operational control of divisions. Others will operate in direct or general support.

In the defense, engineers reinforce the terrain to anchor the defense in critical areas, to maximize the effects of the defender's fires, and to facilitate the movement of counterattack forces. They also prepare positions and roads or trails for moving reserve, artillery, logistical, and other units.

Denial plans are included in the engineer plan when the commander wishes to prevent or hinder the enemy from occupying or using areas or objects of strategic or tactical value. To the maximum extent possible, all materials of military value to the enemy will be removed or destroyed before retrograde movements.

Maneuver commanders must coordinate their obstacle plans in detail. They must assure that engineers or other designated units destroy or emplace bridges at the proper time, emplace and report flank obstacles, and close gaps left open for friendly maneuver at the right time. All engineer, artillery, and aviation units are responsible for emplacing scatterable mines. Plans must provide for the timely recording of installed obstacles, and key information must be promptly disseminated to all affected units.

COUNTER AIR OPERATIONS

US forces cannot count on unchallenged air superiority. Enemy air forces will contest control of the air, and our operations are likely to be conducted under temporary or local air superiority, air parity, or even enemy domination.

All counter air systems must be integrated to preclude the attack of friendly aircraft and to engage hostile aircraft. The theater air commander is normally the area counter air operations commander. He integrates all units pertaining to counter air operations and establishes counter air rules of engagement and procedures for the theater. Control of theater counter air operations will usually be exercised through a control and reporting center (CRC).

Air Defense Artillery. Air defense units provide the commander with security from enemy air attack by destroying or driving off enemy close air support aircraft and helicopters. Their fires can degrade the effectiveness of enemy strike and reconnaissance aircraft by forcing them to evade friendly air defenses. Short-range air defense (SHORAD) systems normally provide forward air defense protection for maneuver units whether they are attacking, delaying, withdrawing, or repositioning in the defense. Air defense secures critical facilities, such as command posts, logistic installations, and special ammunition supply points. It also protects convoys and lines of communication. In conjunction with Air Force elements, Army air defense plays a significant role in protecting friendly air maneuver and in attacking enemy air maneuver units.

Corps and divisions have organic SHORAD units. High-to-medium altitude air defense (HIMAD) units may also be assigned or attached to corps when higher echelons are not providing them.

Commanders locate their air defense units to protect high priority assets, units, and facilities. Priorities must be assessed first in terms of the operational significance of the functions performed by assets, units, and facilities and then by their tactical significance because air defense systems will always be scarce. Priorities vary with each operation, but ordinarily include—

- Massed and moving maneuver forces.
- Command posts.
- Logistic facilities.
- Airfields.
- Artillery units.
- Bridges, choke points, or defiles along important routes.
- Reserves (especially on the move).
- Forward arming and refueling points.

The unit air defense officer organizes the air defense based on the commander's guidance for each operation. In so doing, he must consider all available counter air capable weapons, not merely those specifically dedicated to air defense. Passive defensive measures will also remain important since there will rarely be enough ADA weapons to provide complete protection.

Like field artillery, ADA must provide continuous coverage of protected units during mobile operations. Movements must be carefully planned, firing positions must be cleared with sector or zone commanders, and plans must be flexible enough to accommodate changes. FM 44-1 and Joint Chiefs of Staff Publication 8 contain detailed discussions of air defense operations.

COMMUNICATIONS

Reliable communications are the heart of command and control. General Omar Bradley once said "Congress can make a general but only communications can make him a commander." It has long been Army doctrine that communications responsibilities go from "higher to lower" from "supporting to supported," and from "left to right."

Commanders should comply with this to the extent possible, but also do what they can to ensure communications are adequate in the other directions. This is essential when working with allies and with sister services.

Signal support plans must be made for each specific operation. Commanders and staffs at all echelons must understand the capabilities and limitations of their systems. They must be actively involved in ensuring adequacy. Atmospheric conditions, terrain, enemy EW efforts, and nuclear electromagnetic pulse (EMP) can all affect electronic signal equipment. The key to survivability is establishing communications procedures that—

- Provide redundancy of communications.
- Eliminate unnecessary reports.
- Ensure that subordinates know what to do during communications interruption.
- Limit the use of electronic communications.
- Minimize use of the most vulnerable means.
- Stress operations security and communications security.

AIRSPACE COORDINATION

Airspace coordination maximizes joint force effectiveness without hindering the combat power of either service. Friendly aircraft must be able to enter, to depart, and to move within the area of operations free of undue restrictions, while supporting fires and remotely piloted vehicle (RPV) flights continue uninterrupted. The tempo and complexity of modern combat rule out a system that requires time-consuming coordination. To be simple and flexible, our airspace coordination system operates under a concept of management by exception.

Each service is free to operate its aircraft within the theater airspace. Army aircraft at low altitudes operate under the control of the Army Airspace Command and Control (A^2C^2) System. Air Force aircraft at medium and high altitudes operate under control of the Tactical Air Control System. Navy and Marine Corps aircraft may also provide mission support to the force. The boundary between low- and medium-altitude regimes is flexible and situation-dependent. Coordination between services is continuous but it is especially important when aircraft pass from one regime to another. Generally, Army aircraft operate with fewer restrictions below coordinating altitudes forward of the division rear boundary. Passing information about major movements or high concentrations of fire helps to avoid conflicts.

In practice, Air Force support of strategic and operational plans is flown within airspace procedures established by theater or joint force commanders. These may include aircraft of any service or ally, all using rules and procedures appropriate to operational plans. Aircraft supporting tactical plans (usually Army aviation) will adhere to theater-wide procedures as augmented by the tactical commander being supported. All airspace management rules and procedures will be standardized to the extent possible, but will ultimately be applied in a particular theater in accordance with operational direction.

The G3 or S3 is responsible for the unit's operation in the A^2C^2 system. The G3 Air or S3 Air ensures that staff elements in the A^2C^2 cell conduct the necessary coordination.

DECEPTION

Any operational plan must seek to achieve surprise. An integral part of any plan of campaign or major operation is the deception plan. During the Normandy operations of WWII, the Germans believed that a large allied force under General Patton would land in the Pas de Calais area long after the beachheads were consolidated on the Normandy coast and refused to move significant reserves to counter the landings until too late. Every successful operation in WWII devoted a significant effort to deception. As the war progressed, the Russians became masters of operational deception.

Deception is a vital part of tactical operations as well. It masks the real objectives of tactical operations and delays effective enemy reaction by misleading the enemy about friendly intentions, capabilities, objectives, and the locations of vulnerable units and facilities. Tactical level deceptions must be coordinated with operational level deception plans so they reinforce rather than cancel each other.

A sound deception plan is simple, believable, and not so costly that it diverts resources from the main effort. Because deception seeks an enemy response, it must be targeted against that enemy commander who has the freedom of action to respond appropriately.

Generally speaking, the most costly, difficult, and least promising form of deception is convincing an opponent to alter his intended course of action. It is far easier to convince an opponent to believe what he wants to believe anyway—that his current course of action is correct. Easiest of all is the creation of ambiguity concerning the friendly force's own intentions—and frequently, that will suffice to create an exploitable weakness.

The G3 assembles the deception plan, making use of every unit and asset available to protect a plausible deception story designed to elicit a specific enemy reaction. He may use combat units; CEWI units; elements of the signal, support, command, and aviation units, as well as civil affairs staff and other forces. The deception effort may include demonstrations and ruses as part of offensive or defensive maneuver plans.

A demonstration is a show of force in an area where a decision is not sought; unlike a feint, a demonstration avoids contact with the enemy. Ruses are tricks designed to deceive the enemy by deliberately exposing false information to his collection means. FM 90-2 provides additional details on deception operations.

ELECTRONIC WARFARE

Electronic warfare uses the electronic spectrum to deceive the enemy, locate his units and facilities, intercept his communications, and disrupt his command, control, and target acquisition systems at critical moments. EW is conducted concurrently at both the operational and tactical levels, and these efforts must be synchronized with each other and with other activities—maneuver, fire, and air support—to obtain maximum benefit.

Staff officers have specific responsibilities for EW. The G3 or the S3 has the overall responsibility for EW, but focuses his primary effort on offensive EW. He implements the commander's guidance by integrating EW with the rest of the plan. The G2 or the S2 develops targets for interception, jamming, or destruction. The communications-electronics officer manages defensive electronic warfare.

The supporting military intelligence unit provides an electronic warfare support element (EWSE) to assist the G3 or the S3 in coordinating EW. The EWSE usually collocates with the fire support element (FSE) to facilitate target acquisition, fire planning, and coordination.

Military intelligence units (combat electronic warfare intelligence (CEWI)) detect and identify important enemy communications nets and intercept their traffic to provide the commander with intelligence. They also direct electronic countermeasures, primarily jamming, against enemy fire direction and command and control communications, air defense radar, and electronic guidance systems. This capability to locate the enemy, to intercept his messages, and to hamper his operations at critical periods contributes both directly and indirectly to the effectiveness of combined arms operations.

When developing his concept of operation, the tactical commander should treat EW assets much as he treats artillery assets. He should deploy EW assets to committed units in the light of their missions, the capabilities of available systems, and potential enemy actions. Plans should reflect the relative scarcity of EW weapons, their limitations, and the transient nature of their effects.

Enemy nets which routinely pass information of intelligence value should be identified and monitored. Those which have high tactical value to the enemy but little or no intelligence value should be attacked with jammers or with fire. Enemy jammers and radars should be located, reported, and destroyed. Guidance for jamming, destroying, or exploiting enemy electronic emitters should be reviewed before each tactical operation.

Jamming should interrupt or disrupt the enemy's communications at decisive moments in the battle—when key information needs to be passed or new instructions are required. Jamming may be effective only for the short periods of time the enemy needs to take evasive action or to execute countermeasures.

Jammers support other combat actions—

- By disrupting key command and control nets, thus slowing or disorganizing the enemy in critical sections.

- By denying the enemy the ability to react to changes on the battlefield.

- By reducing the effectiveness of enemy fire support and air control nets.

- By denying the enemy the use of his air defense fire control nets.

- By disrupting the enemy's flow of critical supplies, such as ammunition and POL.

Jammers should be used judiciously and moved often enough to avoid destruction. The G3 or the S3 coordinates the positioning of jammers and other electronic warfare assets.

The G3 or the S3 is also responsible for electronic deception activities. These must be a coordinated part of the overall deception plan and may include imitative communication deception (ICD) and manipulative electronic deception (MED). ICD is the controlled entry of an enemy net by operators posing as enemy stations to disrupt the enemy's operations by passing false reports or by confusing the transmission of information and orders. MED is the transmission of false information on friendly communications nets to deceive the enemy.

RECONSTITUTION

Sustained combat, heavy casualties, and massive destruction of equipment will require commanders to rebuild units during operations. Reconstitution is focused action to restore ineffective units to a specified level of combat effectiveness. Reconstitution may include replacement of personnel, supplies, and equipment; reestablishment or reinforcement of command and control; and conduct of mission-essential training. When the responsible commander determines that a unit is not sufficiently effective to meet operational requirements, reconstitution of that unit should begin as soon as feasible. Reconstitution requires coordinated planning by G3/S3, G1/S1, and G4/S4 staffs.

Commanders have two options available for reconstituting units: *reorganization* and *regeneration*. Reorganization is action taken to shift resources within an attrited unit to increase its level of combat effectiveness. Reorganization consists of measures such as internal redistribution of equipment and personnel and the formation of composite units. Regeneration is the rebuilding of a unit through large-scale replacement of personnel, equipment and supplies; the reestablishment of command and control; and the conduct of mission-essential training for replacement personnel. Usually a unit undergoing regeneration must be withdrawn from contact with the enemy.

These options can be used separately or in combination. Their application depends upon current and anticipated situations, command priorities, and resources and time available. Reconstitution does not automatically require unit withdrawal. However, a reconstituted unit should ideally be allowed time to stabilize and begin reestablishing internal cohesion before it is committed to battle again.

The commander's decision to reconstitute a unit is normally based on—

- The unit's personnel losses, including MOS shortages or shortages in leadership structure.

- The unit's equipment status including shortages of mission-essential items, low operational ready rates of major items, or lack of maintenance and repair parts.

- The unit's psychological condition, including its internal cohesion and the physical and mental condition of its soldiers.

- The impact of releasing the unit on the operations of the parent force, including the time and resources available to reconstitute it.

Based on an analysis of these considerations and any others which may be relevant, the staff determines a unit's level of combat effectiveness and recommends to the commander measures to correct identified problems. No single report will provide the commander and staff with the necessary level of detail to determine relative combat effectiveness. Commanders must determine their unit's capabilities, taking into consideration both objective and subjective combat effectiveness indicators. Objective indicators include a comparison of personnel and equipment authorizations with on-hand strengths. Subjective indicators include evaluations of the levels of leadership, cohesion, training, and morale.

PSYCHOLOGICAL OPERATIONS

Psychological operations (PSYOP) are an important component of the political, military, economic, and ideological actions that support both long-term and immediate objectives. Propaganda and other PSYOP techniques for changing the attitudes and behavior of target groups provide the commander with his primary means of communication with opposing military forces and civilian groups. When effectively integrated with other operations, PSYOP contribute significantly to combat power. They can—

- Reduce the combat effectiveness of enemy forces.
- Promote support for friendly forces among local populations and external groups (including in some cases the enemy's own population).
- Reduce the effectiveness of enemy PSYOP directed toward friendly forces and supporting civilian groups.

PSYOP must be coordinated from the theater to the division level. Based on levels of employment, objectives, and targeted groups, each of the following categories is part of an integrated theater PSYOP effort:

- Strategic PSYOP, conducted to advance broad or long-term objectives and to create a psychological environment favorable to military operations.
- Operational PSYOP, conducted to achieve mid-term objectives in support of campaigns and major operations.
- Tactical PSYOP, conducted to achieve relatively immediate and short-term objectives in support of tactical commanders.

At any level, PSYOP may be consolidative, conducted to facilitate military operations, to reduce interference by noncombatants, and to obtain the cooperation of the civilian population in the area of operations. Or it may be divisive, intended to lower the efficiency and fragment the loyalty of military forces which directly oppose the objectives of a command.

The G3 is responsible for integrating psychological and combat operations. The supporting PSYOP unit commander plans and executes PSYOP. He normally provides a small PSYOP staff element to the supported G3.

Effective integration of PSYOP is based on the following fundamental principles:

- Planning should begin early, concurrently with operational planning.
- PSYOP must begin early in an operation.
- Scarce resources for conducting PSYOP should be targeted against groups most critical to success.
- Divisive and consolidative PSYOP conducted at the strategic, operational, and tactical levels of war must be thoroughly coordinated and mutually supportive. PSYOP should also be integrated with operational deception effort.
- All PSYOP units are part of a PSYOP command to ensure integration and consistency of operations.
- PSYOP must respond to the changing requirements of the battlefield.

AMPHIBIOUS OPERATIONS

An amphibious operation is an attack launched from the sea by naval and landing forces against a hostile shore. It may be conducted to—

- Prosecute further land combat operations.
- Obtain a site for advanced bases.
- Deny the use of an area or facilities to the enemy.

An amphibious operation constitutes one of the more potent capabilities available to a theater commander, as the invasions of Normandy and Inchon demonstrated. Its usefulness stems from the mobility and flexibility of the amphibious task force and its potential to achieve surprise. The US Army has a collateral responsibility for planning and executing joint amphibious operations.

An amphibious operation confronts difficulties not normally encountered in land combat operations. These include natural forces, such as unfavorable weather, seas, surf, and features of hydrography; technical problems of the logistics involved in loading troops and equipment on ships and aircraft so that they can be landed in the proper sequence on open beaches or landing zones that are contested; and the inherent vulnerabilities of landing forces while embarked on naval vessels and aircraft whose maneuverability is restricted to relatively fixed locations during the actual assault and while conducting ship-to-shore operations. As a result, detailed planning and the closest cooperation among all participating forces in a joint amphibious operation are essential for success.

In addition to direct participation in joint amphibious operations, the Army may also become involved in supporting operations, special operations, or separate operations in conjunction with amphibious operations. These could include—

- Airborne operations to seize air bases for the subsequent introduction of follow-on forces.

- Air-transported operations.

- Isolation of the objective area by interdicting enemy forces.

- Psychological and unconventional warfare operations.

A detailed discussion of amphibious operations is found in FM 31-11.

SPECIAL OPERATIONS FORCES

Unconventional warfare (UW), conducted by US Army Special Forces, other special operating forces (SOF), or native insurgents, takes place deep in the enemy's rear area. US Army Special Forces and other SOF can disrupt the enemy's operations by conducting either unconventional warfare or unilateral operations in his rear areas. Normally, preestablished command arrangements will determine how the unified commander assigns missions to his SOF. Special forces can also provide support to lower level commanders when their elements are located in such a commander's area of interest.

Unconventional warfare operations in a theater concentrate on strategic and operational goals. They may seek either immediate or long-range effects on the conflict. They include interdicting enemy lines of communications and destroying military and industrial facilities. SOF conduct PSYOP to demoralize the enemy and to collect information in the enemy's rear areas. Ranger units can be used for strike missions of special importance Special forces organize, train, equip, and advise resistance forces in guerrilla warfare, evasion and escape (E&E), subversion, and sabotage. Their greatest value to commanders of conventional forces is in adding depth to the campaign, forcing the enemy to deploy significant numbers of combat forces to protect his rear area.

Special forces elements can deploy unilaterally into the enemy's rear area to assist in the attack of uncommitted enemy forces by locating, identifying, and destroying targets of operational value. Special forces detachments may have the following missions:

- Intelligence collection.

- Target acquisition.

- Terminal guidance for strike aircraft and missile systems.

- Interdiction of critical transportation targets.

- Destruction of nuclear storage sites and command and control facilities.

- Personnel recovery.

CIVIL-MILITARY OPERATIONS

Commanders must expect to fight in or near populated areas. Such areas contain supplies, facilities, services, and labor resources which US commanders can use to support military operations. Conversely, uncontrolled and uncoordinated movement of civilians about the battlefield, hostile actions by the population, or failure to cooperate with friendly forces can significantly disrupt military operations.

Civil-military operations (CMO) seek to influence the relationship between a military command and the civilian population. They include activities conducted to assist civil authorities and to control the population in the operational area. To obtain the co-operation of the civilian population, CMO integrate psychological operations and civil affairs operations.

The G3 supervises PSYOP, but the G5 coordinates those PSYOP directed against civilian populations. PSYOP support CMO through political, military, and economic actions planned and conducted to mold the opinions, attitudes, and behavior of foreign groups to support US national objectives. They also counter enemy PSYOP. The target audience need not be under US control.

The G5 or the S5 staff supervises civilian affairs activities. Civil affairs are those activities which involve US military forces and civil authorities and people in a friendly country or area or those in a country or area occupied by US military forces. This relationship may be established before, during, or after military action in time of hostilities or other emergencies. In a friendly country or area, US forces coordinate activities with local agencies or authorities when possible. Normally these relationships are covered by a treaty or other agreement. In occupied territory, a military government may have to exercise executive, legislative, and judicial authority. Civil-military activities—

- Identify the local resources, facilities, and support available for US operations. In theaters where US forces are forward deployed in peacetime, such support may be prearranged through negotiated Host Nation Support (HNS) agreements.

- Coordinate the use of local resources, facilities, and support such as civilian labor, transportation, communications, maintenance or medical facilities, and miscellaneous services and supplies.

- Minimize interference by the local population with US military operations.

- Assist the commander in meeting legal and moral obligations to the local population.

CHAPTER 4
Sustainment Planning and Execution

As the scale and complexity of warfare have increased, the importance of logistics to success in battle has likewise increased. An army's ability to marshal, transport, and distribute large quantities of materiel and to maintain the men and equipment of large units can make the decisive difference between victory and defeat in high- or mid-intensity conflict. In low intensity conflict, logistical operations are conducted differently, but are just as vital.

Today the US Army's ability to sustain its operations is more important as an element of combat power than ever before. To fight effectively in any type of operation with any combination of light and heavy units, Army forces must field an adequate, well-operated combat service support system. Deployed Army forces will also be expected to furnish supporting Air Force units with a variety of logistical services.

Sustainment is equally vital to success at both the operational and tactical levels of war. Campaigns will often be limited in their design and execution by the support structure and resources of a theater of war. Almost as commonly, the center of gravity of one or both combatants will be found in their support structures, and in those cases major operations or even entire campaigns may be mounted to destroy or defend those structures. Operational maneuver and the exploitation of tactical success will often depend critically on the adequacy of a force's sustainment.

At the tactical level, a unit's flexibility, its ability to maneuver or to mass fires extensively, and its capacity for prolonged operations and operations in depth will all

CONTENTS

rely heavily on its sustainment system. The differences in firepower, agility, and endurance which can decide battles all derive as much from the combat service support system as they do from any of the other systems that support fighting forces.

To realize their units' full potential, commanders must support their operations with rugged, flexible, self-sufficient combat service support forces. They must protect their sustainment systems from disruption or interdiction at critical junctures, train their combat service support (CSS) units to the same standards of toughness and competence as the rest of the force, and operate their CSS systems effectively before, during, and after battle.

This chapter describes the principles of sustainment planning and operations and provides general guidance for the application of those principles at the operational and tactical levels of war.

SUSTAINMENT CHALLENGE

Sustaining large forces in combat has become an extraordinary challenge. Even in World War II, the challenge was considerable. During its August 1944 pursuit across France, for example, the US Third Army consumed 350,000 gallons of gasoline every day. To fulfill this requirement and to meet similar demands from First Army, the Communication Zone organized the famous "Red Ball Express," a conveyor belt of trucks connecting the Normandy depots with the field armies. At its peak, the Red Ball Express ran 6,000 trucks day and night in an operation that became more difficult with every mile the armies advanced. To meet the demands of logistics, three newly arrived infantry divisions were stripped of their trucks and left immobile in Normandy.

The Red Ball Express itself consumed 300,000 gallons of precious gasoline every day—nearly as much as a Field Army. Today, it is estimated that *one* armored division equipped with M1 tanks will consume over 600,000 gallons of fuel per day, more than twice the consumption of Patton's entire army.

The sole measurement of successful sustainment has always been the generation of combat power at the decisive time and place. As the environment for this has never been more demanding, today's units must be as simple and as rugged as possible. They must also use complex weapons and consume large stocks of materiel to fight a sophisticated enemy. High- and mid-intensity operations will therefore be characterized by *high consumption of military materiel*; by a *great diversity of equipment types*; by the *expansion of the battle area* resulting from both sides employing sophisticated weapons, communications, and sensors; and by *extended lines of support* within and outside the theater of operations. Sustainment on this enlarged, material-intensive, electronically sensitive, and lethal battlefield presents an unprecedented challenge.

KEY SUSTAINMENT FUNCTIONS

Sustaining operational and tactical efforts in this environment comprises six key sustainment functions: manning, arming, fueling, fixing, and transporting the supported force, and protecting the sustainment system itself from attack.

MANNING

The first challenge of sustainment is to assure the uninterrupted flow of fighting men to the battle area and to provide necessary personnel services during operations.

To support operations, units must be assembled, transported, and distributed as the commander requires, and their fighting strength conserved. Health services, administrative support, chaplain activities, morale support, replacement operations, and above all, leadership are part of maintaining strength and spirit in a fighting force.

ARMING

The weapons and implements of war have never been more diverse and complex. Today's weapons consume large amounts of ammunition and depend on high quality electronic and optical devices for accuracy and coordination. In most recent wars, replenishing arms, ammunition, and equipment required extraordinary efforts. Today, given the large variety of ammunition and weapons in use and the expected fluidity of battle, arming the soldier has become an even greater challenge. In periods of intense combat, arming the fighting units will be the largest, most time-sensitive task of the sustainment system.

FUELING

While the high-performance air and ground vehicles of the Army furnish great potential mobility for both heavy and light forces, they also consume large quantities of fuel. Wheeled vehicles use less fuel than tracked vehicles and heavy equipment but will still make great cumulative demands on the sustainment system. To assure adequate support of operations, commanders will have to set clear priorities for fueling, plan consumption accurately, and economize whenever possible. Logisticians will have to operate a high volume fuel system merely to support routine consumption rates. In peak consumption periods, victory may depend on the ability of the sustainment system to increase the flow of fuel.

FIXING

In all operations, time will be critical and replacement equipment will be scarce. The force which is better able than its opponent to recover damaged equipment and return it to service rapidly will have a clear advantage in generating and concentrating combat power. For the force operating at a numerical disadvantage, the capability to maintain, recover, and repair equipment will be even more important. Good maintenance practices in all units, forward positioning of maintenance units, stocks of repair parts and replacement equipment, and well understood priorities for recovery and repair may spell the difference between tactical success or failure. Similarly, theater facilities for repair and replacement of materiel and theater policies on repair and evacuation of equipment will strongly influence the outcome of campaigns.

TRANSPORTING

Men, equipment, and supplies must be moved rapidly and in quantity to support operations. Operational and tactical actions require timely concentration of units and materiel and will often demand short notice movement of sizable forces and major shifts in direction of movement. At the tactical level, units, supplies, and important facilities must be moved as battles progress to assure responsive support of committed units as large as corps. At the operational level, the number, location, and quality of lines of communication may well determine the very structure and tempo of a campaign. Planning, controlling, and executing transportation operations in a theater of war or in the course of a battle require detailed preparation and extensive training of CSS staffs and units. The complicating effects of terrain, weather, and enemy interdiction will demand great flexibility of transportation planners and operators.

PROTECTING

Protecting the sustainment effort is an integral part of all combat operations. Because sustainment is necessary to every operation, the support system will be a prime target of enemy operations both in the forward areas and in depth. Enemy air, missile, ground, and unconventional warfare forces will attack the support system as part of a coordinated battle or campaign plan. Passive and active measures must therefore be combined to protect the sustainment effort. To the greatest degree possible, combat service support forces must seek protection in dispersion, concealment, and self-defense. Nevertheless, commanders may frequently have to take active steps to defend their sustainment system and prevent disruption of support functions, especially at decisive stages of combat.

SUSTAINMENT IMPERATIVES

To meet these challenges, sustainment of AirLand Battle operations confronts five fundamental imperatives: *anticipation, integration, continuity, responsiveness, and improvision.*

ANTICIPATION

The agility of a force, its ability to seize and retain the initiative, and its ability to synchronize its activities in depth all depend to a great extent on how well its support operations anticipate requirements. Neither sustainment nor operations planners can predict the exact course of events, but both must foresee future operations and demands as accurately as possible.

For sustainment planners, anticipation means maintaining or accumulating the assets necessary to support the commander's operation at decisive times and places. Anticipation also demands that sustainment operations be flexible enough to accommodate any likely operational or tactical contingency. At the tactical level, this may mean rapid readjustment of basic loads, prescribed loads, and expenditure rates to assure that shortages of fuel, ammunition, and parts do not limit the force's conduct of battle. At the operational level, anticipation requires that sustainment planners visualize the entire course of a major operation or campaign while planning specifically for the phase that is under way. Planners must assure that base facilities, priorities of support, lines of communication, and troop movements in the theater can effectively support the main line of operations, yet adjust rapidly to any branches or variations that are likely to be developed. Planners must also anticipate shifts in demand based on the changing nature of operations; for example, a shift from high ammunition to high petroleum consumption as exploitation begins.

INTEGRATION

Neither tactical nor operational plans can succeed without fully integrated combat service support. The commander must assure that his overall operation is supportable at every stage of its execution. Support unit commanders must plan their own activities to give the operational or tactical commander the greatest possible freedom of action throughout the campaign or battle. They must be bold and innovative in their support operations to contribute to surprise by allowing the supported force to do more than the enemy thinks possible. In this regard, sustainment operations must also be thoroughly integrated into any deception plan.

CONTINUITY

Sustainment cannot be interrupted for long without directly diminishing the combat power of a force. During operations, committed forces—combat, combat support, and combat service support—must receive continuous supply and service to sustain their fighting strength. If the commander expects units to be isolated by enemy action as a result of his own tactical plan, he must arrange for those units to be sustained throughout the operation either by accompanying CSS forces or through specially planned replenishment operations.

While operations and sustainment both vary in intensity, operations may enter inactive periods; sustainment does not. In fact, periods of operational inactivity usually coincide with efforts by both combatants to rebuild their units and bases of support. Sustainment planners and commanders must take advantage of every opportunity to increase sustaining capabilities. When the pace of combat activity diminishes, they must redirect their efforts to replenish the sustainment base while continuing support to combat units. Since such efforts require CSS units to operate constantly, commanders must make special provisions for resting, retraining, and reequipping them.

Finally, continuity requires that the sustainment effort never become hostage to a single line or mode of support. Temporary or permanent losses of key ports, airheads, and LOC nodes must be expected and hedged through forward stockage, alternate facilities, or a combination of both. Since the price of such hedging is a reduction in current consumption, the commander must constantly balance that cost against the risk of interruption.

RESPONSIVENESS

In crises or when fleeting opportunities arise, the sustainment system must react rapidly. Such quick reaction to increased demand is only possible if CSS units are trained to respond on short notice and to "surge" their support for brief periods. Such efforts may temporarily upset the support system, but are often necessary to winning. At the operational level of war, the sustainment system must be able to meet similar extraordinary demands on an even greater scale. Efforts to reestablish a ruptured defense or to exploit a tactical success may call for relocation of support bases,

major redirection of supply flows, reallocation of transportation means, or short notice transfer of units from one part of the theater to another. The mental and physical agility to cope with such requirements must be built into the sustainment system ahead of time by effective organization, careful planning, and solid training.

IMPROVISATION

No matter how carefully commanders and planners try to anticipate events, unforeseen contingencies arise in every conflict. Enemy action, interruption of sealift or airlift, and natural disasters can all upset plans and require improvisation. In cases such as the Battle of the Bulge of 1944 and the Tet Offensive of 1968, CSS planners and operators have had to improvise to meet unanticipated emergencies. In such situations, normal operating procedures must be suspended, unusual sources of supplies and transportation exploited, and exceptional risks accepted. Tactical vehicles may have to be pressed into service as supply transporters, equipment in uncommitted units cannibalized for parts, or emergency supply points established.

Less dramatic emergencies, such as unexpected maintenance failures in a particular type of equipment, loss of support equipment, or unanticipated peaks in workload also require improvised solutions. Such improvisation has long been one of the American soldier's greatest strengths and should be viewed as an advantage in meeting emergencies. It should be seen not as a substitute for anticipation, but rather as a necessary complement to it.

ORGANIZATION FOR SUSTAINMENT IN A THEATER OF WAR

Because future conflicts will most likely be some distance from the United States, organization and planning for sustainment of operations will be strongly influenced by the nature of the theater and the circumstances in which US forces are committed. Among the most important considerations

influencing theater sustainment organization and planning are the following:

- *Forces available.* The forces available for sustainment operations will critically influence the time needed to create a sustainment base in the theater and the preparation of that base for operations. Since a large proportion of the Army's CSS units are in the reserve components the preparedness of those units and the time necessary to mobilize and deploy them will be a significant factor in planning the establishment of an overseas theater of war. If reserve component forces are not readily available, the scope and nature of theater sustainment will be seriously affected.

- *Theater infrastructure.* The difficulty of establishing the theater sustainment base will depend greatly upon the extent and nature of the civil and military infrastructure existing in the theater before hostilities begin. When ports, airfields, depots, repair facilities, supplies, and transportation facilities are well developed and operated by friendly governments, US forces can begin operations quickly without having to establish a wholly new base of support. When facilities and supplies are not present or available, Army units may have to operate for a considerable period from austere, in-theater bases. In such an event, CSS and construction units will be needed early and in substantial numbers, and operations may initially be restricted accordingly.

  In some cases, the required support infrastructure, while not available in the theater of operations, may be present elsewhere in the theater of war. In this case, combat operations can be supported from an intermediate forward staging and sustainment base until a communications zone (COMMZ) can be organized in the theater of operations itself.

- *Host nation support (HNS).* In a theater of operations in which US forces are deployed in peacetime, such as Korea or Europe, pre-established arrangements for HNS can significantly reduce the requirement for early augmentation of US sustainment assets. Such HNS arrangements can include operation, maintenance, and security of ports and airheads; management of routes, railways, petroleum pipelines, inland waterways, and bulk storage facilities; and operation of existing communications networks. HNS can also supply transportation, civilian labor, and local security and police forces in some cases.

- *Establishment of the sustainment base.* Even in a developed theater, operational and logistical planners will have to make early but far-reaching decisions about their principal and supplementary bases of support. Whether sustainment facilities are available or must be developed from scratch, the choice of where to establish the initial support base or bases may influence the course of the entire campaign. Such bases should allow easy access to strategic sealift and airlift, offer adequate space for storage, facilitate transshipment of supplies, and be accessible to multiple lines of communication. They should provide the greatest possible protection from both natural hazards and enemy action. Most importantly, their location should give the operational commander the greatest possible freedom of action. They must therefore be able to support more than a single line of operation.

In practice, these features may not all be attainable. The base locations most accessible to sealift, for example, may be poorly sited to support the preferred line of operations or may be excessively vulnerable to enemy action. Campaign planners may have to make difficult choices as they organize a theater for operations and sustainment. The dominant considerations should be responsive of support to the fighting units and maximum flexibility for the operational commander.

- *Major sustainment systems.* Wherever it is established, the theater sustainment base must be capable of supporting the five functional systems of the sustainment effort: transportation, maintenance, supply, personnel, and health services.

OPERATIONAL SUSTAINMENT

Operational sustainment comprises those logistical and support activities required to sustain campaigns and major operations within a theater of operations. Operational sustainment extends from the theater sustaining base or bases which link strategic to theater support functions, to the forward CSS units and facilities organic to major tactical formations.

The central organizational framework for operational sustainment is the theater army, described more fully in FM 100-16. However, depending on the nature of the contingency and the organization of the theater, field armies, corps, and even divisions may find themselves responsible for planning and conducting sustainment at the operational level. At whatever level conducted, planning for operational sustainment will involve several critical decisions concerning the interface of combat and sustainment activities.

LINES OF SUPPORT

Maintenance of uninterrupted sustaining support throughout all phases of the operation or campaign is the central challenge of operational sustainment. Such continuity is provided in large part by establishing lines of communication linking the theater base or bases to the forward tactical formations. Depending on the geography of the theater, the availability of transportation assets, and the threat, ground lines of communication (LOC) may be supplemented by air lines of communication (ALOC), sea lines of communication (SLOC), or both. More usually, ALOC and SLOC will serve as strategic LOC, linking with a predominantly land LOC network at the theater base.

Whatever the composition of theater LOC, their relation to intended lines of operation will be crucial to the quality and continuity of sustainment. Generally speaking, the fewer the sustaining assets and the less certain the forecast of future operations, the more advantageous it will be to sustain along lines of communication interior to projected lines of action, that is, behind and centered on the supported force.

Such interior lines of support permit collocation of key sustaining facilities at central points, maximizing the capacity of the support system at minimum cost in resources. Interior lines of support also allow the rapid shift of support priorities from one zone of action to another, allowing the operational commander maximum flexibility.

On the other hand, since interior lines of support originate from central points, they are more vulnerable to enemy disruption, especially in the early phases of an operation or campaign. Such enemy

INTERIOR LINES OF SUPPORT

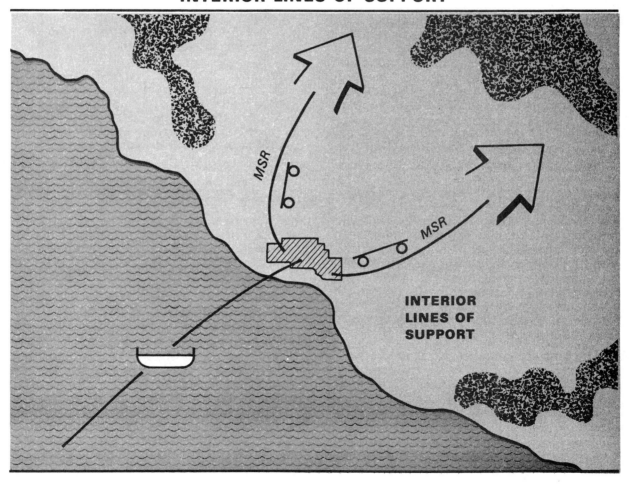

interdiction is facilitated by the enemy's ability to concentrate on the nodal points from which LOC originate. Moreover, while interior lines of support tend to converge in the defense and retrograde, they tend to diverge as offensive operations unfold. Initial establishment of interior lines of support may therefore eventually force the commander to proliferate forward support bases.

Exterior lines of support originate from multiple theater bases, and require both additional in-theater base facilities (ports, airheads, transshipment points) and sufficient

sustaining resources to maintain multiple simultaneous flows. Because the total sustaining effort is divided among several functionally independent LOC, the risk of interruption is reduced by the enemy's need to disperse his interdiction efforts. Moreover, in the offense, exterior lines tend to converge on the objective, becoming more versatile as operations progress. However, until they converge, their very separation makes it more difficult to shift the sustainment flow. Thus loss of an LOC, unanticipated tactical reverses, or rapid changes of the friendly main effort are less easily accommodated.

EXTERIOR LINES OF SUPPORT

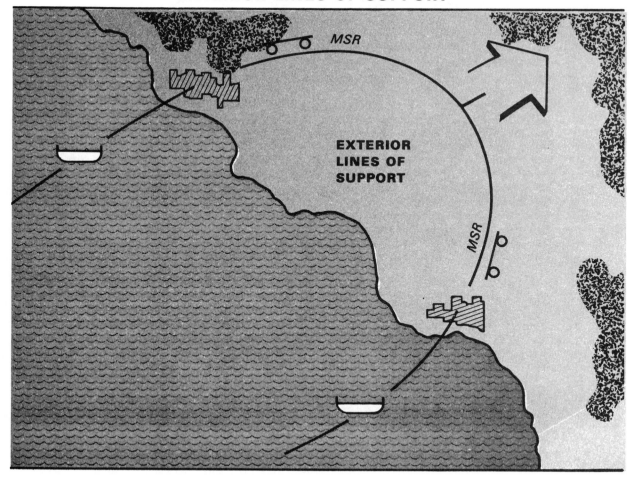

Whether supported on interior or exterior lines, a campaign or major operation should never depend on a single line of communication. Moreover, where austere sustaining resources limit the number of LOC which can be supported simultaneously, special care must be taken to secure LOC from air and ground interdiction. Geographic features, friendly civil security forces, and uncommitted combat units should all be employed to maximize LOC security at minimum cost to committed combat formations. Occasionally, it may even be necessary to conduct major operations simply to secure the lines of communication required to support subsequent phases of a campaign.

STAGING

During a campaign, LOC will often become overextended. This may require the staging of sustaining bases forward as the combat forces advance; or the rapid evacuation of those bases if friendly forces withdraw. Routes, rail lines, airfields, ports, and pipelines of the LOC will also be affected by such moves. Additional construction, route improvement, and movement control measures will accompany any staging of bases forward or withdrawal to the rear. In either case, the commander has to establish limits on how far he can move from his bases and how close to the battle he will bring his bases. Control of the airspace, transportation limitations, requirements of the force, and the availability of CSS units and military police all affect the location and movement of bases and LOC.

The operational commander must understand the relationship between time, LOC extension, and forward combat power. Time spent in deliberate preparation— moving units and stockpiling resources— can result in a greater operational capability in the future. These advantages, however, must be weighed against current operational requirements. Similarly, the length of the LOC directly affects combat power. Longer LOC consume more resources themselves, making fewer resources available to combat units. Long LOC are more susceptible to interdiction, need more transportation and

maintenance support, and require earlier forecasting of requirements and longer lead times for delivery. Longer LOC also require more engineer effort, traffic control, and protection. The operational commander must therefore seek to support each phase of his campaign efficiently, and as the campaign progresses, adjust his LOC and support bases. If the attack continues, forward staging will provide readily available stocks forward and reserve stocks at intermediate locations. If a retrograde action is required, stocks may be attrited through consumption.

Operational planners assist the commander and his CSS planners in deciding when to stage bases forward or to the rear by providing them with estimates of friendly and enemy future actions. CSS planners, in turn, must keep the commander and operational planners informed about logistical factors that affect the conduct of the campaign. These include current equipment densities, supply levels, personnel strengths, support relationships, availability of LOC, and the status of support facilities. The continuous exchange of operational and logistical information assists the commander in maintaining adequate sustainment for his operations.

CSS planners must provide projections of requirements for each campaign phase or major operation and then determine whether the next phase can be supported by existing bases and LOC. The necessary support may be available from internal resources, higher or adjacent units, or host nation support. Upon completing the analysis of both requirements and capabilities, the CSS planner must again report to the commander on the CSS system's ability to support operations, highlighting any risks associated with the support plan.

Staging logistics forward or to the rear will not normally interfere with slow-moving operations. In a rapid operation, though, staging may act as a brake, and must be timed to minimize disruption of operational tempo. The full extension of a sustainment system will often bring an attacking force to its culminating point and require a temporary halt.

ALTERING LINES OF COMMUNICATION

On a fluid battlefield, lines of operation may change with startling rapidity. Unexpected threats may require the rapid redeployment of combat power to block or counterattack. Unexpected opportunities may develop which will require a significant reorientation of the main effort and which will disappear unless instantly exploited. Ideally, lines of communication will be located so that such shifts in operational direction can be accommodated without major adjustment of the sustaining effort. More frequently, however, shifts in the line of action will require a corresponding

change in LOC. Such a change may also be necessary to compensate for damage to or interruption of existing LOC.

Unless carefully planned and intensively managed, alteration of a key LOC for whatever reason can easily unravel the support structure of an operation, resulting in dangerous shortages at the worst possible moment of the battle. A decision to shift LOC is thus a critical operational as well as sustainment decision and must be weighed in terms of the overall operational situation.

Third Army's counterattack from Lorraine north into Belgium in December 1944 furnishes one of the best examples of a

COUNTERATTACK FROM LORRAINE NORTH INTO BELGIUM

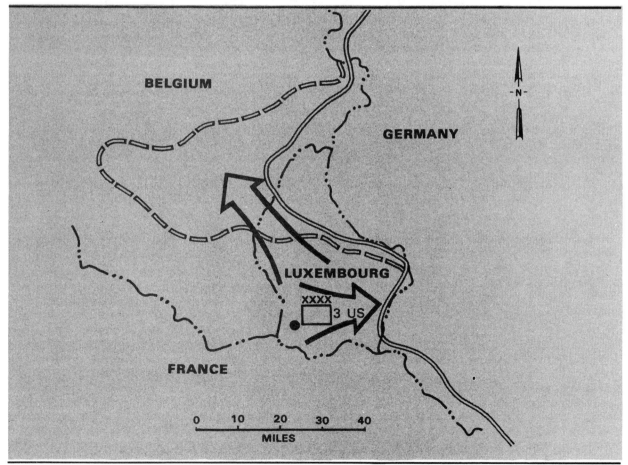

major shift in direction. With little warning and in less than 3 days, priority of sustainment was shifted from an eastward direction along existing LOC to a northward axis involving the establishment of an entirely new support network. Eastward movement was curtailed. Temporary depots were established from which stocks could be redirected northward. Routes were reallocated and priorities for their use ruthlessly enforced. Maintenance, supply, transportation, and service units were reallocated across corps without regard for habitual support relationships. And all this was accomplished in adverse weather and under enormous time pressure.

On an air-land battlefield, such alterations are more apt to be the rule than the exception. To accomplish them with minimum confusion and delay, versatility must be built in the sustaining system. Terrain and route reconnaissance, assignment and reconnaissance of alternate transshipment and supply point areas, development and rehearsal of rapid relocation procedures, and continuous contingency planning can all help to diminish the risks associated with shifting LOC. Careful integration of intratheater airlift, use of host nation support, and temporary expropriation of tactical support assets can all be used to prevent sustainment shortfalls during the actual relocation of facilities and traffic.

Most important, commanders and planners must attempt to anticipate those events—intended and otherwise—which could require significant adjustment of lines of support. They must estimate the time required to make those adjustments and begin the relocation process early.

SUSTAINMENT PRIORITIES

In all operations, commanders will have to conserve sustaining resources and establish priorities for support. These priorities will normally be given to the most vital units for successful accomplishment of the mission.

Once support priorities are established, they must be disseminated as quickly as possible. At this point, it becomes the responsibility of the CSS planners and operators to develop and implement a support plan. The support plan must provide the mobility and flexibility that will enable the commander to change priorities to take advantage of the situation.

Priorities may shift between units or to a different area. When priorities are shifted to a new operational area, the ports of debarkation (POD) within the area must be evaluated and analyzed to ensure they are capable of providing the necessary support to the operational area.

Any shifting of priorities may require the relocation of certain supply, service, maintenance, or personnel units to ensure full support. While relocating, the operational capability of the force will be temporarily reduced. Also transportation and other CSS assets will have to be diverted from support of combat units to move the support base.

Priorities may be altered to exploit an operational situation, to conduct reconstitution efforts, to prepare for future battles, or to continue current operations. When the commander changes a support priority, it is important that the operational and CSS planner alike review the affected support relationships.

FORCE EXPANSION

As the force in a theater is enlarged, the commander must assure an appropriate balance of combat, combat support, and CSS forces at all stages of the expansion. In the effort to maximize combat effectiveness by introducing the greatest possible number of combat forces, he must take care not to exceed the support capacity of his logistics base. Any necessary acclimatization, reequipping, or in-theater training must be reflected in plans to build up forces in a theater. CSS units require the same time as any other units to organize for operations.

While each newly assigned unit is being integrated into the force, a detailed analysis of the CSS system must be completed. This analysis should result in a revised CSS support plan which assigns missions to newly assigned CSS units, adjusts the missions of CSS units already in operation, and cross-levels supplies as necessary.

Using information provided in the logistics estimate, the CSS planners must ensure that appropriate measures are taken to meet the increased demands for supplies and services resulting from the expansion of the force. Both CSS and operational planners must also be prepared to meet the increased demand for terrain on the battlefield. Units to be relocated will have to be given adequate terrain to enable them to prepare for the accomplishment of future missions.

With the integration of each new unit, the commander must reevaluate his sustainment priorities and adjust them if necessary. Each time the force is expanded, the requirement for new facilities and lines of communication must be reviewed to ensure that they are adequate to accomplish the mission.

TACTICAL SUSTAINMENT

Tactical sustainment includes all the CSS activities necessary to support battles and engagements and the tactical activities which precede and follow them. Tactical units from corps to battalion are sustained by organic or supporting CSS which provide for their routine requirements and which can be reinforced to give them additional strength for operations.

Tactical commanders can only realize the full combat potential of their units and achieve synchronization in their operations by effective use of their sustainment system. They must assure that their tactical plans realistically reflect logistic limitations and fully exploit their CSS capabilities. Ammunition, fuel, food and water, maintenance, transportation, personnel services, and medical support must all be provided to support the operations.

Commanders must strike a balance in their tactical sustainment operations. While assuring adequate support to the force, so that nothing needed for combat is lacking, they must simultaneously conserve all the assets possible for future operations. They must make specific provisions for the support of their main effort and for the associated close, deep, and rear operations. Like all supporting operations, CSS operations must be capable of rapid adjustment to changes in the tactical situation. As a minimum, they must be capable of responding to the major tactical contingencies foreseen by the commander. They must also be able to react to logistical contingencies which could affect support of an operation.

CSS planners advise commanders and tactical planners on the status, capabilities, and limitations of the sustainment system supporting the force. They assist in formulating courses of action in an operation. After the commander's decision, they adjust support operations to conform with his concept of operation. CSS staff officers and commanders assist in preparing the force for operations, support it during battles and engagements, and play a leading role in rebuilding its strength following combat.

Among the critical factors to be considered in planning support for tactical operations are—

- Number and types of support units and quantities of resources available.

- The commander's priorities for support.

- Consumption factors for the type of operation being planned.

- Critical weapons systems whose continuous operability is crucial to the success of the battle.
- The threat to CSS operations in the rear and forward areas.
- Major tactical contingenices that may have to be supported.
- The locations of supporting and supported facilities.
- The effects of terrain and weather on support activites.
- Future operations.

In applying these factors, commanders and their planners should be guided by the following broad principles:

- Support must be continuous and adequate.

- CSS functions should be performed as far forward as possible.
- Roads, airlift, and other means of transportation must be fully exploited and controlled to overcome interdiction and congestion.
- Committed units must be supported by "push" packages rather than by requisition.
- CSS units and facilities must be positioned to support the operation, afford priority of support to the main effort, and must survive.
- Protection of CSS units should be planned in detail with self-protection and passive protective measures receiving special emphasis.

SUSTAINMENT CONTROLS

A variety of management controls are available to assist commanders in applying and adjusting sustainment priorities. These include methods of supply distribution, basic loads, expenditure controls, and operational measures of support.

SUPPLY DISTRIBUTION

Normally, CSS elements provide support on an area basis. When providing this support, CSS organizations use a varying combination of unit distribution and supply point distribution procedures.

When *unit distribution* is used, the supporting unit *delivers* supplies to the supported unit's area in transportation arranged by *the supporting unit*. Throughput is a form of unit distribution in which shipments bypass intermediate supply organizations or installations.

When *supply point distribution* is used, the supporting unit *issues* supplies from a supply point to the supported unit. The supported unit uses *its own transportation* to move the supplies to its area.

When determining the type of distribution to be used to support combat forces, the CSS planner should consider—

- The availability of personnel and equipment to deliver and pickup supplies.
- The missions of the supported forces.
- The adequacy of road networks in the area of operations.
- The priorities for use of the roads.
- The anticipated distances between supporting and supported forces.
- The locations of the supported forces.
- The threat to road and rail networks.

BASIC LOADS

A basic load is that amount of equipment required by a unit to sustain itself until resupply can be effected. This basic load is normally established by the theater commander. The basic load is not a fixed quantity; it may be altered as situations dictate. For example, a maneuver unit conducting an attack behind a large enemy force may have its basic load of ammunition increased for that particular operation. The term "basic loads" applies to all classes of supply.

One method of easing the resupply requirements of supported units is tailoring of the basic loads. Units whose missions require greater than average movement, expenditure of large amounts of ammunition, or extended operations away from the main force can be given larger or different basic loads of fuel, ammunition, parts, or other necessary supplies.

RSR AND CSR

Two other sustainment controls apply uniquely to ammunition resupply: required supply rate (RSR) and controlled supply rate (CSR). The RSR is the estimated amount of ammunition needed to sustain a combat force without restriction for a particular type of operation for a specific length of time. It is expressed in rounds of ammunition per weapon per day. The tactical commander uses the RSR to forecast his ammunition requirements. The RSR is normally computed by the S3/G3 based on the most current usage data and the projected tactical situation. If current data are not available, consumption estimates from FM 101-10-1 should be used as a guide.

The CSR is the rate of ammunition expenditure that can be sustained with available supplies. Like the RSR, the CSR is also expressed in rounds per weapon per day. The theater commander announces a CSR for each item of ammunition. CSR are disseminated through G4 channels. They are normally published in operation orders or in their fire support annexes. They represent the higher headquarter's statement of what ammunition will be made available to support operations. In developing CSRs, planners consider the RSRs, the amounts of ammunition on hand, the availability of assets to move it to using units, and the issuing organization's daily handling capability. CSRs may be reallocated internally by subordinate commanders to match their priorities for support.

OPERATIONAL MEASURES OF SUPPORT

Commanders must be concerned not only with support of current operations, but also with the sustainability of future operations. A comprehensive and meaningful picture of the sustainment condition of the force must constantly be available to the operational planners and to the commander during planning.

To provide that picture, CSS personnel must express the condition of personnel, materiel, and equipment in terms which have operational significance. For example:

- How far the commander can expect to be able to move the force or how long he can expect a particular type of equipment to operate in projected tactical conditions.

- How much barrier material is available, expressed in terms of linear or area measurements.

- How much roadway can be constructed with available resources.

- How many company-sized units can be issued new protective clothing.

- How many days of rations, fuel, parts, and ammunition are in the system, by type and by unit.

The current and projected maintenance posture must also be available in operational terms. It is more useful for operational planners to know that the maintenance posture of a reserve division will allow it to counterattack in 24 hours than to know that the maintenance posture of the force as a whole will improve by five percent over the next 24 hours.

The CSS system must keep the operational planners constantly appraised of the status of key supply items in operational terms. Additionally, operational planners must know the current storage sites of each supply class to assist in planning. Any class or item of supply whose status will adversely impact on the mission must be highlighted to the commander and to operational or tactical planners, together with recommended options to compensate.

Effective support of the soldier also affects combat power. CSS planners must monitor such aspects of field service as—

- The health, morale, and welfare of soldiers.

- The availability of field services such as showers, laundry, and graves registration units.

- The impact of the field service capabilities on the fighting capacity of units.

The final expression of operational sustainability by the CSS planner or operator must be a judgment regarding the extent to which the mission can be supported.

COMBAT SERVICE SUPPORT AS A DECEPTION INSTRUMENT

CSS elements must be integrated into both operational and tactical deception plans. As with all deception planning, both operational and CSS planners must consider the resources required to execute the deception story and the risks involved in committing them.

CSS resources can contribute to deception plans in a number of ways. They can—

- Establish new or bogus CSS facilities for which there is no immediate need to project false intentions to the enemy.

- Create dummy storage sites.

- Close or give the appearance of closing existing facilities.

- Position materiel in and provide support out of unusual or unorthodox positions.

- Change CSS movement patterns.

- Alter positioning of units to mislead the enemy.

- Transmit bogus reports and orders on administrative-logistical communications nets.

Sustainment is a central, potentially decisive aspect of operations, not an adjunct to them. It is as important to success as any other part of the commander's operational plan. To meet the sustainment challenge, commanders must grasp both the operational and logistical possibilities and limitations of their situations. The most successful commanders have been those who pressed their operations to the very limit of their sustaining power—but not one step further.

CHAPTER 5
Environment of Combat

Weather, terrain, and the day-night cycle constitute the basic setting for all military operations. These physical conditions significantly affect the movement, employment, and protection of units in campaigns and battles. Commanders must understand the operational and tactical implications of the physical environment as well as its effects on their soldiers, equipment, and weapons.

Commanders must also recognize the moral and physical effects of combat itself. These are as much a part of the setting of battle as the natural environment and are equally responsible for the "friction" of war. The danger, destruction, and confusion of combat; the alteration of the terrain by weapons and obstacles; and the inevitable occurrence of the unexpected contribute substantially to that atmosphere in which, as Clausewitz said, "the simplest things become difficult."

This chapter discusses weather, terrain, special environments, battlefield stress, and the effects of nuclear and chemical weapons and electronic warfare (EW). Although it treats each of these topics separately, all combine in combat to produce the stressful, resistant environment of battle.

CONTENTS

EFFECTS OF WEATHER AND VISIBILITY

Weather and visibility conditions create advantages and disadvantages for opposing forces. To fight effectively, commanders must acquire weather information about their entire area of operations. They and their staffs must also know how to exploit the opportunities offered by the weather while minimizing its adverse effects on their operations. They must also understand the seasonal weather patterns that influence the campaign as a whole.

Weather affects soldiers, equipment, operations, and terrain. Cloud cover, wind, rain, snow, fog, dust, light conditions, and temperature extremes combine in various ways that affect human efficiency and limit the use of weapons and equipment.

Control of soldiers is more difficult in bad weather and in low visibility conditions. Security of positions and formations is more difficult to maintain. Generally, inclement weather favors an attacker by concealing his movement and making enemy air support less effective, even though it also degrades his mobility. Defending troops tend to be less alert during inclement weather.

Weather conditions also affect equipment and weapon systems. Cloud cover reduces air support, degrades airborne sensors, limits airborne and air assault operations, and affects terminally guided weapons. Wind and precipitation also affect the performance of nuclear and chemical weapons and the extent of their downwind hazards.

Seasonal climatic conditions influence the conduct and support of large unit operations. Heavy rain, snow, and freezing and thawing cycles restrict cross-country movement. Poor trafficability increases fuel consumption, reduces range, increases maintenance requirements, and impedes tactical and logistical movement.

Freezing temperatures may improve trafficability, but also increase maintenance problems. Extreme heat, especially at high altitudes, reduces aircraft load limits; and heat waves from the earth's surface can make optical systems less effective. Sandstorms in the desert can disable or immobilize equipment.

Limited visibility also affects operations. Night, fog, and smoke reduce the useful ranges of most weapons. Despite technical advances in night vision equipment, these conditions usually require a change in tactics. The blinding effect of nuclear fires is greater at night. Generally, limited visibility favors the attacker. The defender's observation and the effectiveness of his ground based weapons and air support are reduced. The movements of the attacker are more easily concealed, making it easier to achieve surprise.

Successful operations under adverse conditions or during periods of limited visibility require thorough planning. Simple schemes of maneuver should be rehearsed and then executed aggressively.

Three general observations summarize the effects of weather and visibility on operations:

- Good physical condition, acclimatization, and discipline at the small-unit level can help offset the adverse effects of weather and visibility. In adverse conditions, a well-prepared force has an even greater advantage than usual over an ill-prepared enemy.

- The leadership time and effort required to care for soldiers increases proportionately with the severity of weather.

- Adverse weather impedes the air operations of both sides. Such weather is therefore most advantageous to the side inferior in air support, especially in offensive operations.

EFFECTS OF TERRAIN

Terrain forms the natural structure of the battlefield. Commanders must recognize its limitations and possibilities and use it to protect friendly operations and to put the enemy at a disadvantage. Terrain analysis, intelligence preparation of the battlefield (IPB), and engineer operations are key to the operational use of terrain.

TERRAIN ANALYSIS

Understanding the limitations and opportunities of terrain is a fundamental military skill. Terrain analysis varies among levels of command. Leaders of small tactical units concentrate on woodlines, streams, and individual hills. Division and corps commanders analyze road nets, aerial avenues of movement, drainage patterns, and hill systems.

At the operational level, campaign planners consider terrain from an even broader perspective. Ports, transportation systems, natural resources, major land forms, and regional characteristics are significant in the planning and direction of campaigns. Features, such as coastal plains, mountain ranges, marshlands, and river deltas, must be considered as obstacles and avenues of movement for armies.

Commanders perform terrain analysis in the light of their units' missions. They evaluate the terrain's potential for cover and concealment, its impact on their own and enemy mobility, and its use for observation and direct fire effect. The able commander recognizes the battlefield's natural structure and acts to improve or overcome it as necessary to accomplish the mission. Such analysis must include a unit's assigned area of responsibility, the surrounding terrain which may affect operations, and the airspace immediately over it. Fire, maneuver, and obstacle plans are designed as an integrated whole fitted to the terrain on which the operation is to be conducted.

The commander must consider the terrain in depth as well as in the area of his immediate operations. Terrain analysis extends into the territory through which the enemy must move to attack or to concentrate defensive forces. Areas of interest and operations must be evaluated to determine the areas and routes the enemy is most likely to use. Surveillance, interdiction, and deep operations depend upon that estimate. Destroying bridges, blocking defiles, or obstructing routes in depth can separate enemy echelons, isolate enemy positions, and create lucrative targets for ground or air attack.

Analysis of the terrain to the front, flanks, and rear of the assigned area is also necessary. Such analysis facilitates changes in the direction of friendly movement and assists in anticipating threats created by enemy maneuver during an operation.

After studying the area in detail, staff officers provide the commander with an assessment, including the ground's general organization, dominant features, chief avenues for movement to include low-level air approaches and key terrain. Intelligence and operations officers identify significant features, air and ground avenues of approach, and defensible terrain. The staff

or commander specifies named areas of interest (NAI) as a means of focusing the surveillance and interdiction efforts of the unit.

The key elements of terrain analysis are summarized in the traditional mnemonic OCOKA: Observation and fields of fires, Cover and concealment, Obstacles and movement, Key terrain, and Avenues of approach.

Observation and Fields of Fire. Contour and vegetation affect observation and fire. Where visibility is limited, direct fire weapons are less effective and movement entails less risk. Remote sensors can be used to cue artillery and to cover some of the space which cannot be observed directly. Large forests, jungles, built-up areas, and tracts of broken ground limit observation and the effects of fire.

Fields of observation and fire differ according to weapon characteristics. Hilltops and the tops of buildings make excellent observation posts or radar sites, but are rarely satisfactory positions for direct fire weapon positions. Tanks, missiles, and machine guns must be sited where their effects will be the greatest and dead space will be minimized.

The terrain should also be analyzed in terms of air observation and fire. In many cases, Army aircraft can overwatch from flanking positions in woods and valleys which are inaccessible to ground troops. Conversely, the enemy can also be expected to exploit aerial avenues of approach for air reconnaissance and attacks.

Cover and Concealment. Terrain can protect a unit from observation and fire or it can hide forces. Cover is protection from observation and fire. The cover afforded by slopes, folds, and depressions is critical because it preserves the strength of the force. Covered positions are as important to command posts, indirect fire units, reserves, combat support units, and combat service support units as they are to close combat units. While nuclear and chemical fires can overcome some of the protection the ground affords, prudent dispersion of units among multiple covered positions can provide considerable cover even in active nuclear-chemical environments. Whether maneuvering on the ground or in the air, all forces should seek the protection of covering terrain to the greatest degree possible.

Concealment is protection from observation. Urbanized terrain, broken hills, high ground, and forested areas can be used to hide forces, but in operations against sophisticated forces, terrain alone cannot conceal a force or facility. Limiting electronic and thermal emissions must also be used to conceal units and headquarters, camouflage used to conceal men and equipment, and movement limited to help prevent the detection of hidden units. Even in fluid conditions, there will be opportunities to conceal forces for short periods.

Concealment of maneuver forces can be a great tactical advantage. Defenders can use it to draw the enemy deep into prepared defensive areas. Attackers can use it to avoid being detected or engaged as they approach defended positions. Stay-behind forces, from patrol to battalion size, can use it to permit bypass by attacking enemy forces.

When nuclear weapons are used, concealment of command posts, artillery units, logistics facilities, and other high value targets is especially important. Urban areas, farm buildings, and other manmade structures can be used to hide these sensitive units or facilities.

Obstacles and Movement. There are few truly impassable areas. The cliffs at Quebec, the tides of Inchon, and the Ardennes forest all appeared impassable to their defenders. Enterprising commanders have often won decisive victories by striking suddenly over unlikely routes. We should actively seek such "impassable" approaches in our offensive operations and protect difficult approaches into our own positions against surprise enemy attacks.

Roads, ridgelines, river valleys, and plains are high speed approaches on which fluid battles may develop rapidly. Combat moves slowly through swamps, thick forests, soft sandy areas, and broken or mountainous terrain that is traversable only through defiles or by dismounted movement. Urban area also can constitute formidable obstacles.

Some areas vary in trafficability with the season or weather. Snow and ice on hills can slow a mounted movement considerably. Thaws or rains can change plains to quagmires within hours. The fires, tree blowdown, and contamination from nuclear or chemical weapons can alter movement conditions radically and rapidly.

Normally, an area of operations will contain a mixture of obstructing terrain and avenues that are suitable for air assault, mounted movement, or dismounted movement. Terrain which canalizes movement allows the defender to economize in difficult ground and to concentrate on the dangerous approaches. In such areas, the attacker must either secure the area before the defender can occupy it or resort to ground or aerial bypass, infiltration, or nuclear fires. In predominantly open areas, the attacker will be able to choose between many different approaches and the defender may be forced to fight a mobile battle in depth.

Natural or man made obstacles which parallel the direction of movement can protect the flanks of attacking or counterattacking forces. When such obstacles cross an avenue of approach, they form lines of resistance for the defender.

Obstacles vary in their effect on different types of forces. Rail lines, small streams, and villages along roads do not significantly impede dismounted operations, but can significantly slow the pace of a mounted operation. Adequately guarded forests and marshes which are difficult for unassisted armored forces to penetrate can be traversed by dismounted infantry or enveloped by air assault forces.

The most promising approaches are often those which appear unlikely. Often it is possible to gain access to a high-speed, ridge approach by crossing difficult

TERRAIN ANALYSIS

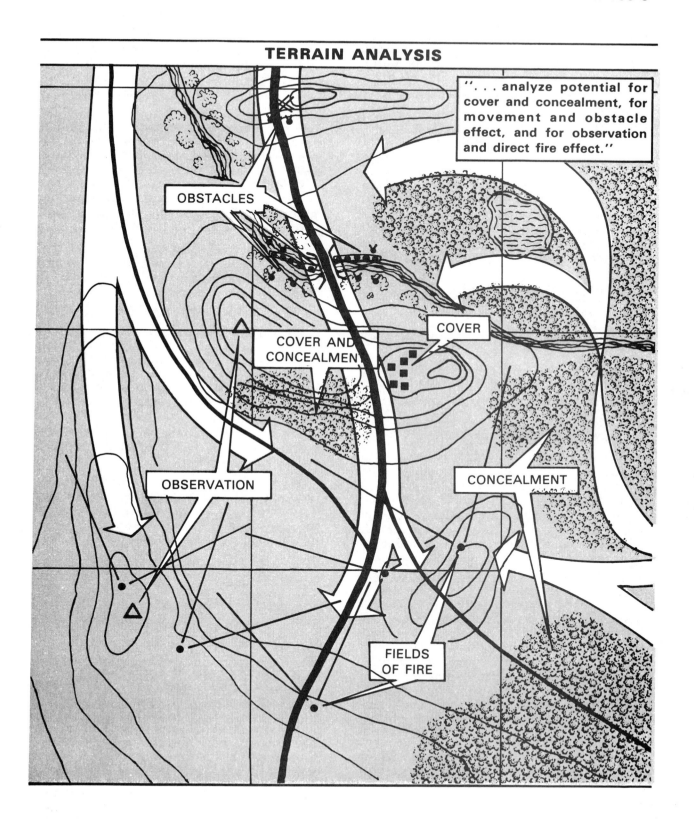

"... analyze potential for cover and concealment, for movement and obstacle effect, and for observation and direct fire effect."

OBSTACLES

COVER

COVER AND CONCEALMENT

CONCEALMENT

OBSERVATION

FIELDS OF FIRE

terrain immediately to its front. Old road beds also offer good movement potential because they follow solid ground and are usually not as well defended as improved routes.

Key Terrain. Key terrain is any feature, locality, or area which affords a marked advantage to the combatant who controls it. Since this advantage is situational, the commander designates key terrain only after he has analyzed his mission. The commander may designate certain key terrain as "decisive terrain" if accomplishment of his mission *depends on* seizing or retaining it. Many battlefields will not have decisive terrain. The commander designates decisive terrain in his concept of operation to communicate its importance to his staff and to subordinate commanders.

Avenues of Approach. Avenues of approach are evaluated in terms of their—

- Potential to accommodate maneuver units of a specified size and type.
- Access to important areas and adjacent avenues.
- Degree of canalization.
- Cover and concealment.
- Effect on line-of-sight communications.
- Obstacles.

A good avenue of approach must allow rapid movement along its entire length. Obstacles should be avoidable or reducible in reasonable time. The obstacle-producing effects of mines, barriers, and conventional, nuclear, and chemical interdiction must also be taken into account. Ideally, an avenue should be broad enough to permit lateral maneuver along its course and afford parallel spurs or branches which can be used to bypass strong defenses. Enough covering terrain should be available to permit part of the force to overwatch the rest. Combat support units and combat service support units must be able to move along the avenue in support of the attacking force. This may also be done over parallel routes or along routes which are uncovered as the attack gains ground.

If the enemy has air superiority, the avenue should provide maximum concealment from the air.

Air avenues for attack helicopters, air assault forces, and close air support differ from ground avenues. A good air approach of any type provides rapid access to the target area, together with terrain-masking from air defense radar and direct-fire air defense weapons.

Analyzing avenues of approach is as important to the defender as to the attacker. The defender must accurately determine the main approaches to his sector and identify the internal avenues which will permit him to maneuver against the attacker.

TERRAIN REINFORCEMENT

The proper use of natural obstacles and the reinforcement of terrain must be an integral part of the commander's plan. Artillery fires, direct fire engagement areas, and obstacles must all be completely meshed in the tactical plan. At the operational level, routes must be built or improved and obstacles and interdiction planned in depth to support the campaign or major operation.

Although the attacker determines the time and place of attack, the defender has a clear advantage in the preparation of the battlefield. He must make the most of his opportunity to study, to organize, and to improve the terrain. The attacker must bear this advantage of the defender in mind and must allow the defender as little time as possible to dig in, to obstruct routes, to prepare counterattack approaches, and to establish solid communications. *Once the defense has occupied a strong position and improved it, successful attack becomes far more difficult.*

Terrain reinforcement and mobility and countermobility improvements are the responsibility of the maneuver commander. Generally, a commander should concentrate his engineer effort in two directions. In one direction, he should develop an obstacle system in depth which enhances his fires and degrades the mobility of the enemy. In the other direction, he should develop covered positions and routes which facilitate the execution of his own scheme of maneuver.

Terrain reinforcement is a combined arms operation in which engineers and other units participate. Engineers install tank ditches, minefields, abatis, craters, and demolitions to canalize enemy movement, to hold the enemy in areas where he can be destroyed by fire, and to protect the flanks of maneuvering forces. Artillery, aviation, and close air support units emplace scatterable mines on targets of opportunity, to suppress threat air defense and artillery units and to interdict follow-on threat formations. Defending units emplace minefields around their own positions and usually construct their own fighting positions. Engineers operating with leading maneuver elements clear obstacles, construct bridges and rafts, and support countermine operations.

The introduction of remotely delivered scatterable mines makes every unit on the battlefield vulnerable to obstruction by mining. All units must therefore be capable of conducting mine-clearing operations.

TERRAIN INTELLIGENCE

The commander must personally acquaint himself with the terrain to the fullest extent possible before combat. Because maps are sometimes inaccurate or incomplete, commanders should conduct detailed personal reconnaissance, issuing orders from vantage points on the ground itself whenever possible. The intelligence staff officer (G2 or S2) is responsible for assembling all available information on the terrain and producing an estimate of its effect on operations. Sources of terrain intelligence include military, civilian, and engineer maps; topographical studies; civilian officials and area residents; prisoners of war; and air, space, and ground reconnaissance units.

URBANIZED TERRAIN

Commanders have always recognized the importance of urban centers as strategic objectives, but conducting operations in defended cities and towns has always been difficult. As the battles in Stalingrad, Aachen, Hue, and Beirut have shown, such efforts require enormous resources, diminish the tempo of offensive operations, restrict maneuver, and consume time. From an operational perspective, therefore, commanders should avoid committing forces to the attack of urban areas unless the mission absolutely requires doing so. Conversely, urbanized terrain may offer great advantages to the defender, provided the attacker is unable readily to avoid or by-pass the urban area.

In the heavily industrialized regions of the world, it will rarely be possible to avoid urban combat altogether. Previously separated centers have expanded to form extensive urban belts in Western Europe, Asia, and North America. Commanders and staff officers must therefore learn to analyze urbanized terrain and to plan effectively for operating in it. They need to learn to work with maps of different scales—maps of lower scale for greater resolution of detail within cities and normal military maps to control the overall battle.

Corps and division commanders may be responsible for major urban areas in their operations. Brigade and battalion commanders will usually have smaller cities, towns, villages, and strip areas in their zones or sectors. Commanders and staff officers at those levels analyze terrain from the standpoint of fighting from, within, or between urban areas.

In urbanized terrain, engagement ranges are shorter and terrain detail is more varied. Structures offer observation, fields of fire, and cover and concealment. When a sewer system is available for communications and small unit maneuvers or when heavily constructed multistory structures are present, they add a vertical dimension to urban combat.

The cover and concealment available in urban areas normally work to the tactical advantage of the defender. Mutually supporting strongpoints in an urban area or village can slow or impede the attacker and provide islands of resistance around which to maneuver and counterattack. They can also create opportunities for offensive maneuver against an attacker who has been halted and lies exposed at the edge of an urban area.

For his part, the attacker will attempt to isolate and bypass most built-up areas. Like the defender, the attacker can take advantage of urban cover and concealment to position command posts, supplies, and combat service support units. Both forces will be affected by the presence of the population and its sympathies in the conflict.

Urban areas impede the operations of armored and mechanized forces, restricting their mobility, maneuverability, and the effectiveness of their long-range weapons. Infantry forces including light forces are best suited to combat in built-up areas. In such areas, they can hold well-protected positions while minimizing their vulnerabilities to heavy weapons.

For details of how to fight on urbanized terrain, see FM 90-10.

SPECIAL ENVIRONMENTS

MOUNTAINS

Light forces (infantry, airborne and air assault) can operate effectively in mountainous regions because they are not terrain-limited. In such regions, light forces move primarily by air and on foot. Heavy forces must necessarily operate in passes and valleys which are negotiable by vehicle. Aviation units will be important for reconnaissance, antitank fire, and troop movement. Even then, dismounted infantry and aviation units will be needed to secure the high ground along the flanks.

Mountainous terrain significantly influences the use of weapons and equipment. Direct fire is generally less effective there because rocks and cliffs offer good natural cover. Aerial and long-range fires, however, will be effective because of the good observation the elevation affords, even though slopes limit grazing fire and create large dead spaces. Weapons with a high angle of fire, such as field artillery and especially mortars, and grenade launchers, take on added importance because they can reach into dead space.

Ground mobility in mountains is extremely difficult. Highways usually run in the valleys; existing roads and trails are normally few and primitive; and cross-country movement is particularly arduous. Helicopters, however, can normally overcome these difficulties. Although limited by unfavorable weather, density-altitude considerations, and enemy air defense, helicopters are extremely useful for moving troops and equipment, for reconnaissance, and for command and control during mountain operations.

From an operational perspective, mountain combat lacks the unity that is characteristic of combat in level or rolling terrain. The compartmented nature of the terrain induces isolated contests which are difficult for higher commanders to control. Typically, major engagements occur at the entrances and exits of passes.

Mountainous terrain tends to favor the defender and provides him with excellent observation and firing positions. Man made obstacles reinforce the natural ruggedness of mountainous terrain. The defender can easily deceive the enemy as to his strength and dispositions. Because the defender normally has more time to develop lateral trails, he can usually shift forces on the ground more rapidly than the attacker. Delaying actions are particularly effective in the mountains and can be accomplished by smaller-than-ordinary forces. Nonetheless, an aggressive attacker can sometimes traverse mountains rapidly, as the US campaign through the Eifel and the German attack through the Balkans demonstrated. A detailed discussion on how to fight in mountains is in FM 90-6.

JUNGLES

Jungle warfare has been common throughout the world in this century. Central Africa, Southeast Asia, the Pacific Islands, and Central and South America have all seen jungle combat at varying levels of intensity.

Jungles vary from tropical rain forests and secondary growth forests to swamps and tropical savannas. The dominating features of jungle areas are thick vegetation, constant high temperature, heavy rainfall, and humidity. These features combine to restrict movement, observation, fields of fire, communications, battlefield surveillance, and target acquisition. However, they also provide excellent cover and concealment.

Operations in jungles tend to be isolated actions because of the difficulties of movement and of maintaining contact between forces. Divisions can move cross-country slowly, but aggressive reconnaissance, meticulous intelligence collection, and detailed coordination are required to concentrate forces in this way. More commonly, large forces operate along roads or natural avenues of movement and, as in the mountains, this is where decisive battles will occur for the most part. Both combatants normally try to support or reinforce their committed forces by air and ground once fighting begins, and jungle combat has historically seen active deep operations of interdiction by air and ambush.

Large unit actions are usually surrounded by very active security areas in jungle operations. Patrolling and other surveillance operations are especially important to assure security of larger forces in the close terrain of jungles. This produces frequent engagements between small forces fighting for control of the security area. When security forces succeed in making contact with a larger force, they may be reinforced as their commander tries to bring on decisive battle.

Air operations are also highly important in the jungle because of the difficulties of ground movement. Reconnaissance, maneuver, fire support, and CSS can all be greatly assisted by air operations. A force without effective air support may make its major operational effort in the area's rainy season and concentrate on night tactical operations throughout the year to nullify its disadvantage. When the area of operations lies in a coastal or island area, naval support can be used for many of the same purposes as air support.

Short fields of observation and fire and thick vegetation make maintaining contact with the enemy difficult. The same factors reduce the effectiveness of indirect fire and make jungle combat primarily a fight between infantry forces. Support by air and mechanized forces can be decisive in jungle battles or engagements, but it will not always be available or effective. A detailed discussion of how to fight in jungles is found in FM 90-5.

DESERTS

Forces of all types can be employed in the desert. Armor and mechanized infantry forces are especially suitable to desert combat except in rough mountainous terrain where light infantry may be required. Air assault and motorized forces can also be advantageously employed to exploit the vast distances characteristic of desert warfare. Amphibious and airborne forces may be valuable to secure a lodgement in desert areas, but the former will normally be unable to operate far inland while the latter will require additional tactical mobility to conduct operations outside the lodgment area.

Deserts are semiarid and arid regions that contain a wide variety of soils in varying relief. Weather conditions can change rapidly. Temperatures may range from 30 to 130 degrees Fahrenheit in a 24-hour period. A clear day with unequaled visibility and flight conditions may quickly change to a raging sandstorm that can halt all military operations. Long periods of drought can be interrupted by sudden rains that bring flash floods and mud but little relief from water shortages. Large areas of excellent trafficability are often interspersed with rugged mountains, dunes, deep ravines, bogs, and sand seas. The availability of water will be a prime factor in planning and executing desert operations. The selection of locations for supporting logistics facilities and selection of objectives will frequently be based on water supply.

Flat desert areas alter the conduct of military operations. Because the terrain does not canalize large forces, large scale use of mines and obstacles becomes necessary. The lack of prominent features complicates land navigation and requires the use of dead-reckoning and celestial navigation. Although the lack of relief diminishes the influence of key terrain, small indentations and folds in the ground can provide cover for small units and individual vehicles. Because of the sparse vegetation, concealment in the desert is more difficult than in many other environments. Concealment, however, is not only possible, it is *absolutely necessary*. To survive, forces must use camouflage nets, pattern and mud painting, covers for reflective surfaces, and similar techniques. In general, easy observation makes undetected advances and withdrawals difficult.

Deception measures of all types (feints, ruses, decoy equipment, for example) thus become mandatory for success. Movement at night or during sandstorms while maintaining strict communication security assumes enormous importance in positioning units. Engagements are often fought at long ranges, and this places a premium on accurate gunnery at maximum range.

The desert environment has a debilitating effect on troops who have not been properly acclimatized or trained. Continuous exposure to the sun causes profuse sweating, sunburn, dehydration, cramps, heat exhaustion, and even heat stroke. The environment induces mental fatigue, impaired perception, and depression which, coupled with the pressures of combat, can overwhelm unprepared soldiers.

The desert has an even more adverse effect on machines. Intense supervision is required to ensure continuous availability of clean air, fuel, and lubricants. Vehicle cooling and electrical systems are vulnerable to extremes of temperature. Tracks, tires, and suspension systems wear out rapidly in the desert. The intense desert heat can also cause communication equipment to overheat and malfunction. A detailed discussion of how to fight in desert areas is in FM 90-3.

WINTER ZONES

In regions such as the polar ice cap, survival of forces requires so many resources that few may remain to accomplish anything militarily useful. Therefore, the likelihood is small that large forces will be committed to such an extreme environment. Nevertheless, the Army must be able to employ small combined arms forces in the arctic regions if required.

Larger forces, however, might well have to operate in a number of less severely cold environments worldwide. In areas which experience extremely cold winters, troops will have to be specially trained and equipped if they are to fight on equal terms with a well prepared enemy. Commanders in such areas will have to pay special attention to the protection, mobility, and tactics of their units.

When the temperature remains below zero for an extended period of time, troops will require special clothing, larger than usual rations, and more rest. They will have to be trained and acclimated to move, fight, and maintain themselves and their equipment in a hostile environment.

Special training in operation of weapons, land navigation, prevention of cold weather injuries, and the use of special tools and equipment may be necessary for troops deployed to winter zones. Good physical conditioning and proper psychological preparation are indispensable in such areas.

Although frozen ground and water can improve trafficability in winter, vehicles require special care to remain in operation. Batteries lose their charges rapidly. Engines need lighter weight lubricants. Water-based cooling systems need antifreeze. Track, tires, and suspension systems are subject to special strains when the temperature remains low and when the ground is frozen. Weapons also need special attention and maintenance because of the stiffening of recoil mechanisms and the increased brittleness of metal parts. Special gunnery techniques and computations may also be required to compensate for the effects of deep cold on propellants and the reduced effectiveness of ground bursts in snow.

Forces fighting in extreme winter conditions will have to learn special techniques of camouflage and of constructing fighting positions on frozen ground. They will almost always need to be well-prepared for night operations since winter days are short. Air support for friendly maneuver and vulnerability of friendly forces to air attack will be affected by icing conditions, winds, and snow storms. Commanders will have to take these limitations of aviation into account when planning tactical actions, troop movements, reconnaissance, and supply operations.

Terrain conditions vary widely in winter operations and tactics will have to be adapted to the specific conditions of the theater. The usual capabilities and limitations of units will apply in winter zones depending on the character of the ground. In open terrain, armored and mechanized forces will be effective although they will have to plan and train for special conditions such as ice-impeded maneuver, ice fog formed by their weapons, weather effects on their fire control equipment, and difficulties of maintenance and supply. In broken terrain, forests, and mountains, light forces will predominate as usual. They will, however, have to be equipped for cross-country mobility over ice and snow and their movement rates will be slower than in warmer conditions.

Finally, the winter environment significantly increases the time required for the performance of all tasks in the open. Construction of fighting positions, installation of obstacles, performance of maintenance tasks, and movement of units on foot can take five times the normal time in severe cold. *The highest caliber of leadership is required to assure that all necessary tasks are performed, that security is maintained, and that troops and their equipment are protected from the physical effects of extremely low temperatures.*

A detailed discussion of how to fight in winter is in FM 90-11.

EFFECTS OF NUCLEAR AND CHEMICAL WEAPONS

Soviet doctrine emphasizes the principle of mass and seeks victory through relentless offensive operations. If nuclear and chemical weapons are required to ensure success, they will be used. Soviet planners recognize that the employment of nuclear or chemical weapons may alter tactics, force requirements, and rates of advance. However, they expect little deviation from their basic doctrine, and equip, arm, and train their own forces and their allies to fight with nuclear and chemical weapons. Our own forces can therefore do no less.

The immediate effects of nuclear weapons are blast, thermal radiation, initial nuclear radiation, and electromagnetic pulse (EMP). These effects can cause significant personnel and materiel losses. Nuclear weapons can also cause tree blowdown, urban destruction, fires, radiological contamination and, in some cases, flooding. The EMP from a nuclear explosion can burn out unshielded electronic equipment. Long-term residual radiation from fallout or rainout can injure or kill soldiers. It may also contaminate supplies, facilities, equipment, terrain, and uncovered food or water.

Chemical weapons also produce immediate and delayed effects. They contaminate individuals, terrain, equipment, and supplies. Prompt use of protective equipment and shelters will significantly reduce casualties, but it also reduces individual and unit efficiency.

On a nuclear or chemical battlefield, heavy casualties could occur very quickly. Such heavy and sudden losses are likely to shock and confuse inadequately trained or psychologically unprepared troops.

In addition to taking immediate casualties, units suffering such attacks will be weakened by long lasting effects. Soldiers exposed to different levels of radiation will lose varying effectiveness. Wearing chemical protective clothing or operating for long times in contaminated environments will also degrade performance. Commanders must apply the proper mission-oriented protective posture (MOPP) to balance protection with mission accomplishment.

The use of chemical and nuclear weapons will dramatically affect the control of forces. Command posts will be prime targets for attack. Even within small units, control will be difficult. Soldiers and leaders who are wearing protective equipment will be difficult to recognize. Leaders will have to cope with the additional burden of their protective equipment while they perform their duties. *Only cohesive, disciplined, and well-trained units can function in such an environment.*

Together, these conditions could radically alter the tempo and structure of battle. Accordingly, when fighting an enemy with a nuclear or chemical capability, our forces must operate in full awareness that such weapons could be used at any time. Commanders must act to accomplish the mission with the least risk; the enemy cannot be allowed to win through the surprise use of nuclear or chemical weapons.

Units survive by anticipating nuclear or chemical attacks. They must take the following measures to avoid becoming lucrative targets:

- *Maintain alertness.* Commanders at all levels must be continually alert to nuclear or chemical attack. They have to balance the risk to their units against mission requirements, adjusting their dispersion and MOPP without losing momentum.

- *Instill discipline.* Units must continue their missions in spite of nuclear or chemical attacks. Troops should be physically conditioned by frequent training in protective clothing and psychologically prepared for the effects of nuclear and chemical weapons.

- *Avoid detection.* Units must use active and passive measures to defeat enemy target acquisition capabilities.

- *Retain mobility.* Tactical mobility gives the commander the best chance for survival. Commanders must consider displacing whenever they suspect that their units have been detected.

- *Disperse forces and installations to limit damage.* Units and facilities must be kept dispersed to the maximum degree consistent with mission performance. Proper dispersal is based on the characteristics of enemy weapons and must include provisions for massing on short notice. The degree of acceptable dispersal will depend on the tactical situation, enemy capabilities, and available terrain.

- *Seek terrain shielding and cover.* Natural terrain shields troops from the effects of nuclear and chemical weapons. Foxholes with overhead cover and simple shelters are usually preferable to elaborate shelters which take a long time to construct and are easily detected.

- *Ensure logistical preparedness.* The logistical system must continue to function in a nuclear or chemical environment. Logistical facilities should be dispersed, concealed, and redundant. Units must have sufficient combat supplies, protective clothing, decontamination, and medical supplies to fight without immediate support.

- *Plan for rapid reconstitution.* Commanders must be prepared to continue the mission after a nuclear or chemical attack. The commander who can reconstitute or replace lost units rapidly will have the advantage in the continuing battle. Prompt damage assessment following an enemy strike and early implementation of contingency plans are the keys to rapid reconstitution.

EFFECTS OF ELECTRONIC WARFARE

Opposing armies possessing electronic warfare capabilities will attempt to deny their enemies the use of the electromagnetic spectrum. They will analyze their opponent's communications, radar, and data processing systems and act to destroy or disrupt them at critical times.

Using countermeasures to cope with enemy electronic warfare may mean the difference between tactical success and failure. The commander should take the following steps to conceal emitters or to deceive the enemy as to their identities and locations:

- Change radio frequencies often.

- Use directional antennas.

- Issue emission control (EMCON) orders to restrict use of the electromagnetic spectrum.

- Employ manipulative electronic deception (MED) to alter their electromagnetic profiles or to portray notional units.

- Use wire or cable communications whenever possible.

Operators must be trained to work in spite of EW. Commanders should make their tactical training in EW as realistic as possible.

Continued operations in an EW environment require—

- Training operators to use communications-electronics operations instructions (CEOI) and to make short transmissions.

- Operation on the lowest power possible.

- Masking emitters with terrain.

- Finding and attacking enemy EW assets.

- Establishing alternate communications means.

- Training subordinates to act independently in support of the overall mission when communications fail.

EFFECTS OF SMOKE AND OBSCURANTS

Opposing forces will use smoke to increase their effectiveness while reducing their vulnerability. Specifically, smoke can—

- Deny the enemy information.

- Reduce the effectiveness of enemy sensors, range finders, and target designators.

- Restrict nap-of-the earth and contour approaches for enemy aircraft.

- Disrupt enemy movement, operations, and command and control.

- Create conditions to surprise the enemy.

- Mask the use of chemical weapons.

- Deceive the enemy.

In US tactical operations, each level of command plans the use of smoke to support its overall plan. When planning smoke operations, commanders must weigh how smoke will degrade enemy combat effectiveness against how it might adversely affect friendly command and control and target acquisition. Units employing smoke must coordinate with adjacent, higher, and lower headquarters to avoid disrupting their operations. During darkness and other periods of reduced visibility, smoke can degrade enemy observation capability further, particularly the capability of enemy electro-optical devices. It can increase the effectiveness of conventional and scatterable mines and chemical munitions. Similarly, smoke can intensify the effects of electronic warfare on enemy command and control.

SMOKE OPERATIONS IN THE OFFENSE

Commanders can maneuver units behind or under smoke screens. This denies the enemy information about our strength, position, activities, and movement. It also facilitates breaching obstacles and bypassing enemy strongpoints, and reduces the effectiveness of enemy observers and weapon systems.

Deception screens enhance surprise and prevent the enemy from concentrating his defense against the main attack. Obscuration smoke against enemy defensive positions in depth helps isolate forward enemy positions for assault.

SMOKE OPERATIONS IN THE DEFENSE

Smoke employed with other munitions impedes and disrupts the movement of enemy formations. It obscures suspected enemy observers, conceals defensive positions, screens disengaging forces, or conceals counterattacking forces. Smoke screens can silhouette assaulting forces and prevent enemy aerial surveillance of assembly, marshaling, staging, and logistic areas. Smoke operations should not interfere with friendly target acquisition, adjustment of fires, or maneuver.

BATTLEFIELD STRESS

Commanders must bear in mind the stressful effects of combat as they plan and conduct operations, for the pressures that battlefield chaos and destruction place on soldiers have always been very great. Unit discipline, realistic field training, deliberately fostered unit cohesion, and solid bonding between leader and lead can diminish the effects of this stress in part, but nothing can wholly eliminate it. The commander who understands this and protects his soldiers through strong, positive, and caring leadership, proper mental, physical, and training preparation, and simple decisive plans will win.

The lethality of modern weapons, the disruption of control through enemy use of EW, the physical expansion of the danger area around battlefields, and the threat or use of nuclear and chemical weapons are all mentally corrosive, and commanders must act to protect their units accordingly. Leaders at all levels must be able to recognize the signs of battlefield stress and deal with it quickly and effectively. Prompt treatment of stress casualties in forward areas can rapidly return most soldiers to duty. Further, constant effort to protect the force and an observable concern for the soldier's personal welfare will help troops cope with stress, and thus maintain fighting effectiveness. Finally, deliberate actions to maintain and enhance unit cohesion through effective integration of replacements, shared responsibilities among the leadership, and sustainment of small unit teams will pay handsome dividends.

While shielding their own troops from stress, commanders should attempt to promote terror and disintegration in the opposing force. Aggressive patrolling, raids, and sudden, violent actions which catch the enemy by surprise and do not permit him to recover should be commonly used as tools to magnify his battlefield stress. Coupled with attacks on his command structure, the use of artillery, air-delivered weapons, EW, smoke, deception,

psychological warfare, and special operations forces, stress-creating actions can hasten the destruction of his combat capability.

Historically, even the psychological stress of victory has been considerable. Much of the difficulty of initiating or sustaining exploitations or pursuit has been connected with overcoming the exhaustion of troops and junior leaders. In such cases, commanders must make a realistic appraisal of their soldiers' actual capabilities and drive them on even in the face of great resistance to gain the full advantage of their success. Such determination is even more critical with defeated or retreating troops, who are harder to rally.

PART II

OFFENSIVE OPERATIONS

CHAPTER 6

Fundamentals of the Offense

The offensive is the decisive form of war—the commander's ultimate means of imposing his will upon the enemy. While strategic, operational, or tactical considerations may require defending, defeat of an enemy force at any level will sooner or later require shifting to the offensive. Even in the defense itself, seizure and retention of the initiative will require offensive operations. The more fluid the battle, the more true this will be.

HISTORICAL PERSPECTIVE

From Yorktown in the Revolutionary War to the Yalu River in the Korean war, the US Army has a history of successful offensive campaigns. Sherman, Jackson, MacArthur, Bradley, and Patton are names which stand out from a long list of American leaders who were expert in the attack. General Grant also understood the essence of offensive operations. Although he could fight direct and bloody actions when necessary, he also was a master of maneuver, speed, and the indirect approach. His operation south of Vicksburg fought in the Spring of 1863 has been called the most brilliant campaign ever fought on American soil. It exemplifies the qualities of a well-conceived, violently executed offensive plan.

After 6 months of fruitless fighting north of Vicksburg, Grant moved his army south of the fortress and crossed to the eastern bank of the Mississippi early in May, masking the move with demonstrations and raids. That move turned the Confederates' Vicksburg defenses and put the Union Army

CONTENTS

within reach of the enemy's rear. It was risky, however, because it separated Grant from his base of operations and placed him in enemy territory against an army of equal strength.

Nonetheless, Grant retained the initiative. Rather than moving north on the most obvious approach to his objective, he avoided the defenses south of Vicksburg and used the Big Black River to protect his flank as he maneuvered toward Jackson,

THE VICKSBURG CAMPAIGN

Mississippi. By threatening both Jackson and Vicksburg, Grant prevented the Confederates from uniting their forces against him, and by swinging to the east of the fortress, he interdicted its main line of support. His speed of movement and his

THE VICKSBURG CAMPAIGN (Continued)

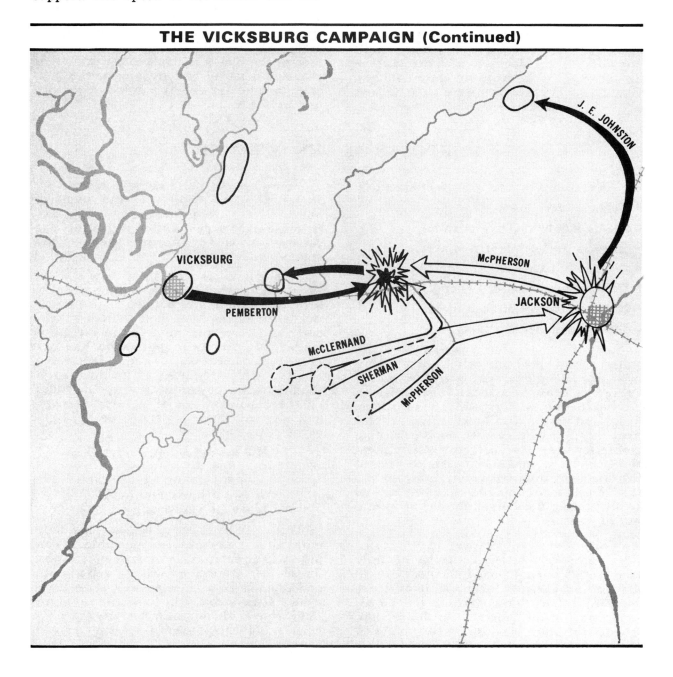

refusal to establish conventional lines of supply added to the effect of his attack, confusing the enemy and frustrating Confederate attempts to strike at his rear.

Setting a pace of operations so rapid that his enemies could not follow his activities, Grant defeated the forces of Generals Johnston and Pemberton in five successive engagements. He covered 200 miles in 19 days, capturing Jackson and driving the defenders of Vicksburg into their trenches. Grant's 4,000 casualties were only half as great as his enemy's. Within 6 weeks the 30,000 men of the Vicksburg garrison surrendered, giving the Union uncontested control of the Mississippi and dividing the Confederacy.

The same speed, surprise, maneuver, and decisive action will be required in the campaigns of the future. Sensors and long-range weapons, the mobility of ground and air units, and the concentration of forces and fires at the time and place of the attacker's choosing must all be harnessed to the task of collapsing the enemy's defenses rapidly and in depth.

PURPOSES OF THE OFFENSE

Offensive operations are undertaken to—

- Defeat enemy forces.
- Secure key or decisive terrain.
- Deprive the enemy of resources.
- Gain information.
- Deceive and divert the enemy.
- Hold the enemy in position.
- Disrupt an enemy attack.

Because the offensive requires the attacker to expose himself by movement, offensive operations usually require the attacker to achieve a local superiority in combat power at the point of the attack. That, and the need to have sufficient force available to exploit success, imply accepting risk elsewhere. A successful attack must therefore be pressed relentlessly to prevent the opponent from recovering from the initial shock, regaining his equilibrium, and reconstituting a cohesive defense or attacking in his turn.

While offensive operations may have as their objective the destruction or neutralization of an enemy force, inflicting physical damage is frequently incidental to offensive success. Rather, large gains are achieved by destroying the coherence of the defense, fragmenting and isolating enemy units in the zone of the attack, and driving deep to secure operationally decisive objectives. Historically, the most successful offensive operations have produced more enemy prisoners than casualties, reflecting the corrosive impact of offensive shock on the enemy's will to resist.

Such results are most likely from attacks which avoid the enemy's main strength, turn him out of his defensive positions, isolate his forces from their sources of support, and force him to fight in an unintended direction over ground he has not prepared. Successful commanders have consistently attempted to produce such conditions, thereby shifting to the defender all the disadvantages of fighting exposed and surprised. Field Marshal Viscount Slim put it concisely:

> Hit the other fellow
> As quick as you can,
> As hard as you can,
> Where it hurts him most,
> When he isn't looking.

There will be times, of course, when only more direct attacks are possible. Even MacArthur, a master of maneuver, was forced into frontal attacks to seize Buna and Gona in New Guinea. Such attacks are nearly always costly in lives and materiel. They should therefore be undertaken only when no other approach is possible or will accomplish the mission.

While most attacks seek the outright defeat of the opposing force, offensive operations may also be conducted for related purposes. Attacks may be mounted to seize key terrain for use in defense or subsequent attack, or to secure or protect vital lines of communication. The Israelis' capture of the Mitla Pass in 1967, for example, provided the springboard for their subsequent drive to the Suez Canal. Attacks may also be conducted to secure critical war-supporting resources, as in Germany's effort in 1941 to seize Great Britain's oil fields in the near east.

Sometimes an attack may be launched simply to force the enemy to disclose his strength, dispositions, or intentions. Such a *reconnaissance in force* may develop into a major attack if the inital probe discloses an exploitable weakness in the enemy's defenses. Attacks may also be used to deceive or distract the enemy. Used in conjunction with other deception measures, such *diversionary attacks* can delay the enemy's identification of and reaction to the main effort, and may actually induce him to shift forces away from critical areas. Alternatively, an attack may be designed to fix an enemy force in position, thereby preventing its interference with a friendly maneuver elsewhere. *Feints* and *demonstrations* are special forms of diversionary attack.

Finally, once hostilities have begun, attacks may be used by a defending force to disrupt an expected enemy attack, upsetting its preparation and thus buying time and information. As in the case of the reconnaissance in force, such a *spoiling attack* may develop into a major offensive operation if the attack reveals an exploitable weakness. *Raids* are a special form of spoiling attack, designed to destroy installations or facilities critical to the enemy's operations. Raids may also be mounted prior to or in conjunction with other offensive operations to confuse the enemy or divert his attention.

CHARACTERISTICS OF OFFENSIVE OPERATIONS

Whatever their purpose, all successful offensive operations are characterized by surprise, concentration, speed, flexibility, and audacity.

SURPRISE

Commanders achieve surprise by striking the enemy at a time or place, or in a manner, for which he is unprepared. Surprise delays enemy reactions, overloads and confuses his command and control, reduces the effectiveness of his weapons, and induces psychological shock in soldiers and leaders. By thus radically diminishing enemy combat power, surprise enables an attacker to succeed with fewer forces than he might otherwise require.

Achieving outright surprise once hostilities have begun has never been easy, and modern surveillance and warning capabilities have made it even more difficult. Surprise can still be achieved, however, by operating in a manner contrary to the enemy's expectations—for example, by attacking over a more difficult, therefore less obvious, avenue of approach or in adverse weather. Germany's precipitate defeat of France in May, 1940, for example, resulted in large measure from the surprise created by attacking through the "impassable" Ardennes Forest. Four years later, German armies surprised American forces by attacking in the dead of winter over the very same ground.

Surprise can also be created by radically altering the structure or tempo of the battle. For example, the insertion of airborne, airmobile forces or special operating forces deep in the enemy's rear can sharply and suddenly increase the enemy's sense of threat, sowing fear and confusion, and in the extreme case, inducing outright paralysis. British and American airborne attacks the night before the Normandy invasion had just such an effect on defending German forces. Similarly, deep ground attacks can achieve surprise simply through the rapidity with which they move, by confronting rearward enemy forces with a wholly unanticipated threat. The Israeli attack in the Sinai in June, 1967, illustrated such surprise-gaining agility.

Finally, surprise can be achieved by manipulating the enemy's expectations through deception, feints, and ruses. Egypt's attack across the Suez Canal in 1973 owed its success in part to a succession of demonstrations and maneuvers conducted in the months prior to the attack—actions which led Israeli commanders to believe that preparations for the actual attack were merely part of the same pattern. More recently, British forces in the Falkland Islands used deception effectively to surprise Argentine forces defending Port Stanley.

While surprise can radically degrade enemy combat power, the effect is usually only temporary, as the events of the Battle of the Bulge demonstrated. Unless enemy forces or their leaders are inherently fragile, they will sooner or later recover from the initial shock. History affords countless examples of armies including our own which recovered from initial surprise to achieve final victory. To reap the benefits of surprise, therefore, the attacking commander must exploit its initial shock ruthlessly, allowing the enemy no time to regain his equilibrium.

To sum up, surprise can be a vital ingredient of successful offensive operations. But it can never be guaranteed, and, even when achieved, rarely lasts. While always seeking surprise, therefore, the commander must also hedge against the loss of surprise and plan for the aggressive exploitation of surprise whenever it is achieved.

CONCENTRATION

While surprise may often contribute to offensive success, concentration of effort is invariably essential to both achieving and exploiting it. Virtually all modern offensive operations have been characterized by sudden concentrations followed by rapid,

deep exploitations. Germany's attack through France in 1940, the Soviet attack into Manchuria in 1945, MacArthur's counteroffensive in Korea in 1950, and Israel's seizure of the Sinai in 1967 all illustrate the rapid concentration of combat power to penetrate or envelop, then shatter the enemy's defenses. In all but the Manchurian case, the attacker enjoyed little overall numerical advantage. Rather, each succeeded by achieving overwhelming local superiority, then preserving that initial advantage by rapid and relentless exploitation.

Modern technology has made the process of concentration both more difficult and more dangerous. While advances in ground and air mobility enable the attacker to concentrate more rapidly, they also enable the defender to react more quickly. Moreover, the lethality of modern weaponry—especially nuclear weapons—radically increases the threat to concentrated formations.

To overcome these difficulties, the attacking commander must manipulate both his own and the enemy's concentration, first dispersing to stretch the enemy's defenses and to avoid presenting lucrative targets for the enemy's deep fires, then concentrating rapidly along converging axes to overwhelm enemy forces at the point of attack, then dispersing once again to exploit initial success and shatter the enemy's defenses in depth.

Achieving this pattern of rapid concentration and dispersal requires flexible leaders, agile units, and careful synchronization of combat, combat support, and combat service support activities. Commanders at all levels must designate a main effort, focus resources to support it, and be prepared to shift it rapidly without losing synchronization as the attack unfolds. Units making the main attack must be allocated enough combat support and combat service support to adjust to changing circumstances without time consuming and potentially confusing reorganizations. At the same time, the commander must retain control of sufficient assets to shift his main effort to a supporting attack if the latter appears more promising.

At every level, but especially at division and higher, special effort must be devoted to concealing concentration until it is too late for the enemy to react to it effectively. Units must avoid or mask patterns of movement and preparatory activity which might reveal the direction or timing of attack. Logistical build-ups, patrolling activities, communications, and indirect fires must be monitored to preclude a visible change in the attacking force's operating pattern. Speed, security, and deception are essential to successful concentration for attack.

On an air-land battlefield, concentration will require the careful prior coordination of other service support—especially air support. Tactical air operations will be vital at every stage of the attack—offensive and defensive counter air to protect the concentration from detection and attack, reconnaissance and interdiction to delay and disrupt enemy counterconcentration, and close air support to weight the main effort and especially, sustain the momentum of the attack. The flexibility of airpower makes it a powerful instrument of rapid concentration, but its full advantages cannot be realized unless ground and air operations are effectively synchronized.

SPEED

The attack must move rapidly. Speed is absolutely essential to success; it promotes surprise, keeps the enemy off balance, contributes to the security of the attacking force, and prevents the defender from taking effective countermeasures. Properly exploited, speed can confuse and immobilize the defender until the attack becomes unstoppable. Finally, speed can compensate for a lack of mass and provide the momentum necessary for attacks to achieve their aims.

Attacking forces move fast and follow reconnaissance units or successful probes through gaps in enemy defenses. They must shift their strength quickly to widen penetrations, roll up exposed flanks, and reinforce successes. The attacker tries to carry the battle deep into the enemy rear to break down the enemy's defenses before he can react. The enemy must never be permitted to recover from the shock of the initial assault, never be given the time to identify the main effort, and above all, never be afforded the opportunity to mass his forces or supporting fire against the main offensive effort.

Speed is built into operations through careful planning. Commanders must identify the best avenues for attack, plan the battle in depth, provide for quick transitions to exploitation and pursuit, and concentrate and combine forces effectively. Speed depends on the violent execution of the plan by fire and maneuver units, but it will also depend on—

- Full understanding of the commander's intent.

- Availability and positioning of engineers.

- Use of air and ground cavalry.

- Maintenance of effective air defense.

- Responsive logistic support of the force.

- Effective use of military intelligence (MI) and electronic warfare (EW) assets.

- Effective command and control.

- Effective air support.

FLEXIBILITY

The attack must be flexible. The commander must foresee developments as far ahead as possible. However, he must also expect uncertainties and be ready to exploit opportunities. To preserve synchronization on a fluid battlefield, initial planning must be detailed. Subordinates must understand the higher commander's aims so well that they can properly exploit battlefield opportunities even when communications fail. The corps or division must coordinate and support all arms and control operations that may cover 50 to 80 kilometers daily and change direction frequently. Brigades and battalions must sustain themselves in such an environment and maintain the ability to change direction quickly without losing their concentration or synchronization.

The plan must use routes which permit the maximum possible opportunities for maneuver around strongpoints. A major offensive operation must provide—

- Branches from the main approach.

- Plans for reversion to the defense and for exploitation.

- Control measures that facilitate changing the direction or location of the main effort.

- Provisions for combat at night or in limited visibility.

Even if nuclear and chemical weapons do not support the attack, commanders must plan to protect the force from their use by the enemy. Planning for maximum dispersal, using multiple routes, and having reserves assume major missions are all basic to an attack.

AUDACITY

Audacity has always been a feature of successful offensives. More attacks have been defeated because of lack of audacity than for any other reason. To the overly cautious around him, General George S. Patton, Jr., warned, "Never take counsel of your fears. The enemy is more worried than you are. Numerical superiority, while useful, is not vital to successful offensive action. The fact that you are attacking induces the enemy to believe that you are stronger than he is." In short, the key tenets of AirLand Battle doctrine—initiative, agility, depth, and synchronization—also apply to any successful attack.

PHASES OF OFFENSIVE OPERATIONS

All offensive operations tend to occur in roughly sequential phases, although the length and nature of each phase, and whether it even occurs at all, will vary from situation to situation. The four general phases of offensive operations are *preparation, attack, exploitation, and pursuit.*

PREPARATION

The preparatory phase of an offensive operation involves the concentration of attacking forces and associated support and their movement into contact with the enemy. It may also include the conduct of preliminary diversionary actions and delivery of preparatory fires. The extent and nature of the preparatory phase will depend on whether or not opposing forces are already in contact and on the posture of the enemy.

A central feature of the preparatory phase is the *movement to contact*, conducted to gain or reestablish contact with the enemy. While normally associated with mobile operations in which both sides are contesting the initiative, movement to contact occurs at some level in virtually all attacks where forces are not in immediate proximity. It is characterized by rapid movement along multiple axes, decentralized control, and rapid deployment of combined arms formations from the march to attack or to defend.

In a fluid situation where both opponents have freedom of maneuver, movement to contact will frequently produce a *meeting engagement* in which each side attempts to seize the initiative and either overwhelm the other or force it into the defensive. The Soviets consider this a likely event, especially in nuclear or chemical warfare, and assiduously practice rapid attack from the march. More frequently, movement to contact occurs when a defending enemy has disengaged or is attempting to do so. Here the objective of the movement to contact is to force the enemy to battle before he can reestablish a cohesive defense.

Even in less fluid conditions, movement to contact will be necessary whenever opposing forces are beyond immediate observation. In a division attack, for example, battalions or even brigades may need to conduct a movement to contact prior to deploying for attack if the situation to their front is ambiguous and enemy positions have not been clearly located. Such situations are especially characteristic of wide envelopments.

In either case, the critical elements of the movement to contact will be security to the front and flanks, smooth and rapid deployment into the attack when contact is made, and prior coordination of supporting fires, both ground and air, to produce the fastest possible buildup of combat power superiority at the point of contact. Seizure of the initiative is the overriding imperative, and will require aggressive action by leaders at every level without waiting for detailed orders.

ATTACK

Unless contact reveals an overwhelmingly superior enemy force, movement to contact will normally be followed immediately by a *hasty attack*, launched with the forces at hand and with minimum preparation to destroy the enemy before he is able either to concentrate or to establish a defense. Such an attack may also be employed to seize a fleeting opportunity or regain the initiative quickly after a successful defense. In the defense, hasty counterattacks may recapture lost positions before the enemy has had time to consolidate his success. In World War II, German units down to platoon level were renowned for the rapidity and effectiveness with which they could mount such hasty counterattacks.

At higher echelons, hasty attacks are often anticipated through the use of contingency plans. Large formations attack from the march using hasty attacks by subordinate units or covering forces.

Regardless of its purpose or the echelon at which it is conducted, a hasty attack purchases agility at the risk of losing synchronization. To minimize this risk, units conducting hasty attacks must make maximum use of standard formations and well understood and rehearsed battle drills, and supporting arms and services must be able to react quickly using prearranged procedures. The more closely combat and supporting units have worked together prior to the attack, the easier and more successful such implicit coordination will be. Hasty attacks accordingly place a premium on habitual relationships among supported and supporting units at every level.

In contrast to hasty attacks, *deliberate attacks* are fully synchronized operations which employ every available asset against the enemy defense. Because such synchronization requires careful planning and extensive coordination, deliberate attacks take time to prepare. During this time, the enemy can improve his defenses, disengage, or launch a spoiling attack of his own. Deliberate attacks should therefore be reserved for those situations where the defense can neither be outflanked nor overcome with a hasty attack.

Whether hasty or deliberate, successful attack depends on concentrating the maximum possible shock and violence against the enemy force. The objective is to shatter the enemy's nerve, ruin his combined arms synchronization, and destroy his units' cohesion and the willingness of his soldiers to fight. The most successful attacks leave defending units incapable of further resistance.

EXPLOITATION

Attacks which succeed in annihilating a defending enemy are rare. More often, the enemy will attempt to disengage, withdraw what he can, and reconstitute an effective defense as rapidly as possible. In large-scale operations, he may attempt to draw forces from less active areas, or bring forward reserves heretofore uncommitted. Every attack not restricted by higher authority or lack of resources should therefore be followed without delay by bold exploitation designed to keep the enemy under pressure, compound his disorganization, and erode his will to resist. The ultimate object of the exploitation is disintegration of enemy forces to the point where they have no alternative but surrender or flight.

While exploitation is integral to every attack, it is especially important in a deliberate attack in which concentration for the attack may require accepting risk elsewhere. Failure to exploit success aggressively may permit the enemy time to detect and exploit that weakness, and thus regain both initiative and advantage.

PURSUIT

If it becomes apparent that enemy resistance has broken down entirely, either attack or exploitation may give way to pursuit. The object of the pursuit is annihilation of the opposing force. It is conducted as a series of encirclements in which successive portions of the fleeing enemy are intercepted and captured or destroyed. Large-scale pursuits are rare in modern war, but they occur, as in the US Eighth Army's pursuit to the Yalu River in 1950. Like the exploitation, the pursuit is normally characterized by broad decentralization of control and rapid movement. Unlike the exploitation, however, the pursuit rarely can be anticipated, and forces are not normally reserved for it.

Exploitations and pursuits test the audacity and endurance of soldiers and leaders alike. Typically, an attack will disorganize the attacker nearly as much as the defender. Attacking forces will be tired,

units will have suffered losses of men and materiel, and as the exploitation or pursuit unfolds, lines of communication will become increasingly tenuous. Extraordinary effort will be required to sustain the momentum of the attack and thus translate tactical success into operational or even strategic victory.

Although history reveals offensive operations in which all four phases occurred in the sequence just described, most offensive operations deviate from this pattern in one way or another. Attacks—especially counterattacks—may take place with little preparation, or following the unintended collison of forces at a time and place neither had foreseen. The battle of Gettysburg resulted from just such an unintended collision. Successful attack may give way directly to pursuit, bypassing exploitation altogether. Such a pattern was typical of engagements in Vietnam, in which enemy forces attacked by US forces simply sought sanctuary in Laos or Cambodia. In conventional war, in contrast, pursuits are rare, and exploitation is more than likely to end short of annihilation, curtailed either by insufficient sustaining capability or by deliberate strategic restriction.

Some offensive operations intentionally exclude one or more phases. Spoiling attacks and feints, for example, rarely envision full exploitation, although unusual circumstances may convert either into a full-scale attack. Demonstrations seek no real contact whatever, and are in effect no more than an elaborate preparatory phase designed to deceive the enemy into expecting an attack.

Finally, phases may run into each other with no abrupt and discernible break. This is especially true of the exploitation and pursuit. Nevertheless, these phases constitute significantly different problems, and each must be dealt with differently in planning and execution.

FORMS OF MANEUVER

Just as similar phases are common to all offensive operations, so similar forms of maneuver are common to all attacks. These forms of maneuver include envelopment, the turning movement, infiltration, penetration, and frontal attack. While frequently used in combination, each attacks the enemy in a different way, and each poses different challenges to the attacking commander.

ENVELOPMENT

Envelopment is the basic form of maneuver in any doctrine which seeks to apply strength against weakness. Envelopment avoids the enemy's front, where his forces are most protected and his fires most easily concentrated. Instead, while fixing the defender's attention forward by supporting or diversionary attacks, the attacker maneuvers his main effort around or over the enemy's defenses to strike at his flanks and rear. Flank attacks are a variant of the envelopment, in which access to the enemy's flank and rear is furnished by the enemy's own forward movement. Single envelopments are directed against only one flank of the defending forces, while double envelopments attack both flanks. Either variant can develop into an encirclement if the attacking force is able to sever the defender's lines of communications (LOCs) and prevent his reinforcement or escape.

ENVELOPMENT

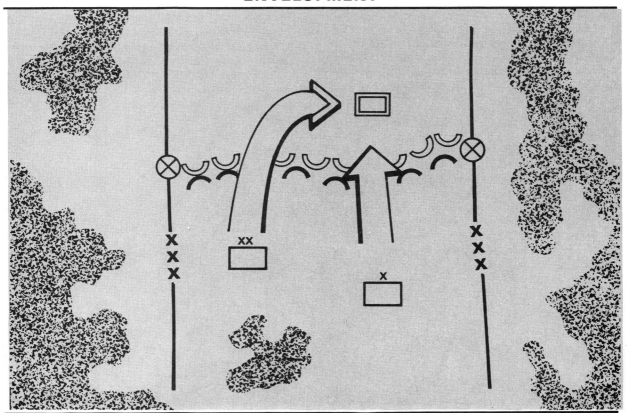

Successful envelopment requires discovery or creation of an assailable flank. In meeting engagements and counterattacks, this may actually be the flank of the enemy force. In less fluid conditions, it is more likely to be a gap or weak point in the enemy's defense. Such gaps can be created by conventional, nuclear, or chemical fires, or by penetration prior to envelopment.

Envelopment typically requires less initial combat power than other forms of maneuver, since the attacker need not push through heavily defended prepared positions. However, envelopment places a premium on agility, since its success depends on reaching the enemy's vulnerable rear before he can shift his forces and fires.

TURNING MOVEMENT

The turning movement is a variant of the envelopment in which the attacker attempts to avoid the defense entirely, instead seeking to secure key terrain deep in the enemy's rear and along his lines of communication. Faced with a major threat to his rear, the enemy is thus "turned" out of his defensive positions and forced to attack rearward at a disadvantage.

TURNING MOVEMENT

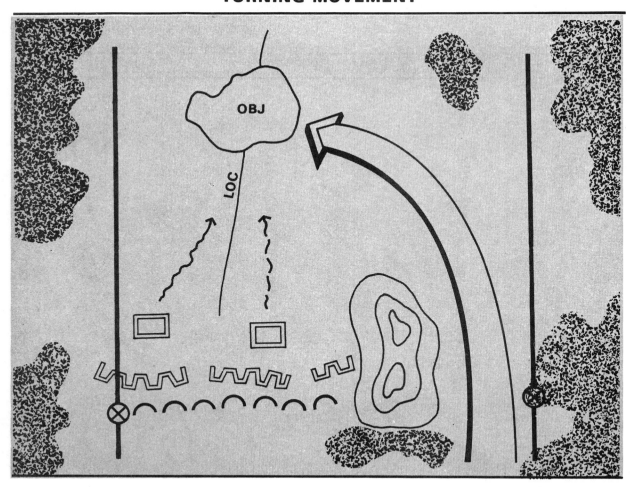

MacArthur's invasion at Inchon was a classic turning movement. Amphibious, airborne, and air assault forces are uniquely valuable for conducting turning movements. However, because they will have to fight beyond supporting distance of other ground forces, they will require heavy and continuous air and/or naval support.

INFILTRATION

Infiltration is another means of reaching the enemy's rear without fighting through prepared defenses. It is the covert movement of all or part of the attacking force through enemy lines to a favorable position in their rear. Successful infiltration requires above all the avoidance of detection and engagement. Since that requirement limits the size and strength of the infiltrating force, infiltration can rarely defeat the defense by itself, but rather is normally used in conjunction with some other form of maneuver.

Infiltration is most feasible in rough terrain and reduced visibility, or in areas poorly covered by observation and fire. It may be used to attack lightly defended positions, or stronger positions from flank

INFILTRATION

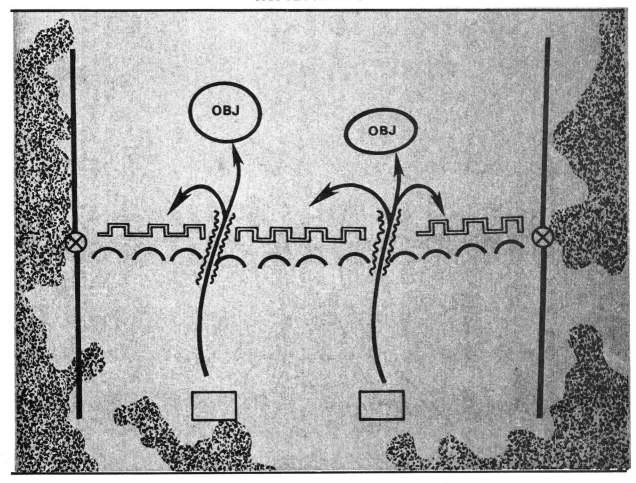

and rear; secure key terrain in support of the main effort; or disrupt enemy rear operations.

PENETRATION

Penetration is used when enemy flanks are not assailable and when time does not permit some other form of maneuver. It attempts to rupture enemy defenses on a narrow front and thereby create both assailable flanks and access to the enemy's

PENETRATION

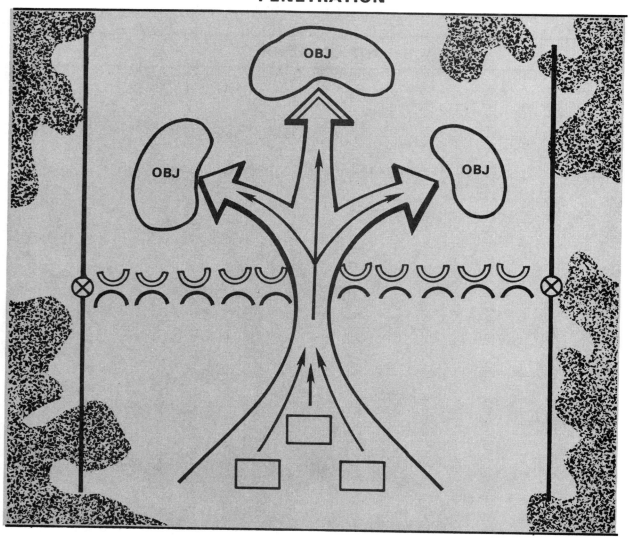

rear. Penetrations typically comprise three stages: initial rupture of enemy positions, roll-up of the flanks on either side of the gap, and exploitation to secure deep objectives. Because the penetration is itself vulnerable to flank attack, especially in its early stages, penetrating forces must move rapidly, and follow-on forces must be close behind to secure and widen the shoulders. Fire support must concentrate on suppressing enemy defenses quickly, then shift to protect the flanks of the attack.

Penetration may be attempted on one or several axes depending on the forces available. When feasible, multiple penetrations are desirable, since they disperse the enemy's fires and complicate commitment of his reserves.

FRONTAL ATTACK

A frontal attack strikes the enemy across a wide front and over the most direct approaches. For deliberate attacks, it is the

FRONTAL ATTACK

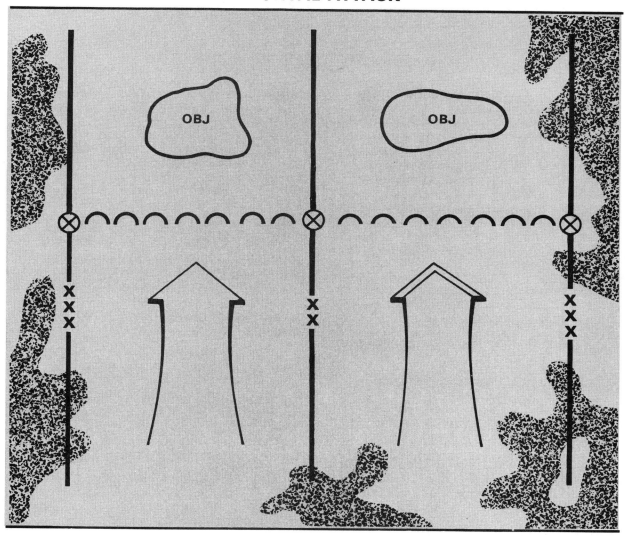

least economical form of maneuver, since it exposes the attacker to the concentrated fire of the defender while simultaneously limiting the effectiveness of the attacker's own fires.

As the simplest form of maneuver, however, the frontal attack is useful for overwhelming light defenses, covering forces, or disorganized enemy forces. It is often the best form of maneuver for a hasty attack or meeting engagement in which speed and simplicity are paramount, or for exploiting the effects of nuclear or chemical fires. Frontal attack may also be used during exploitation or pursuit, and by subordinate elements of a large formation conducting an envelopment or penetration.

Like many aspects of war, the forms of maneuver have seen little change in modern history. They are understood by potential adversaries as well as by American soldiers. Offensive success will therefore depend less on the choice of forms than on their creative combination and, especially, on the skill and audacity with which they are executed.

OFFENSIVE FRAMEWORK

A simple, complete concept of operation is the basis of all tactical offensive actions. The concept should permit rapid transition between offensive phases.

Corps and divisions make use of five complementary elements in fighting their offensive battles:

- A main attack with supporting attacks as required.

- Reserve operations in support of the attack.

- A reconnaissance and security operation forward and to the flanks and rear of main and supporting attacks.

- A continuous deep operation in vital parts of the zone of attack.

- Rear area operations necessary to maintain offensive momentum.

While some deep and rear activities conducted by higher echelons affect, and must therefore be coordinated with, brigade and subordinate units, the latter normally do not conduct separate deep and rear operations. These echelons, however, look for and anticipate enemy uncommitted forces which may affect accomplishment of the mission. They also provide all around security to include protection of logistic trains in the rear.

The commander organizes elements of the offensive framework for complementary functions in the conduct of his attack. In the *close operation*, reconnaissance and security forces—covering forces and advance, flank, or rear guards—locate the enemy and find gaps in his defenses, protect the force from surprise, develop the situation, and give the commander time and space in which to react to the enemy. The main and supporting efforts maneuver around or through enemy defenses to occupy objectives that permit the defeat of defending forces.

Reserves are positioned to weight the main effort. They exploit success, reinforce or maintain momentum, deal with enemy counterattacks, provide security, complete the destruction of enemy forces, secure deep objectives, or open the next phase of a campaign or major operation by seizing objectives beyond the defended area.

Deep operations isolate enemy defenses, disorganize enemy reserves, disrupt enemy support, and complicate the reconstitution of the defense during withdrawal.

Rear operations assure freedom of action of committed and uncommitted forces and protect necessary combat support and combat service support from disruption.

Corps, divisions, and maneuver brigades can perform any type of tactical offensive operation. Divisions, brigades, and battalions may also be employed as security forces, as elements of main or supporting attacks, as reserves, or, in some cases, as elements of deep or rear operations.

Maneuver battalions and companies attack, defend, delay, or move as part of

their parent unit's operation. They form their own security elements and reserves as necessary.

All elements of an attacking force must be able to move quickly, change orientation rapidly, mass and disperse on the move, and accept new missions without loss of time or momentum. Synchronization must be preserved in spite of rapid movement, battle losses, and changes in the main effort. Units in all elements of offensive tactical operations must be prepared to defend when they are finally halted.

THE OFFENSIVE FRAMEWORK

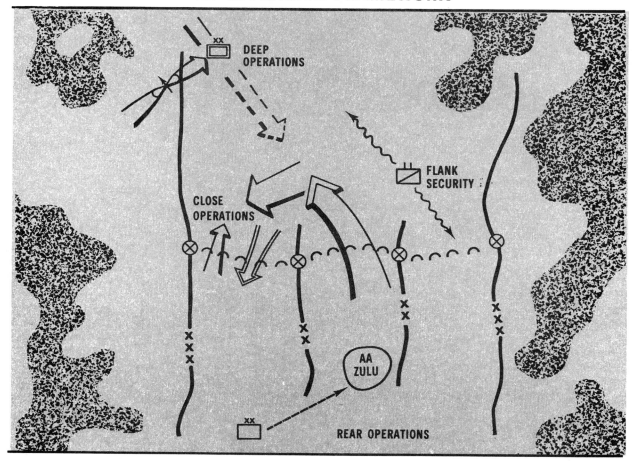

CHAPTER 7

Conducting Offensive Operations

Offensive operations are characterized by aggressive initiative on the part of subordinate commanders, by rapid shifts in the main effort to take advantage of opportunities, by momentum, and by the deepest, most rapid destruction of enemy defenses possible. The ideal attack should resemble what Liddell Hart called the "expanding torrent." It should move fast, follow reconnaissance units or successful probes through gaps in enemy defenses, and shift its strength quickly to widen penetrations and to reinforce its successes, thereby carrying the battle deep into the enemy rear. Forces or areas that are critical to the enemy's overall defensive organization should be destroyed or brought under control rapidly before the enemy can react to the attack.

OFFENSIVE CAMPAIGNS AND MAJOR OPERATIONS

The key to success in an offensive campaign is to defeat the enemy before the offensive reaches what Clausewitz called its "culminating point." This culminating point is achieved when a force on the offensive expends so much of its strength that it ceases to hold a significant advantage over the enemy. At that point the attacker either halts to avoid operating at a disadvantage or goes on and risks becoming weaker than the defender.

Culminating points occur because the attacker must consume resources and commit forces as he moves into enemy territory fighting successive battles and engagements. He must protect his flanks and rear area, sustain his momentum with reserves, and extend his line of supply. Constant actions are likely to occur in his rear areas and to draw resources away from his main effort. The defense is apt to become harder to defeat as its own lines of supply shorten

CONTENTS

and the space to be defended contracts. Finally, the natural friction of war acts to slow the attacker and bring him to the culminating point of his operation.

Napoleon's Russian campaign, Rommel's advance into Egypt, and the Allied "Operation Market-Garden" of World War II exemplify operations that reached their culminating points before achieving victories. Operational level offensive planning must take into account the influence of friction and make a realistic estimate of friendly capabilities. When complete success cannot be attained in a single operation, the campaign should be separated into phases that allow the attacker to regain the advantage before continuing. When forces are inadequate for the complete occupation of the theater, the commander may have to assume the defensive when he has reached his culminating point. Appendix B discusses the culminating point in more detail.

Offensive campaigns are oriented on a decisive theater objective whenever possible. The enemy's center of gravity may rest on a particular physical feature necessary to defense of a theater, a certain force which is key to the defense, or a combination of such forces and features.

The campaign plan identifies this center of gravity and establishes objectives that will lead to the enemy's defeat. Usually there will be more than a single phase to a campaign. If an enemy force delays or avoids decisive combat, it will have to be defeated in a series of battles. Eisenhower's operations in early 1945, for example, amounted to a series of army frontal attacks which aimed first at engagement of German reserves, then at penetration of the enemy's defensive line, and finally, at deep exploitation of the penetration. In Korea, MacArthur dislocated the entire North Korean Army by his amphibious operation at Inchon and then pursued the withdrawing enemy in a series of attacks all the way to the Yalu River.

In their offensive campaigns, large unit commanders will use all types of tactical actions. They will commonly have to defend in some parts of a theater to mass the necessary strength to attack elsewhere. Divisions or corps may have to defend flank

or rear positions as part of army-level offensives. In rare cases, the entire force may fight predominantly defensive battles after seizing key positions that force the enemy to attack or withdraw.

In any offensive campaign, the commander should try to collapse enemy defenses throughout the theater as rapidly as possible while protecting himself from unnecessary losses. Offensive campaigns should seek to retain the initiative, to strike enemy weaknesses, to attack the enemy in great depth, and to create fluid conditions which prevent the enemy from organizing a coherent defense.

Airborne, air assault, or amphibious operations, deep penetration of armored or mechanized forces, coordinated conventional and unconventional operations, and upon approval by National Command Authorities, nuclear fires, all promote this fluidity. Their use should be synchronized throughout the theater to disrupt the defense. Air interdiction actions should also contribute to the theater campaign and must be synchronized effectively with ground operations.

Battles should also be used to maintain fluidity in the theater. Initially, they may be necessary to disorganize the defender. Thereafter, battles should be used to keep the enemy from reestablishing a workable defense. Concurrently, attacking commanders should maneuver to avoid battles sought by the defender to slow or weaken the offensive.

The campaign should attempt to defeat the enemy in a single operation when possible. When all of the defending forces are well forward or when a theater of operations is relatively shallow, it may be possible to penetrate or envelop the defense quickly. In such cases, operational reserves may be kept out of battle and maneuvered through, around, or over the battle area. Their mission will be to occupy the theater in depth and to preempt the enemy's attempts to establish supplementary defenses. Germany's campaigns in France and Poland early in World War II and the Soviet Manchurian campaign of 1945 illustrate this type of campaign.

In larger areas and when the defense is organized in depth, offensive campaigns will halt periodically for logistical reasons or because of effective defense. In these cases, static and dynamic conditions alternate. The attacker may then have to shift his main effort, re-mass against vulnerable areas, and fight deliberate battles to restore fluidity to the theater. In World War II, operations in North Africa, Eastern and Western Europe, and the Pacific followed this pattern. The Persian Gulf war of the 1980's suggests that linear stalemate is still possible if the attacker fails initially to disrupt the defense in depth.

Whatever its design and objective, the campaign plan must be flexible enough to accommodate change. In particular, the commander should be capable of shifting his main effort or lines of operation in response to change or opportunity. The initiative is of vital importance in offensives. Large unit commanders should be sufficiently flexible to avoid unprofitable battles or to initiate unanticipated battles that contribute to the attainment of the objective.

Offensive campaigns may be fought against either concentrated or dispersed enemy forces. Facing a concentrated enemy, large unit commanders should attempt through maneuver to force the enemy to abandon his position or fight at a disadvantage. In practice, this means directing operations against the enemy's flanks or rear or penetrating his defenses through weak areas. It also implies operating on converging lines of action, a technique that requires close coordination and can expose the separated forces to defeat in detail. Sherman's Atlanta campaign epitomizes a successful campaign against a concentrated enemy force.

When enemy forces are widely separated, the attacker can operate on interior lines, fighting each enemy force in turn. Operating on interior lines permits the attacker to keep his own forces united while giving him an opportunity to isolate and defeat separated enemy forces before they can join to organize a stronger defense. The attacking commander's campaign plan should be designed to defeat the enemy's apparent center of gravity—that portion of the defending force which, if defeated, will cause the overall defense to fail. Manstein's campaign in the Crimea exemplifies the use of interior lines to defeat an enemy force in detail. Appendix B discusses lines of operation in greater detail.

In each phase of the campaign, large unit commanders anticipate battle of a general type—an envelopment, for instance—and dispose their forces accordingly. To attack effectively, a large force should deploy its divisions or corps in ways which facilitate the most likely type of maneuver in battle. Some forces must be held in depth as reserves during operational maneuver. The force as a whole moves in zones of attack orienting on enemy forces or major geographical features.

Because of the enemy's reconnaissance and the length of time which may pass before battle, Army and corps formations should mask the commander's intention as well as possible. Friendly intentions can be concealed by adopting flexible dispositions which do not limit the force to a single form of maneuver. Active deception and security operations also help to conceal friendly intentions.

Covering forces should operate well forward during operational maneuver to give the force notice of the enemy's presence and time and space in which to act. As battle is joined, large unit commanders adjust the final movement of their forces and look for opportunities to defeat the enemy's defense in depth. In particular they seek ways to employ operational reserves decisively.

The choices for employing corps or divisions held in reserve will be between using it to annihilate the enemy in the battle area or pushing it through the defended area to secure deep objectives. Seizing objectives in operational depth is preferable since that will set the terms for the campaign's next phase or may even gain the objectives of the campaign.

In a meeting engagement between large units, the commander will be closely involved in the battle. His options for employing operational reserves will also be more numerous.

In a deliberate attack against an established defense, the commander will have to position operational forces where they can exploit tactical success. In such actions, a large battle—a tactical action—precedes

the operational commitment of reserves to move beyond the defended area into the depth of the theater of operations.

In an offensive campaign, the commander must take care to preserve synchronization and the strength of his force. If his force becomes dispersed or overextended, or if his activities become unsynchronized, he may have to assume the defensive temporarily, especially if the enemy remains capable of offensive action. All offensive campaigns end in a defense of either the theater of operations or that part of it under the attacker's control when he reaches his culminating point. This defensive phase must be foreseen and planned for.

TACTICAL OFFENSE

As part of either offensive or defensive campaigns or major operations, corps, divisions, and smaller tactical level units may be given missions requiring movement to contact, hasty attack, deliberate attack, exploitation, or pursuit.

MOVEMENT TO CONTACT

The purposes of the movement to contact are to gain contact with the enemy and to develop the situation. Movements to contact should be conducted in such a manner as to maintain the commander's freedom of action once contact is made. This flexibility is essential to maintaining the initiative and is based on the following principles:

- The commander must lead with a mobile, self-contained covering force to locate and fix the enemy, but he must also hold the bulk of his force back far enough so that he can maneuver without inadvertently becoming decisively engaged. He fights through light resistance with lead units whenever possible to maintain the momentum of the operation.

- The commander must organize his unit into combined arms forces that are ready

to deploy and attack rapidly in any direction with the support of accompanying air and artillery.

- The formation must provide for all-around security—that is, to the flanks and rear and against air attack, as well as to the front.

- The force must move aggressively and with maximum speed. A slow or overly cautious advance will be dangerous, because slow-moving forces are easy to outflank or to target.

- The commander must decentralize execution of the movement to leaders on the front and flanks. However, he should maintain sufficient control to assure that long-range supporting fires are effective and that forces in depth can be employed promptly when the unit makes contact.

Organization and Planning. A corps and its divisions usually organize a covering force, an advance guard, and a main body for movements to contact. The main body normally provides flank and rear security forces.

The composition, size, and operation of the covering force may influence the entire course of the battle. It must include the fire support, combat support, and combat service support (CSS) necessary to enable it to fight independently. It must especially include engineer assets—bridging for hasty gap crossing and dozers and plows to reduce obstacles.

The covering force should be mobile and well balanced, and it should be employed far enough forward of the main body to give the overall commander space and time in which to react to enemy contact. The

missions assigned the covering force are to reconnoiter the zone ahead of the main body, develop the enemy situation, and provide security for the main body to deploy and fight on the best possible terms. Covering force operations may include attacking to destroy enemy resistance, securing or controlling key terrain, and containing large enemy units.

The advance guard is a security force provided by the main body. It operates forward of the main body to ensure its uninterrupted advance and protect it from surprise attack. The advance guard protects

ORGANIZATION FOR MOVEMENT TO CONTACT

the deployment of the main body when it is committed to action and facilitates its advance by removing obstacles, repairing roads and bridges, or locating bypasses.

The advance guard moves as fast as possible, but unlike the covering force, remains within supporting distance of the main body. It performs continuous reconnaissance to the front and flanks and pushes back or destroys small enemy groups before they can hinder the advance of the main body. When the advance guard encounters large enemy forces or heavily defended areas, it takes prompt and aggressive action to develop the situation and, within its capability, to defeat the enemy. Its commander reports the location, strength, disposition, and composition of the enemy and tries to find the enemy's flanks and gaps in his position. The main body may then have to join in the attack. The advance guard must be far enough in front of the main body to ensure that the commander of the protected force has freedom of action. However, it must not be so far in front that it can be destroyed before assistance can reach it. The force commander usually specifies how far in front of his force the advance guard is to operate. At night, in close terrain and under conditions of low visibility, those distances are reduced.

The advance guard normally advances in column until it makes contact. It may move continuously or by bounds. It moves by bounds when contact with the enemy is imminent and the terrain is favorable. Mechanized infantry, cavalry, and armored units are most suitable for use in the advance guard. Engineers should move with the advance guard, but other support can normally be provided by the main body.

The main body consists of combined arms elements prepared for immediate action on contact. Companies prepare by cross attaching. Battalions and brigades prepare by cross attachment and the direct support of artillery, engineers, air defense, and other units necessary to maintain momentum. Attack helicopter units will normally remain

under division and corps control until contact is made. Air reconnaissance, close air support (CAS), battlefield air interdiction (BAI), and counter air operations are essential to the success of large-scale movements to contact. Local air superiority, or at a minimum, air parity will be vital to success.

Combat service support must be decentralized and readily available to sustain the elements of the main body without interruption. Aerial resupply may also be necessary to support large-scale movements to contact or to maintain their momentum.

Brigades, divisions, and corps move over multiple parallel routes with numerous lateral branches to remain flexible and to reduce the time needed to initiate maneuver. The speed, momentum, and dispersal of the formation and its limited electromagnetic emissions make targeting by the enemy difficult. However, once the force makes contact and concentrates to overcome the enemy, it becomes vulnerable to nuclear and chemical strikes. It must concentrate, attack rapidly, and disperse again as soon as it overcomes resistance.

Main body units normally provide flank and rear security elements. Air cavalry can be used to assist the covering force, advance guard, and the flank and rear guards.

In a movement to contact, maneuver unit commanders must be well forward. The force commander must be able to move quickly to the area of contact. There, he must size up the situation promptly, act quickly and aggressively, and report the situation accurately.

To provide the commander with the earliest possible warning of enemy movement in his area of interest, long-range surveillance should support a force that is moving to contact. The information-gathering system, especially at corps and division levels, should provide current information as continuously as possible.

Elements of the force maintain continuous coordination with each other. The advance guard maintains contact with the covering force. The lead elements of the main body maintain contact with the advance guard. The rear guard and flank guards maintain contact with and orient on the main body. The main body keeps enough distance between itself and forward elements to maintain flexibility for maneuver. This distance varies with the level of command, the terrain, and the availability of information about the enemy.

Open terrain provides maneuver space on either side of the line of march and thus facilitates high-speed movement. It also allows greater dispersal and usually permits more separation between forward elements and the main body than does close terrain. The main body should never be committed to canalizing terrain before forward elements have advanced far enough to ensure that the main body will not become trapped. As the enemy situation becomes better known, the commander may shorten the distance between elements to decrease reaction time or he may begin to deploy in preparation for contact.

Movement should be as rapid as the terrain, the mobility of the force, and the enemy situation will permit. The commander must determine the degree of risk he is willing to accept based on his mission. In a high-risk environment, it is usually better to increase the distance between forward elements and the main body than to slow the speed of advance.

The force must attempt to cross obstacles in stride. When possible, bridges are seized intact in advance of leading elements. Lead elements bypass or clear obstacles as quickly as possible to maintain the momentum of the movement. If lead elements cannot overcome obstacles, follow-on elements may bypass and take the lead. Follow-on forces remove obstacles which will hinder the flow of sustainment to the force.

Meeting Engagements. A movement to contact often results in a meeting engagement. Such encounters often occur by chance in small unit operations and when reconnaissance has been ineffective in brigade or larger unit operations. But a meeting engagement may also occur when each opponent is aware of the other and both decide to attack without delay to obtain positional advantage, gain a decisive terrain feature, or assert moral dominance. A meeting engagement may also occur when one force deploys hastily for defense while the other attempts to prevent it.

At any level of command, success in a meeting engagement depends on effective actions on contact. The commander must—

- Seize the initiative early.
- Develop the situation and initiate maneuver rapidly.
- Attack violently and resolutely.
- Maintain momentum by synchronizing the actions of combat, combat support, and combat service support elements.

A commander should determine quickly whether he can bypass the enemy or whether he must attack him. Usually, the available intelligence and the concept of operation will indicate which course the commander should follow. Bypassed enemy forces must be reported to the next superior headquarters, which then assumes responsibility for their destruction or containment. Inferior enemy forces cannot be allowed to delay the movement of the force. Hasty attacks are usually necessary to overcome enemy attempts to slow the main force's movement. If hasty attacks fail to defeat enemy defenses, the commander must consider making a deliberate attack or assume the defense himself.

HASTY AND DELIBERATE ATTACKS

The opportunity to attack may arise during the course of battle or it may be created by skillful tactical leadership. Attacks may be launched from a movement to contact, from a defensive posture, from behind a friendly defending force or during exploitation or pursuit. They may be part of a larger defense, such as counterattacks or spoiling attacks. Whatever its nature or purpose, the attack must be fast, violent, resolute, shrewd, and synchronized.

Attacks are of two basic types: hasty and deliberate. The two are distinguished chiefly by the extent of preparation.

Hasty attacks result from meeting engagements or successful defenses. In a hasty attack, the commander attacks quickly from his existing dispositions to gain the upper hand or to keep the enemy from organizing resistance. In moving to contact, the commander must employ formations that permit him to attack effectively on short notice. When defending, he must foresee offensive opportunities and dispose his forces in ways that facilitate the launching of hasty attacks. Hasty attacks are not planned in detail, but commanders should anticipate such attacks and plan their dispositions and fires so as to facilitate them. Speed of attack can offset a lack of thorough preparation, but, from the early moments of the meeting engagement or decision to attack, every available element of combat support must be committed to the attack as rapidly as possible.

For small units this may be a matter of battle drill, but the action taken must always be appropriate to the situation. In some instances, attacking with one unit and supporting with two units will be more advantageous than automatically adopting the opposite standard configuration. Deep operations—air maneuver, long-range surveillance, extended range artillery fires, scatterable mines, and, when authorized, nuclear fires—can materially assist hasty attacks provided these activities can be effectively synchronized without significant delay. Hasty attacks are initiated using fragmentary orders. These brief orders establish an objective, concept of operation, main effort, and tasks for subordinates.

Synchronization is achieved by use of standing operating procedures (SOPs) supplemented by brief amendments. Both synchronization and agility can be enhanced by including "on-order" objectives and zones of attack in the plan for the movement to contact or defense.

Deliberate attacks are usually necessary when the defender is well organized and cannot be turned or bypassed. Deliberate attacks are thoroughly planned. They are characterized by—

- High volumes of fire.
- Timely intelligence.
- Extensive preparation of attacking troops.
- Well-developed deception plans.
- Complete exploitation of electronic warfare.
- Unconventional warfare.
- Psychological operations.

The attacker must be organized in depth to provide for flexibility in the attack. His committed forces should use indirect approaches to gain surprise and to avoid the enemy's concentrated fire. Reserves must be in covered or concealed positions and prepared to replace lead units or to exploit success wherever it is achieved. Commanders of reserve units should identify high-speed routes with the best concealment possible that will allow them to move anywhere in the zone of attack. Whenever possible, deliberate attacks should be rehearsed.

Deep operations are also of great importance in deliberate attacks. Corps and divisions plan to attack the enemy throughout their areas of operations by blocking the movement of his reserves, destroying his command posts, neutralizing his artillery, and preventing the escape of targeted units.

Counterattacks and *spoiling attacks* may be either hasty or deliberate. In the latter case, they are planned based on reasonable assumptions about the enemy and anticipated battlefield contingencies. Once the conditions of a contingency are met or nearly met, the commander launches the attack.

Counterattacks and spoiling attacks are usually part of a defense or a delay. The first attempts to defeat an attacking enemy or regain key terrain, the second to preempt the attack before it gets underway. When the balance of power on the battlefield changes, the commander can exploit the situation by counterattacking to seize the initiative. Plans for all necessary maneuver and support should be made in advance to assure timely execution and maximum possible impact.

The same principles apply to both hasty and deliberate attacks. The effect sought is the same. The differences lie in the amount of planning, coordination, and preparation prior to execution—in other words, how *thoroughly* the principles can be applied, not whether they apply. In practice, a clear distinction seldom exists between a hasty attack and a deliberate attack. Once the commander decides to attack, any unnecessary delays or preparatory movements before execution of the plan allow the defender additional time to react and make his defeat more difficult. Therefore, because the hasty attack may be the rule rather than the exception, commanders, staffs, and units should be trained to react quickly.

EXPLOITATION AND PURSUIT

Exploitation and pursuit proceed directly from the attack and are initiated from attack dispositions. Exploitation is the bold continuation of an attack following initial success, pursuit, the relentless destruction or capture of fleeing enemy forces who have lost the capability to resist.

Offensive operations of corps and division should seek the earliest possible transition from attack to exploitation. Exploitation forces drive swiftly for deep objectives, seizing command posts, severing escape routes, and striking at reserves, artillery, and combat support units to prevent the enemy from reorganizing an effective defense. Exploitation forces should be large and reasonably self-sufficient. Well supported by tactical air, air cavalry, and attack helicopters, they should be able to change direction on short notice. The commander must provide his exploiting forces with mobile support, including air resupply to move emergency lifts of POL and ammunition.

Exploitation is planned as an integral part of the attack. The commander tentatively identifies forces, objectives, and zones for the exploitation before his attack begins. Subordinates watch for indications of enemy's withdrawal or reduced resistance. When they occur commanders issue rapid orders, regroup forces, assign deep objectives, and continue their attacks. Combat service support is reorganized if necessary and follows the exploitation rapidly.

Commanders of committed forces must act fast to capitalize on local successes. Most exploitations will be initiated from the front rather than directed from the rear. When possible, the forces already leading the attack continue directly into the exploitation. More often, fresh forces will need to be passed into the lead.

Commanders normally designate exploiting forces by fragmentary orders issued during the course of an attack. Assigned missions include seizing objectives deep in the enemy rear, cutting lines of communication, isolating and destroying enemy units, and disrupting enemy command and control. The commander of the exploiting force must have the greatest possible freedom of action to accomplish his mission. He will be expected to act with great aggressiveness, initiative, and boldness. His objective may be a critical communications center, key terrain that would significantly contribute to destruction of organized enemy resistance, or simply a point of orientation. It will usually be some distance away.

While exploitation requires decentralization, the overall commander must maintain sufficient control to alter its direction and prevent its overextension. He relies on his subordinates to find the fastest way to their objectives, to deploy as necessary to fight, and to seize all opportunities to damage the enemy or to accelerate the pace of the operation. The major commander uses minimum control measures, but issues clear instructions concerning seizure of key terrain and the size of enemy forces which may be bypassed.

The exploiting commander must be careful not to dissipate combat power to achieve minor tactical successes or reduce small enemy forces. His aim is to reach his objective with maximum strength as rapidly as possible. He must also prevent overextension of either the exploiting force or its sustaining logistics, especially if the enemy is capable of regrouping to attack the command. Available fires neutralize enemy forces that cannot be bypassed or contained. Rapid advances provide security from nuclear attack by keeping enemy forces off balance and degrading their intelligence and surveillance capability. Exploitation continues day and night as long as strength and opportunity remain.

To sustain the exploitation and ensure that supplies and support reach the force safely and on time, commanders must give special attention to the security of logistical units and convoys. Commanders must call them forward and guide them around bypassed enemy positions and obstacles.

Exploitation forces normally advance rapidly on a wide front toward their objectives. Leading elements maintain only those reserves necessary to ensure flexibility of operation, continued momentum, and essential security. Armored and mechanized task forces are best suited for exploitation on the ground. Airmobile forces are useful in seizing defiles, crossing obstacles, and otherwise capitalizing on their mobility to attack and cut off disorganized enemy elements. Attack helicopter units can interdict and harass slowly retreating enemy armored forces.

Commanders conducting exploitations must be aggressive in reconnaissance, prompt to use firepower, and quick to employ uncommitted units. They clear only enough of their zones to permit their units to advance. Enemy pockets of resistance which are too small to jeopardize the accomplishment of the mission are contained, bypassed, or destroyed. Bypassed enemy forces must be reported to adjacent units, following units, and higher headquarters. Enemy formations or positions that are strong enough to pose a threat to the accomplishment of the mission are attacked from the march and overrun when possible. If the enemy is too strong to be destroyed by leading elements of the exploitation force and cannot be bypassed, succeeding elements of the force will mount a hasty attack.

Follow and support forces are usually employed in exploitation and pursuit operations. Such forces—

- Widen or secure the shoulders of a penetration.
- Destroy bypassed enemy units.
- Relieve supported units that have halted to contain enemy forces.
- Block the movement of enemy reinforcements.
- Open and secure lines of communication.
- Guard prisoners, key areas, and installations.
- Control refugees.

The follow and support force is not a reserve. It is a committed force and is provided the appropriate artillery, engineer, and air defense artillery support. In division operations, brigades may be assigned follow and support missions; in corps exploitations, divisions may follow and support other divisions.

Field artillery units should always be available to fire into and beyond retreating enemy columns. In some cases, field artillery battalions are attached to exploiting brigades. When their use has been authorized, nuclear or chemical weapons may be employed to destroy enemy artillery and reserves and close routes of escape.

The exploiting force depends primarily on its speed and enemy disorganization for security. Overextension is a risk inherent in the aggressive conduct of the exploitation. Commanders must rely on aggressive reconnaissance by air cavalry units and supporting aerial systems. In addition, electronic warfare (EW) units can seek out enemy counterattack forces and jam enemy command and control and intelligence nets.

Exploiting forces should be accompanied by mobile air defense units. Air defense arrangements for the initial attack should remain effective for the exploitation. As formations are extended, air defense coverage becomes less effective. Thus, it is particularly important during an exploitation that supporting counter air operations establish and retain local air superiority.

Engineers are integrated into exploiting maneuver forces to help breach obstacles and keep forces moving forward. Engineers also keep supply routes open and unimpeded.

Combat support and combat service support arrangements must be extremely flexible. In deep or diverging exploitations, some combat support and combat service support units will be attached to maneuver forces.

Because troops are frequently tired when the opportunity for exploitation occurs, commanders must exercise aggressive and demanding leadership to keep units advancing. When fatigue, disorganization, and attrition have weakened the force or when it must hold ground or resupply, the commander continues the exploitation with a fresh force.

As the enemy becomes demoralized and his formations begin to disintegrate, exploitation may develop into *pursuit*. Commanders of all units in exploitation must anticipate the transition to pursuit and consider the new courses of action that become available as enemy cohesion and resistance break down.

In the pursuit, the commander attempts to annihilate the fleeing enemy force. Successful pursuit requires unrelenting pressure against the enemy to prevent his reconstitution or evasion. A terrain objective may be designated, but the enemy force is the primary objective. Occasionally, the attacker may be able to launch the pursuit directly after his initial assault if the latter causes massive enemy disintegration. Such a situation could well occur following an attack supported by nuclear or chemical weapons.

To ensure that the momentum of the pursuit continues, commanders position themselves well forward. Because of the enemy's disintegration, pursuit allows greater risks than other types of offensive operations. Pursuit operations are aggressive and decentralized. Troops and equipment are pushed to the utmost limits of their endurance during both daylight and darkness.

In the pursuit, direct pressure against retreating forces is maintained relentlessly while an encircling force cuts the enemy line of retreat. The pursuing force attempts encirclement of retreating enemy forces whenever conditions permit. It makes maximum use of air assault and air maneuver units in the encircling forces. As in the exploitation, artillery, engineers, and combat service support troops are often attached to the maneuver units they support. Pursuit operations require—

- A *direct-pressure force* that keeps enemy units in flight, denying them any chance to rest, regroup, or resupply.
- An *encircling force* to envelop the fleeing force, cut its escape route, and, in conjunction with the direct-pressure force, destroy or capture it.

The direct-pressure force conducts hasty attacks to maintain contact and forward momentum until the enemy force is completely destroyed. The direct-pressure force prevents enemy disengagement and subsequent reconstitution of the defense and inflicts maximum casualties. It should preferably consist of armor-heavy forces. Its leading elements move rapidly along all available roads and contain or bypass small enemy pockets of resistance which follow and support units reduce. At every opportunity, the direct-pressure force envelops, cuts off, and destroys or captures enemy elements, provided such actions do not interfere with its primary mission.

The encircling force moves as swiftly as possible by the most advantageous routes to cut off enemy retreat. If necessary, it organizes a hasty defense behind the enemy to block his retreat so that he can be destroyed between the direct-pressure and encircling forces.

The encircling force must be at least as mobile as the enemy. It must be organized for semi-independent operations. Air assault and airborne forces are ideally suited for this role. The encircling force advances along or flies over routes that parallel the enemy's line of retreat to reach defiles, communications centers, bridges, and other key terrain ahead of enemy forces. If the encircling force cannot outdistance the enemy, it attacks his main groupings on one or both of their flanks. If an attempt to cut the enemy's escape routes fails, a new encircling force is immediately dispatched.

An encirclement resulting from a pursuit can completely destroy an enemy force. Pursuing forces that successfully encircle an enemy must prevent his attempts to break out. If sufficient troops are not available, gaps may be blocked temporarily by fire or with barriers. Maneuver and fires of all forces involved in the encirclement must be coordinated. The enemy must be kept under constant pressure and denied the time to reorganize a cohesive defense. If he is able to form a perimeter, it must be reduced in size by repeatedly splitting it into smaller elements until the encircled force is destroyed or it capitulates. If time is not critical, the commander can keep the encirclement closed, ward off breakout attempts, and weaken the enemy by fire alone.

PLANNING, PREPARING, AND CONDUCTING ATTACKS

When the force receives a mission, the commander issues a warning order to his subordinates and makes an estimate of the situation. He identifies tasks required to accomplish the mission and in most cases translates the mission into specific objectives which when seized will permit him to control the area or to defeat the enemy.

Considerations. As he makes his estimate of the situation for an attack, the commander considers the factors of mission, enemy, terrain and weather, troops, and time.

Mission. Commonly, offensive operations allow subordinate commanders the greatest possible freedom. Whenever possible, subordinates should be assigned an objective and a zone without further restrictions. Some operations require greater control and coordination, however, and it will sometimes be necessary to give subordinates more detailed orders for attacks.

In all cases, commanders need to anticipate likely developments during an attack. They must bear their superior's mission and intentions in mind and make preparations to continue beyond their objectives or assume additional responsibilities.

Enemy. Planners must also consider the dispositions, equipment, doctrine, capabilities, and probable intentions of the enemy. Because of the strength of established defenses, commanders should aggressively seek gaps or weaknesses in the enemy's defenses. Enemy defensive preparations should be studied, obstructed, and frustrated. Commanders plan to penetrate enemy security areas, overcome obstacles, avoid the strengths of established defenses, and destroy the coherence of the defense. This requires active intelligence collection oriented on critical units and areas. Enemy reserves in particular must be identified and located as accurately as possible. Enemy air capabilities and air defenses are also vital aspects of the intelligence estimate since they affect friendly freedom of maneuver.

Terrain (and weather). Attacking forces should select avenues of approach that permit rapid advance, allow for maneuver by the attacking force, provide cover and concealment, permit lateral shifting of reserves, allow good communications, resist obstruction by enemy obstacles, and orient on key terrain. Weather conditions that affect mobility, concealment, and air support should be exploited whenever possible.

Battalion task forces and company teams advance from one covered and concealed position to the next. Divisions and corps move along avenues that provide for rapid advance of all combined arms and supporting forces. To sustain momentum, tank and mechanized task forces must move forward; so must field and air defense artillery, engineers, and combat service support units.

Terrain chosen for the main effort should allow rapid movement into the enemy's rear area. Commanders should normally identify and avoid terrain that will hinder a rapid advance; however, an initial maneuver over difficult terrain may be desirable if the enemy can be surprised. Commanders should personally reconnoiter the terrain, particularly terrain where the main effort is to be conducted.

Special attention should be given to obstacles. Commanders must plan to negotiate or avoid urban areas, rivers, extreme slopes, thick forests, or soft ground between their units and their objective. Such terrain when parallel to the axis of advance can also be used to protect the attacker's own flanks. Light forces can use such areas as approaches and by capitalizing on them for defensive positions, free heavier forces to maneuver.

Key terrain along the axis of advance must be either seized or controlled by fire. When present, decisive terrain becomes the focal point of the attack.

Weather and visibility conditions can have significant effects on offensive operations. Concealment and protection from air attack afforded by weather or light conditions will sometimes be critical to success. Ground conditions will increase or reduce the number of avenues available for maneuver and will affect speed of movement for all forces. Maintenance and logistic support of heavy forces and limitations on aviation operations also increase with inclement weather.

Troops. The number and type of friendly troops available also affect the tactical plan. Relative mobility, protection, and firepower should all be taken into account, and the plan adopted should make full use of the reinforcing effects of combined arms. Dismounted infantry can open approaches for armor and mechanized forces by attacking through heavy cover or by penetrating anti-armor defenses. Air assault or airborne units can seize objectives in depth to block enemy reserves or secure choke points. Armor units can move rapidly through gaps to disorganize the defense in depth. Field artillery, air defense artillery and engineer units all perform critical functions and must be used to support all elements of an attacking force. Aviation units must engage the full range of enemy ground targets as well as enemy helicopters and fixed-wing aircraft.

Time Available. Commanders must bear in mind Clausewitz's warning that *time not used by the attacker benefits the defender.* Offensive actions become harder to conduct as the defender organizes the ground and brings up more troops. Nonetheless, the attacker must take the time necessary to assure that his operation is properly synchronized and that he concentrates all available combat power for the attack.

General Patton, who stressed the efficient use of time in all his operations, carefully distinguished *haste* from *speed*.

"Haste exits," he wrote, "when troops are committed without proper reconnaissance, without the arrangement for proper supporting fire, and before every available man has been brought up. The result of such an attack will be to get the troops into action early, but to complete the action very slowly.

Speed is acquired by making the necessary reconnaissance, providing the proper artillery and other tactical support, including air support, bringing up every man and then launching the attack with a predetermined plan so that the time under fire will be reduced to the minimum. At the battalion level four hours spent in preparation for an attack will probably ensure the time spent under fire not exceeding thirty minutes. One hour spent in . . . preparation . . . will most certainly ensure time under fire lasting many hours with bloody casualties."

Once an attack is underway, time remains critical. The attack can succeed only if it achieves its objective before the enemy recovers his balance, identifies the threat, and masses forces and fires against it. Time is therefore vital to the attacker; he must prolong the enemy's surprise, confusion, and disorganization for as long as possible.

Planning for Attacks. Commanders use mission orders to describe the overall mission of the force, their own intent, the concept of operation, and the missions of their subordinates. Restrictions on subordinates' freedom of action must be minimized.

To avoid pausing or losing momentum after seizing his initial objective, the commander must always anticipate an exploitation. Commanders must plan to overcome the enemy's resistance completely and to exploit successes relentlessly. The plan should facilitate rapid dispersal of concentrated units and the introduction of fresh forces to exploit success.

In designating objectives, the commander must consider the mission, the enemy situation (including enemy dispositions in depth), troops available and their combat effectiveness, the terrain, the weather, and the time-space relationships. After selecting objectives, he develops the scheme of maneuver, allocates available forces, and plans for fire support, combat support, and combat service support.

The scheme of maneuver seeks to gain an advantage of position over the enemy, to close with him rapidly, to overrun him if possible, and to destroy his ability to resist. The attack may strike the enemy's front, flank, or rear and may come from the ground or the air or a combination of both. The commander determines the specific form of maneuver or the combination of forms as part of his estimate of the situation. He selects a scheme of maneuver that facilitates seizing the objective rapidly and positioning the force for subsequent operations.

Surprise and an indirect approach are desirable characteristics of any scheme of maneuver. When a geographically indirect approach is not available, the commander can achieve a similar effect by doing the unexpected—striking earlier, in greater force, with unexpected weapons, or at an unlikely place.

The scheme of maneuver identifies where the main effort is to be made. All of the force's available resources must operate in concert to assure the success of the main effort. The plan of attack must also contain provisions for exploiting success whenever it occurs. Commanders must avoid becoming so committed to the initial main effort that they neglect other opportunities. They must be prepared to abandon failed attacks and to exploit any unanticipated successes or enemy errors. In some cases, the situation may be so obscure that the commander will not designate a main attack initially. In most cases, however, a main attack will be identified.

Commanders concentrate attacking forces against enemy weaknesses. The commander can weight the main attack by positioning reserves, by assigning a narrower zone to the main attack force, by assigning priority of fires to the main attack, or by a combination of these. The main attack normally gets priority of effort from close air support, attack helicopters, combat engineers, EW, CSS, and nuclear, biological, chemical (NBC) defense units. The plan for deep operations, the plan for rear operations, and, when authorized, the plan for nuclear fire will also be oriented on the success of the main attack.

When authorized for such use, nuclear or chemical weapons employment may permit small forces attacking at high speeds to achieve the same success as larger forces supported with conventional fires. Nuclear or chemical fires may so reduce the enemy's strength that multiple simultaneous attacks are possible.

The commander influences the action by shifting air, artillery, engineer, and EW assets during the attack. The reserve, however, is the commander's principal means of influencing the action decisively once the operation is under way.

The reserve reinforces success in the attack or maintains attack momentum. The reserve prepares for a number of specific contingencies which may arise during the attack. It is positioned near the area in which it is most likely to be employed and is re-positioned as necessary to assure it can react promptly.

The reserve's strength and composition vary with the contemplated mission, the forces available, the type of offensive operation, the form of maneuver, the terrain, the possible hostile reaction, and the situation. When the situation is relatively clear and enemy capabilities are limited, the reserve may be small. If the situation is vague, the attacker should lead with probing forces and retain his freedom of maneuver until a gap, a flank, or a weakness appears. When the situation is so obscure that it must be developed before the commander commits himself to a main effort, the reserve may consist of half or more of the available maneuver force.

Commanders should make a distinction between true reserves and trailing forces with subsequent missions. A trailing force may have the mission of moving through a penetration made by another unit and seizing a deeper objective. This mission differs from both the reserve mission and the follow and support mission normally assigned during an exploitation.

Commanders develop a fire support plan that assists and complements the maneuver plan. The fire support plan provides fires in direct support of committed maneuver elements and in general support of the entire force. It also provides for support of the reserve when it is committed. Commanders must decide whether or not to fire a preparation. That decision is based on the likelihood of surprising the enemy; knowledge of the enemy's strength and dispositions; nuclear, biological, and chemical protection; available ammunition; and the results desired. When use of nuclear or chemical weapons has been authorized, the fire support plan assigns such weapons and fires to appropriate executing units.

Deep operations must be synchronized with the scheme of maneuver. Deep operations support tactical offensive operations by isolating the battlefield from reinforcing or counterattacking reserves, disrupting the enemy's combined arms cooperation and operational command and control, and destroying or degrading his sustaining support. Enemy reserves, fire support elements, command and control facilities, and other high value assets beyond the line of contact are potential targets for attack. The primary tools of deep operations are—

- Tactical air support.
- Long-range artillery.
- Attack helicopter units.

- Electronic warfare systems.
- Special forces.
- Ranger units.
- Air assault units.
- Airborne units.
- Armored and mechanized units.

Separately or in combination, these means can block the reinforcement of the enemy defenses; protect the attacking force against counterattack; and disorganize enemy fire support, air defenses, and logistic support. They can slow the reactions of the defender by jamming communications and by destroying command posts. Air assault and airborne forces can divert forces, confuse the enemy, or seize key terrain deep in the enemy's rear area.

Rear operations are of concern in all division and corps level offensive operations. They are of particular concern to divisions and larger units, which must allocate forces and other resources to maintain freedom of action and continuity of operations during and following an attack. Lines of communication, reserves, and displacing support elements are the logical targets of the enemy's own deep operations. Air attack, saboteurs, irregular and regular stay-behind forces, or bypassed enemy units will all present problems during the attack. During attacks of considerable depth, follow and support forces must be provided to protect lines of communications, facilitate the forward movement of supplies, and defeat or contain bypassed enemy forces. Rear operations are treated at length in FM 90-14.

Preparing for Attacks. Time is essential and must be carefully managed. Commanders should use no more than one-third of the available preparation time for planning and issuing orders. Subordinates must be given time to conduct necessary reconnaissance and coordination and to follow troop-leading procedures throughout the force. Warning orders are vital in preparing for attacks.

Attack orders embody the commander's intent and concept of operation. They include measures for coordinating and controlling operations. Control measures describe and illustrate the concept, maintain separation of forces, concentrate effort, assist the commander in the command and control of his forces, and add flexibility to the maneuver plan. As a minimum, they include a line of departure, a time of attack, and the objective. In addition they may assign zones of action, axes of advance, directions of attack, routes, phase lines, checkpoints, and fire control measures. Such control measures support the commander's concept and allow maximum freedom of action for subordinate commanders.

Whenever possible, commanders should issue orders face-to-face. Subordinate commanders must know what the command as a whole is expected to do, what is expected of them, and what adjacent and supporting commanders are expected to do. Subordinate commanders and staffs must have pertinent information and as much time as possible to prepare their plans.

Coordination begins immediately on receipt of a mission and is continuous throughout the operation. When time allows, the commander and/or his staff should review plans of subordinates, giving additional guidance as needed to ensure an overall coordinated effort.

Commanders must integrate support plans with tactical plans during their preparations for offensive operations. They must also ensure that their CSS operators are kept fully informed during the battle.

In the offense, CSS facilities should be positioned as close as possible to the tactical units they support. Only CSS elements that provide essential support (trucks with ammunition and petroleum, oil, and lubricants (POL), for example) should move forward just prior to the attack. If possible, such movements should occur at night.

When the plan calls for the attacking unit to pass through a defending unit, CSS planners should seek assistance from the defending unit. It may be able to assist by providing POL, medical aid, or other support.

Just prior to the attack, units move rapidly into attack positions. This movement must be thoroughly coordinated and planned in detail to avoid confusion and delay. Concentration of the force should take place quickly and should make maximum use of cover and concealment, signal security, and deception. Actions that would alert the enemy to the coming attack must be avoided or masked to preserve surprise.

The attacking force organizes to cope with the environment—to attack across obstacles and rivers, during snow or rain, at night, or to exploit nuclear or chemical strikes. Engineers, nuclear, chemical, and biological reconnaissance units, and air defense artillery and aviation assets must be employed to support maneuver throughout the attack.

Conducting Attacks. The attack must be violent and rapid to shock the enemy and to prevent his recovery until the defense has been destroyed. The attacker must minimize his exposure to enemy fires by using maneuver and counterfire, avoiding obstacles, maintaining security, ensuring command and control, and remaining organized for the fight on the objective.

When a hasty attack fails and the commander decides to resort to a deliberate attack, he must ensure that the force does not become disorganized or vulnerable to counterattack or nuclear and chemical attack during the preparatory period. Positive command and control is imperative. Portions of the force must take up hasty defensive positions; other parts of the force are directed to assembly areas. Rapid dispersal is essential, but it must be orderly enough to allow the attack to continue after the briefest possible period of reorganization, consolidation, planning, and coordination.

Both attack and exploitation often begin with a *forward passage of lines,* an operation in which one friendly unit moves forward through positions held by another. Such a passage must be well planned and coordinated to ensure minimum congestion and confusion. When possible, passage should be through elements that are not in contact.

Specific details of the passage are coordinated between the respective subordinate unit commanders. Normally, the overall commander assigns boundaries to designate areas through which subordinate elements will move. Such boundaries usually correspond to those of the passed force. The passed force mans contact and passage points; provides information concerning the enemy, minefields, and obstacles; and provides guides.

To ensure continuous support without increasing battlefield clutter, the passed unit may provide the passing unit initial logistical support. Once started, the passage is completed as quickly as possible to minimize the vulnerability of the two forces. The passing force must assume control of the battle as soon as its lead elements have moved through the passed force. Artillery supporting the passed force and its own direct fires should be integrated into the fire support plan of the passing unit.

The attack culminates in a powerful and violent *assault* on the objective. The purpose of the assault is to destroy an enemy force or to seize the ground it has occupied. Synchronized fires, maneuver, and combat support are imperative to achieve superior combat power at the point of the assault. Artillery preparation, suppressive fire, isolation of the enemy force, concentration of combat power, and overrunning the enemy all combine to destroy the defending force.

Commanders concentrate all available firepower on the defender's positions at the beginning of the assault. These fires shift to targets beyond the objective as attacking troops begin their assault. This requires detailed planning, precise execution, and considerable discipline in the fire support force as well as in the assault force. Dismounted assault forces should move as close behind their own fires as possible; armored forces should assault under overhead artillery fire.

As the attacker reaches his objective, he must overcome enemy resistance with violent concentrated firepower and a rapid advance. Speed during this phase of the attack is absolutely essential to reduce casualties and to avoid becoming stalled in the enemy's fields of fire. The assault must move completely across the objective. Fortified positions on the objective are then attacked from the flank or rear after the assaulting force has passed around them.

A coordinated effort to suppress enemy field artillery, air defense, radio electronic combat means, and command and control supports the assault. The enemy forces in depth posing the greatest threat to the attacking force are reserves, nuclear or chemical delivery systems, command and control facilities of the force being attacked, and fire support units. They are jammed by combat electronic warfare intelligence units, attacked by artillery or air, or blocked by other maneuver forces during the assault as part of coordinated deep operations.

The exploitation follows immediately either by continuing the attack with the same force or by passing another through. Infantry attacks of fortified defenses are normally exploited by armor and mechanized forces.

OTHER TACTICAL CONSIDERATIONS

Flank Security. The attacking force commander should not ignore the threat to his flanks, which increases as the attack progresses. He must assign responsibility for flank security to attacking units or designated security forces. To maintain forward momentum, it may sometimes be necessary to dispense temporarily with flank protection. The speed of attack itself offers a degree of security, because it makes defensive reactions less effective.

Obstacles overwatched by air or ground cavalry or other security forces can improve flank security. When flank obstacles are emplaced, the commander should be mindful of how they affect both his own maneuver options and those units following his.

Smoke Operations. During offensive operations, smoke may be used to degrade enemy observation. Smoke placed on or near enemy positions blinds gunners and observers. Delivered between friendly and enemy forces, it screens friendly maneuver. Care must be taken, however, to ensure that the use of smoke does not impair the effectiveness of friendly forces.

Smoke may also be used to deceive the enemy as to the attacker's intentions. For example, smoke may be used to attract the enemy's attention to one part of the battlefield while friendly units attack on another.

Protection from Air Attack. Attacking forces are highly vulnerable to enemy air attack. If the enemy dominates the air, attacks will have to use concealment carefully. In that event, cloud cover or limited visibility conditions in conjunction with well-planned, ground-based air defense efforts are a great advantage to an attack.

In a rapid attack, air defense units must seek aggressive control over the airspace from which the attack can be threatened. While SHORAD units provide close-in protection of critical assets such as command and control nodes, artillery, and key mobility features (bridges, and defiles, for example), high- to medium-altitude air defense (HIMAD) assets must be repositioned to reach out and destroy enemy aircraft before they enter the zone of the attack.

Breaching Obstacles. When facing an organized defense, the attacker should expect to encounter obstacles. Natural obstacles should be bypassed, breached, or crossed with the assistance of engineer units in support of the attack.

An attacker should bypass obstacles whenever possible. If he cannot bypass quickly, he should begin breaching operations at once. Since obstacles are usually covered by fire, it is important to act quickly to bypass or to breach.

An assault breach usually occurs under fire, with little opportunity for reconnaissance. When possible, combat engineers, moving with leading companies, perform the breach while tanks and infantry overwatch. Because engineers cannot be everywhere, however, all units must be trained, organized, and equipped to conduct hasty breaches of minefields and other obstacles. In an assault breach, rapid breaching devices clear lanes to the minimum width necessary to allow combat forces to continue the advance.

Combat engineers may conduct a deliberate breach if time permits detailed reconnaissance and planning. Normally, in a deliberate breach, they will clear obstacles completely.

River Crossing Operations. Commanders plan to cross quickly rivers or streams in the path of advance. A river crossing requires special planning and support. The size of the obstacle and the enemy situation will dictate how to make the crossing. Regardless of how they cross the river, attackers try to do so without losing momentum. Only as a last resort should the attacking force pause to build up forces and equipment. FM 90-13 deals with the subject in detail.

Attacks During Limited Visibility. Darkness and other periods of limited visibility offer great advantages to the attacker. Attacks may be conducted at such times—

- To achieve surprise.
- To exploit success.
- To maintain momentum.
- To rupture strong enemy defenses.
- To offset enemy air superiority.

Night vision devices make night combat more feasible and effective than ever before. Because it lights the battlefield for both sides, artificial illumination should be used only when night vision devices are not available in sufficient quantities or when ambient light levels are very low.

When ambient light levels are high, passive night vision devices will overcome many of the limiting effects of darkness. However, limited visibility will still reduce detection and engagement ranges, the length of bounds, and the ability to move on covered and concealed routes.

Snow, rain, fog, or smoke present special problems in navigation, target acquisition, and identification. Special training, use of appropriate sensors, and careful planning can overcome these difficulties.

When a defender occupies positions affording good long-range fields of fire, attackers may choose to wait for a short period to take advantage of darkness or the arrival of bad weather or fog.

Night attacks against strongly defended positions should cover relatively short distances. Leaders at all levels should have the opportunity to reconnoiter the area of the attack as far forward as possible during good visibility. Wire will often be the primary means of communications until the assault begins or surprise is lost. Visual aids for recognition may assist in control of forces. Objectives will usually be smaller than normal, but they must be of sufficient prominence to ensure easy location.

SPECIAL PURPOSE OPERATIONS

While the preceding considerations apply to all offensive operations, some operations, by virtue of their unique purpose or the circumstances in which they are conducted, require special planning. These include the reconnaissance in force, attacks from a defensive posture, diversionary operations, offensive reliefs, and raids.

The *reconnaissance in force* is a limited-objective operation by a considerable force to obtain information and to locate and test enemy dispositions, strengths, and reactions. Even when the commander is executing a reconnaissance in force primarily to gather information, he must be alert to seize any opportunity to exploit tactical success. If the enemy situation must be developed along a broad front, the reconnaissance in force may consist of strong probing actions to determine the enemy situation at selected points. The enemy's reactions may reveal weaknesses in his defensive system. Because reconnaissance in force is primarily an information-gathering operation, commanders must carefully evaluate the risks involved. They must make advance provisions either to extricate the force or to exploit success.

Attacks from a defensive posture include spoiling attacks and counterattacks. *Spoiling attacks* are mounted to disrupt an expected enemy attack before it is launched. A spoiling attack attempts to strike the enemy while he is most vulnerable, during his preparations for the attack in assembly areas, attack positions, or on the move prior to crossing his line of departure. In most respects, it is conducted like any other attack and may be either hasty, when time is short, or deliberate when adequate fore-warning has been obtained. Frequently, the circumstances in which it is conducted will preclude full exploitation, and the attacking force will either halt on its objective or withdraw to its original position. When the situation permits, however, a spoiling attack should be exploited like any other attack.

Counterattacks may be conducted either by a reserve or by lightly committed forward elements to defeat an attack after it has been launched, the enemy's main effort has been identified, and an assailable flank has been created. Counterattacks are conducted much like other attacks, but because they must be synchronized with the overall defensive effort, their timing is especially important. Like spoiling attacks, counterattacks usually revert to a defensive posture after local exploitation rather than full exploitation and pursuit. In some cases, however, the counterattack may be the first step in reverting to offensive operations by the larger defending force. Counterattacks may also be more limited "counterattacks by fire." These are tactical level actions which consist of positioning a force where advantageous flanking or rear fires may be brought against the enemy and enemy positions are not assaulted. Counterattacks are discussed in more detail in Chapter 9.

Diversionary operations include feints and demonstrations. A *feint* is a supporting attack designed to divert the enemy's attention from the main effort. It is normally executed by brigades and smaller units. Feints are usually shallow, limited-objective attacks conducted before or during the main attack. A *demonstration* is a show of force in an area where a decision is not sought. A demonstration threatens attack, but does not actually make contact with the enemy intentionally.

An *offensive relief* is conducted to pass fresh troops into the attack in order to maintain offensive momentum. Such reliefs are most common as the force enters the exploitation or pursuit, but may also be necessary during the attack itself if previously committed units have suffered so severely that they are unable to reach their objectives. Offensive reliefs may be conducted as reliefs in place, but ideally are conducted without a significant pause in offensive tempo.

A *raid* is a limited-objective attack into enemy territory for a specific purpose other than gaining and holding ground. Raids are typically conducted to destroy key enemy installations and facilities, capture or free prisoners, or disrupt enemy command and control or support functions. The raiding force always withdraws from the objective area after completing its mission and unless it is a stay-behind unit, will normally recover to friendly lines.

PART III

DEFENSIVE OPERATIONS

CHAPTER 8

Fundamentals of the Defense

Defensive operations retain ground, gain time, deny the enemy access to an area, and damage or defeat attacking forces. While they can sometimes deny success to the enemy, they cannot normally assure victory. At higher levels, even a defensive strategy designed to deny success will require offensive components to preclude defeat. For this reason, military theorists, such as Clausewitz, Jomini, and Sun Tzu, considered the defense the less decisive form of war, regarding it only as a temporary expedient unless mandated by higher strategic purposes.

While viewing defense as the less decisive form of war, Clausewitz also maintained that it is the stronger one. For one thing, it is easier to deny the enemy his ends than to achieve a positive aim. Moreover, the advantages of cover and concealment, advance siting of weapons, shorter lines of supply, and operations on familiar terrain and among a friendly population generally favor the defense. The only advantage enjoyed by the attacker is the initial choice of when and where to strike. The major challenge of the defense is to overcome this initial offensive advantage.

CONTENTS

HISTORICAL PERSPECTIVE

A successful defense consists of reactive and offensive elements working together to deprive the enemy of the initiative. An effective defense is never purely passive. The defender resists and contains the enemy where he must but seeks every opportunity to go over to the offensive. Early in a campaign or defensive battle, such opportunities will be local and limited. As the situation develops, they will become more numerous. This is especially true when the defender takes steps to uncover enemy vulnerabilities and to confuse or disorganize his force. When the attacker exposes himself, the defender's reserves or uncommitted forces counterattack. The defense that successfully destroys the coherence of enemy operations can ultimately defeat his uncoordinated forces.

While reactive measures may halt the enemy, early counterattacks improve the chances for success. The defense can greatly damage the enemy only when early counterstrokes accompany the reactive phase of the battle. Gettysburg exemplifies a defensive battle of pure reaction. The outcome depended on the errors of the attacker. Although the attacking Confederates erred, their mistakes were not exploited when they occurred. At the battle of Kursk in 1943, the Soviet defense was better balanced. Early counterattacks strengthened the reactive phase, and the entire defending army ultimately went over to the offensive to exploit its defensive success.

A closer parallel to the fluid conditions, rapid maneuver, and calculated risks of contemporary operations can be found in the Battle of Tannenberg fought in East Prussia in August 1914. While the majority of the German Army attacked France, General Max von Prittwitz, commander of the German Eighth Army, defended the province against two Russian armies, Rennenkampf's First and Samsonov's Second, in the north and south respectively. After failing to halt the former with a series of spoiling attacks, Prittwitz notified the high

THE BATTLE OF TANNENBERG

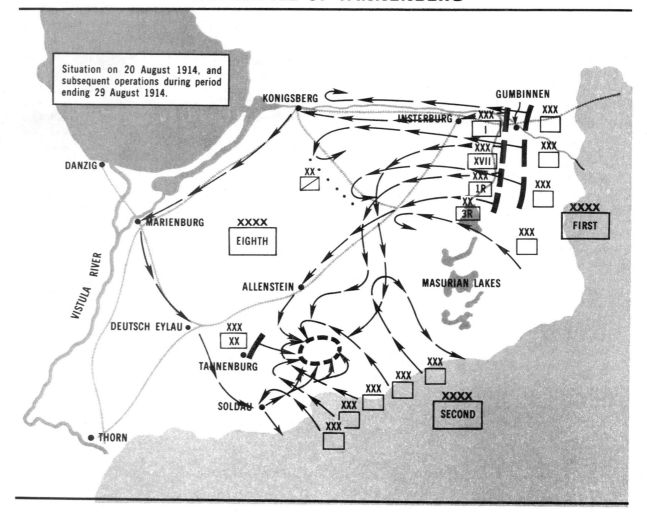

Situation on 20 August 1914, and subsequent operations during period ending 29 August 1914.

command that he intended to evacuate the province to the Vistula River. He was thereupon relieved and replaced by General Paul von Hindenburg.

Upon their arrival in East Prussia, Hindenburg and his Chief of Staff, General Erich von Ludendorff, adopted a plan conceived by Prittwitz's Chief of Operations, Lieutenant Colonel Max Hoffmann, to entrap and destroy Samsonov's Second Army. Leaving only a cavalry screen to confront Rennenkampf's army, Hindenburg began to concentrate his forces in the south. Five days later he first halted, then encircled and destroyed the Second Army near Tannenberg. Samsonov's army broke up in panic, losing 125,000 men and 500 guns from 26 to 31 August.

Turning back to the north, the Germans then concentrated against the Russian First Army, defeating it and driving it out of East Prussia. In this defensive campaign, the Germans lost some 10,000 men while imposing losses of over 250,000 men on their opponents and effectively ending the Russian threat to their eastern provinces. The Tannenberg operation achieved the German theater goal in East Prussia through a defensive campaign characterized by aggressive offensive tactics.

PURPOSES OF DEFENSIVE OPERATIONS

Defensive operations are conducted to—

- Defeat an enemy attack.
- Gain time.
- Concentrate forces elsewhere.
- Control key or decisive terrain.
- Wear down enemy forces as a prelude to offensive operations.
- Retain strategic, operational, or tactical objectives.

The immediate purpose of any defense is to defeat the attack. Other purposes, while important, are ancillary from an operational perspective (they may, however, be overriding from a strategic perspective).

Defense is used to gain time for reinforcements to arrive or to economize forces in one sector while concentrating forces for attack in another. In either case, a defense or a delay may achieve these purposes.

In some instances, a force may defend because it is unable to attack. The defender then uses his advantages of position and superior knowledge of the terrain to cause the enemy to overextend himself. Once the enemy has committed himself against the defense and has been weakened by losses, the defender maneuvers to destroy him with fires or counterattacks.

In other cases, portions of a force may be required to retain key or decisive terrain or essential strategic, operational, or tactical objectives. Even in offensive operations, air assault, airborne, or amphibious forces may need to defend deep objectives until a larger force can link up with them. Whatever its larger purpose, the immediate challenge of any defensive operation is to recapture the initiative and thus create the opportunity to shift to the offensive. All activities of the defense must contribute to that aim.

CHARACTERISTICS OF DEFENSIVE OPERATIONS

Napoleon's *Memoirs* contain his principles for conducting defensive campaigns. They can be summarized as: "The whole art of war consists of a well-reasoned and extremely circumspect defensive, followed by rapid and audacious attack." In any defensive plan *preparation, disruption, concentration,* and *flexibility* are fundamental.

PREPARATION

The defender arrives in the battle area before the attacker. He must take advantage of his early occupation of the area by making the most thorough preparations for combat that time allows. At the operational level, this involves positioning forces in depth, war-gaming campaign plans, organizing the force for movement and support throughout the theater, mounting reconnaissance and surveillance operations forward of the defended area, mobilizing reserves and auxiliary forces, strengthening air defenses in critical areas, coordinating arrangements for joint and combined operations, and preparing deceptions to mislead the enemy.

At the tactical level, commanders plan fires, maneuver, and deep operations in support of their concepts of operations, wargame enemy options, and prepare deceptions to entrap the enemy. They prepare and conceal positions, routes, obstacles, logistical support, and command facilities in detail. Units use available time to train for and rehearse their specific tasks. Preparation of counterattack positions and routes, alternatives for deep interdiction, and measures for maintaining freedom of action in the rear area (traffic control, air defense, rear operations planning) are as important as siting, protecting, and hiding battle positions.

Initially the defender will ordinarily be outnumbered. In the early stages of battle, he will capitalize on the advantage of fighting from prepared positions of his own choice. As the action develops, however, opportunities will arise for the defender to take the initiative. He must prepare for these opportunities with preconceived maneuver and fire plans by designating counterattack forces and making counterattack plans to support his defense and for eventual reversion of his whole force to the offense.

DISRUPTION

To counter the attacker's initiative and to prevent him from concentrating overwhelming combat power against a part of the defense, the defender must disrupt the synchronization of the enemy's operation. This may be done by separating his forces; by interrupting his fire support, logistical support, or command and control; by breaking the tempo of his operation; or by ruining the coordination of enemy combined and supporting arms.

At the operational level, the commander disrupts the enemy attack with spoiling operations, special operations forces, deception, psychological operations, and air interdiction of critical routes, forces, and facilities. The theater commander may also prevent synchronized enemy action by fighting battles which prevent the junction of separated enemy forces or by taking the initiative temporarily to deny the enemy opportunities to prepare deliberate attacks without interference. The attacker's operational reserves and air forces will almost always be primary objectives of disruptive air and ground attacks.

Tactical commanders disrupt the enemy's synchronization by defeating or misleading his reconnaissance forces, impeding his maneuver, disrupting his reserves, neutralizing his artillery and air support, and interrupting his command and control. Defensive techniques vary with circumstances, but all defensive concepts of operation should aim at spoiling the attacker's synchronization. Deep interdiction, counterattack, counter-battery fires, obstacles, electronic warfare (EW), retention of key or decisive terrain, and, when authorized, nuclear or chemical fires must likewise be used to prevent the enemy from concentrating irresistible strength against portions of the defense.

CONCENTRATION

The defender must concentrate at the decisive time and place if he is to succeed. He will have to mass enough combat power to avoid defeat throughout the battle and, if he is to defeat the attacker, he must obtain a local advantage at points of decision. To do this, the defender must normally economize in some areas, retain (and, when necessary, reconstitute) a reserve, and maneuver to gain local superiority elsewhere. Generally, the defender will have to surrender some ground to gain the time necessary to concentrate forces and fires.

In defensive campaigns, large unit commanders mass against separated enemy forces or concentrate their defenses in the areas of greatest risk. They may concentrate by throwing reserves against the enemy early in the campaign to bring on a quick decision or they may defer concentration for decisive battle until favorable terms of combat can be obtained.

Operational concentration can also be obtained by organizing defenses of great depth which force the attacker to fight a series of battles against echeloned defenses. Theater commanders and their chief subordinates use aerial, cannon, and missile fires to assist and complement the concentration of land forces.

Tactical commanders have less time to respond and will normally have to concentrate combat power repeatedly during battle. Effective reconnaissance and security forces are vital to give the tactical commander time to discern the form of the attack and to concentrate forces and fires against it.

Periods in which the defender can develop superior combat power will be brief, so concentration will have to be rapid and violent. Commanders will have to accept risks in some areas to concentrate for decisive action elsewhere. Obstacles, security forces, and fires can assist reducing these risks. Since concentration increases the threat of large losses from nuclear fires, the massing of forces must be masked by concealment and deception. As quickly as the attacking force has been defeated or halted, defending forces must disperse.

FLEXIBILITY

Defensive operations require flexible planning and execution. In exercising the initiative, the attacker initially decides where and when combat will take place. The defender must be agile enough to counter or evade the attacker's blow, then strike back effectively.

Defensive campaigns depend on branches and sequels to defensive battles for their flexibility. Large unit comanders must be prepared to fight the enemy effectively no matter what the form of the attack. They must anticipate the enemy's offensive moves and prepare counteractions for the likely outcomes of battles. Retention of operational reserves is indispensable to flexibility at the operational level. These forces are usually positioned in depth and assigned contingency missions that they may be called on to perform before, during, or after battle.

Once the campaign is under way, plans must be adjusted to conform to the situation and the commander must be prepared to react quickly to the enemy. The defensive campaign plan should allow the greatest possible freedom of action. It should preserve balance by disposing forces so that the commander can respond to crisis and pass quickly to the attack whenever the opportunity arises.

Tactical flexibility rests on detailed planning, organization in depth, and retaining reserves. The plan must enable the commander to shift his main effort quickly without losing synchronization. Tactical commanders organize their defenses to defeat any approach the enemy might make. They add flexibility to their basic plans by designating supplementary positions in depth and counterattack plans which can be ordered into effect during battle.

Static elements of the defense organize for all-around security and plan alternate and supplementary positions which allow them to move forward, laterally, or to the rear if required. Fire planning covers all approaches and is organized to accommodate changes in priority. Deep operation options are developed for all likely variations on the basic concept of operation. Engineer, aviation, EW, and combat service support are concentrated in support of the main effort, but provisions are also made for shifting that support if necessary. Reserves prepare to move anywhere in sector and make counterattack plans to cover all likely contingencies.

Once the attacker has been controlled, the defender can operate against his exposed flanks and rear. The defender, under the cover of his own field artillery and air defense, can then maneuver over ground he has reconnoitered and prepared against extended elements of the attacking force.

The tenets of AirLand Battle doctrine—initiative, agility, depth, and synchronization—apply to any successful defense. Whatever their specific form, defensive operations—

• Seize the tactical initiative locally and then generally as the entire force shifts from defense to offense.

• Maintain agility and flexibility in using fire, maneuver, and electronic warfare to

set the terms of battle. Once the attacker has committed himself, the defender should adjust his own operation to concentrate all his efforts toward containing, isolating, and defeating the committed enemy force. By interdicting enemy movement in depth and concentrating repeatedly to develop local advantages against the attacker, the defender can win the battle by defeating the enemy piecemeal.

• Fight the enemy throughout the depth of his formations to delay him, to disorganize him, and to create opportunities for offensive action. The defender must organize forces and resources in depth to gain time and space for flexibility and responsive maneuver.

• Synchronize all available combat capability. Violent execution of flexible plans and aggressive exploitation of enemy vulnerabilities can halt the attacking force and offset or overcome the attacker's numerical advantage.

ALTERNATIVE DEFENSIVE PATTERNS

While defensive operations may take a wide variety of forms, traditional usage divides defensive arrangements into two broad categories. *Mobile defenses* focus on the destruction of the attacking force by permitting the enemy to advance into a position which exposes him to counterattack and envelopment by a mobile reserve. *Area defenses* focus on the retention of terrain by absorbing the enemy into an interlocked series of positions from which he can be destroyed largely by fire.

Although these descriptions convey the general pattern of each type of defense, both forms of defense employ both static and dynamic elements. In mobile defenses, static defensive positions help control the depth and breadth of enemy penetration, and assure retention of ground from which to launch counterattacks. In area defenses, mobile reserves cover the gaps among defensive positions, reinforce those positions

as necessary, and are available to counterattack key defensive positions should they be lost to the enemy. Typically, defending commanders will combine both patterns, using static elements to delay, canalize, attrit, and ultimately halt the attacker, and dynamic elements— spoiling attacks and counterattacks—to strike and destroy his committed forces. The balance among these elements will depend on the unit's mission, composition, mobility, and relative combat power, and on the character of the battlefield.

MOBILE DEFENSE

Mobile defenses employ a combination of offensive, defensive, and delaying action to defeat the enemy attack. Their exact design varies from case to case and must be described in detail in each instance. Commanders conducting mobile defense deploy relatively small forces forward and

MOBILE DEFENSE

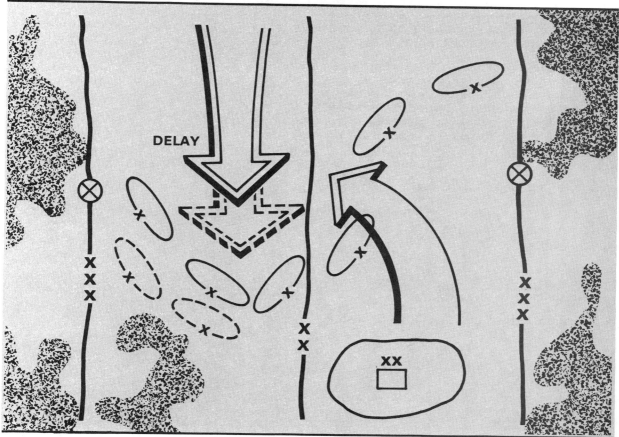

use maneuver supported by fire and obstacles to wrest the initiative from the attacker after he has entered the defended area.

A force conducting a mobile defense must have mobility equal to or greater than the enemy's. It must also be able to form the large reserve which will conduct the decisive counterattack. Since doing so will almost invariably require thinning committed forces, a mobile defense cannot be conducted unless the temporary loss of some terrain is acceptable.

Because of the requirement to form a large reserve, mobile defense is normally conducted by division and larger formations. However, large brigades and cavalry

regiments may be able to conduct this form of defense in some circumstances. In any case, heavy forces are required for the reserve, and may also be used as security forces or to contain anticipated penetrations. Light forces in a mobile defense are usually employed to hold strongpoints in suitable terrain within or adjacent to the area of the enemy's penetration, or in some cases, to stop the enemy during the counterattack.

AREA DEFENSE

An area defense is usually conducted to deny the enemy access to specific terrain for a specified time. Since, unlike the

AREA DEFENSE

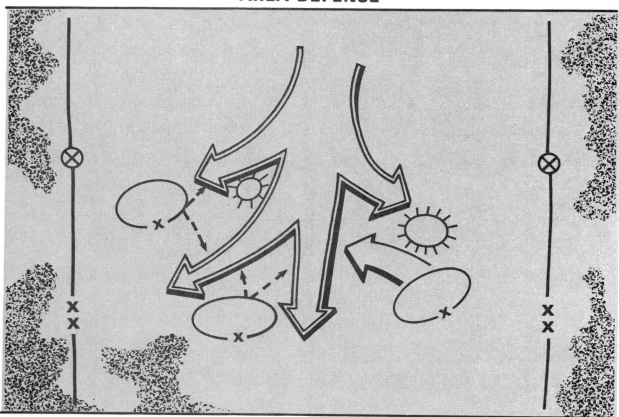

mobile defense, area defense does not promise outright destruction of the attacking force, area defense presumes some other simultaneous or subsequent operation to achieve decisive defeat of the enemy.

In an area defense, the bulk of defending forces are deployed to retain ground, using a combination of defensive positions and small mobile reserves. Commanders organize the defense around the static framework provided by the defensive positions, seeking to destroy enemy forces by interlocking fires or by local counterattack of enemy units penetrating between defensive positions. Both light and heavy forces may conduct area defense. When a defending force is predominantly light, such a defense is usually required.

Unlike mobile defense, for which considerable depth is essential, area defense may be conducted in varying depth, depending on the mission, forces available, and the nature of the terrain. Where necessary, the commander may make his main effort well forward, committing most of his combat power to the forward edge of the battle area (FEBA) and planning to counterattack early, when enemy forces are still along the FEBA or even beyond it. While such a forward defense may often be necessary, it is more difficult to execute than a defense in greater depth. This is because its early commitment to decisive combat makes it less flexible, hence more dependent on rapid identification of and concentration against the enemy main effort.

When the mission is less restrictive, forces are available, and advantageous terrain extends deep into his defensive sector, the commander may organize his defense in greater depth. In extremely wide sectors, divisions and corps may need to defend in depth in order to gain the time to concentrate against the enemy.

When area defense is conducted in depth, elements in the security area identify and control the enemy's main effort while holding off secondary thrusts. Counterattacks on the flanks of the main attack then seal off, isolate, and destroy penetrating enemy forces. In the extreme, therefore, an area defense in depth begins to look much like a mobile defense.

In organization and execution, both defensive patterns vary considerably from the pure form. Each can be visualized as extending across a portion of the defensive continuum. Each uses the same five elements of the defensive framework described below. And each must be fought in the fluid, nonlinear conditions of contemporary combat. Tactical commanders must therefore adapt their defensive arrangements to the requirements of each situation and avoid becoming wedded to rigid patterns in the design of their defensives.

DEFENSIVE FRAMEWORK

A simple, complete concept of operations is the basis of all defenses. Field armies, corps, and divisions fight a unified defensive battle consisting of complementary deep, close, and rear operations. Defenses are organized into five complementary elements:

- Security force operations forward and to the flanks of the defending force.

- Defensive operations in the main battle area (MBA).

- Reserve operations in support of the main defensive effort.

- Deep operations in the area forward of the forward line of own troops (FLOT).

- Rear operations to retain freedom of action in the rear area.

The commander must synchronize all five of these elements in the execution of his defensive plan. If only a screening force is employed, it gives warning of the enemy's approach and harasses advancing enemy forces. If a covering force is used, it meets the enemy's leading forces, strips away enemy reconnaissance and security elements, reports the attacker's strength and locations, and gives the commander time and space in which to react to the enemy.

Defensive operations slow, canalize, and defeat the enemy's major units. The defending commander may do this in a number of ways. In most cases, however, he will have to fight a series of engagements to halt or defeat enemy forces. This will require him to designate a main effort, concentrate in support of it, then shift it to concentrate against another threat, and do so repeatedly. Maneuver units will defend, delay, attack, and screen as part of the defensive battle.

Reserves will be committed throughout the defense and will have to be continually reconstituted as previous reserves enter the battle. Reserves give the commander the means to seize the initiative and preserve his flexibility. Reserves are best employed to strike a decisive blow against the attacker, but they must be prepared to perform other missions as well.

Deep operations will disrupt the enemy's movement in depth, destroy high value targets vital to the attacker, and interrupt enemy command and control at critical times. Forward security elements not forced back by the enemy hold their positions to provide deep observation and target acquisition, and to retain ground from which to launch future counterattacks by maneuver and fire.

THE DEFENSIVE FRAMEWORK

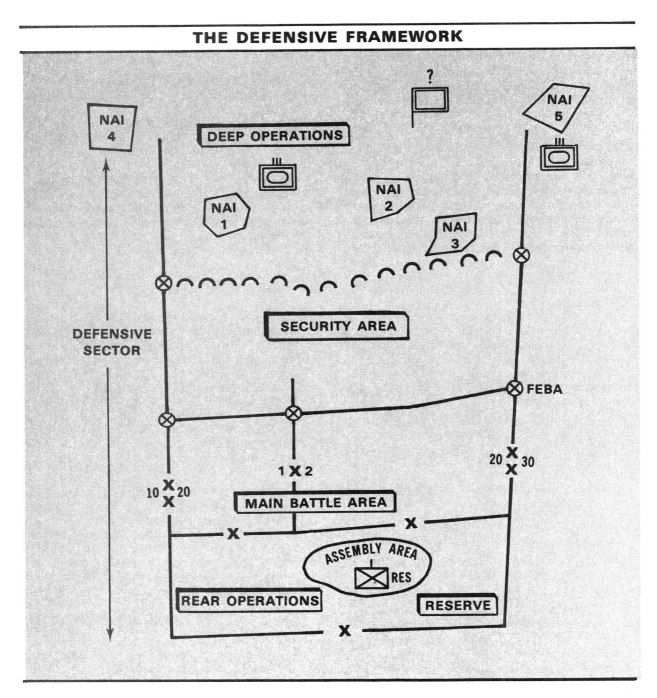

Operations in the rear area protect and sustain command and control and combat service support operations. Their chief function during battle in the MBA is to protect the commander's freedom of action by preventing disruption of command and control, fire support, logistical support, and movement of reserves.

CHAPTER 9
Conducting Defensive Operations

Clausewitz characterized the ideal defense as a "shield of blows." The defender uses his prepared positions and knowledge of the ground to slow the attacker's momentum and to strike him with repeated, unexpected blows. He disrupts the attacker's synchronization, degrades his strength and ability to concentrate, and defeats his force with effective maneuver supported by flexible firepower. The defender need not kill every enemy tank, squad, or fieldpiece; he need only destroy the ability of the enemy force to sustain forward movement.

DEFENSIVE CAMPAIGNS AND MAJOR OPERATIONS

Generally, commanders undertake the defense only when the strategic, operational, or tactical situation makes it impossible to conduct offensive operations or to economize forces to permit an attack elsewhere. To win, they must preserve their own force through successful defense, weaken the enemy, and then take the initiative. In some cases, commanders can secure theater objectives through the tactical offensive actions of a defensive campaign. More commonly, success will require following a successful operational defense with an offensive campaign.

Defensive campaigns are fought to defeat a large attacking force, to retain territory, or to gain time for operations in another theater of operations to succeed or for reinforcements to arrive. Strategic considerations, numerical disadvantage, or the enemy's exercise of the initiative may all require a theater commander to assume the defense.

When possible, a commander conducting a defensive campaign attempts to defer decisive battles until he can win. This may entail exhausting the enemy in protracted

CONTENTS

minor battles, withdrawing into friendly territory, or absorbing the enemy's initial impetus in one area while attacking his lines of communications and bases of support. When strategic direction requires the retention of territory near a political border or the control of vital areas such as political capitals, industrial regions, or population centers, the campaign may have to be fought well forward in the theater. In other cases, a theater may be defended through a series of offensive blows delivered as the enemy masses or approaches a defended area.

As in offensive campaigns, defending commanders try to identify *centers of gravity* as they design their campaign plans. Sources of enemy strength—critical fighting units, command or support facilities, politically significant areas, or allied units—may constitute such centers of gravity. Successful defense of a contested region or the mere denial of success to the enemy over a long period of time may also strike a center of gravity.

Defensive campaigns have varied in form considerably. These forms have included awaiting the enemy's attack in forward positions then striking back immediately after the first battle, preempting the enemy attack with spoiling attacks as soon as he could be reached, fighting a series of inconclusive battles to resist and wear down the enemy, and drawing the enemy deep into friendly territory to exhaust and overextend him.

Whatever the design, commanders conducting defensive campaigns mix offensive with defensive tactical actions and contest the initiative in the theater at every opportunity. They should consider their offensive actions carefully, but should accept calculated risks to avoid becoming excessively passive. As a rule, whatever concept of operation is adopted should reflect the greatest possible use of mobility, surprise, and offensive tactics. The ultimate objective should be to turn to the offensive and to defeat the enemy decisively.

Defenders attempt to defer a decision in the campaign until they can fight on advantageous terms. This means that defending commanders must accurately sense the attacker's culminating point—that time when he has exhausted his offensive potential. The defender tries to hasten the attacker's arrival at that point throughout the campaign. After this has been accomplished through a series of defensive battles (or, occasionally, after a single defensive battle) the defender will be able to shift to the attack himself.

In any defensive campaign, the defender must prevent the attacker from overturning the defense in a single battle. Defensive preparations must therefore stress depth in dispositions and in planning. The retention of some forces in depth is especially vital early in a campaign when flexibility is most important to the defender.

The campaign plan must anticipate likely enemy courses of action and must contain "branches"—variations that enable the commander to cope with them. It must also provide for battles in depth following the first phase of the campaign. This means that logical sequels must be planned as a basis for actions following the first battles. These sequels should assist the commander and his chief subordinates in anticipating actions after a tactical success, a setback, or a stalemate.

Because the attacker will normally attempt to push forces into the depths of the defended theater early in the campaign, the defending commander should hold operational reserves in depth. These may be employed to engage the enemy's operational reserve, to extricate committed units after battle, to exploit tactical success by imposing greater losses on the enemy, or to seize the operational initiative after a defensive victory.

In preparing for a defensive campaign, a commander must consider the logistical base that will support his operation and the limits and vulnerabilities that it imposes on him. He must also take into account the routes and obstacles in the theater, bearing in mind their effects on him and on the attacker. When time permits it, the improvement of routes and obstacles can have a substantial effect on the conduct of the campaign.

Plans for ground operations must be coordinated with air operations to assure that the two are synchronized and that the capabilities of airpower are fully exploited. Similarly, plans for air defense should be made carefully to support the concept of the operation and to allow for the greatest possible operational flexibility.

The campaign plan itself should set clear objectives for the major ground and air forces in the theater. Long-term objectives should be stated and specific objectives should be assigned for the current phase of the campaign. The theater commander should anticipate when and where battles are likely to take place and organize his forces accordingly. Although he will not hold the initiative early in the campaign, he should define for himself and his major subordinates the conditions under which he will accept decisive battle willingly.

The overall concept of operation may take a number of forms, depending on the circumstances of each case. It may exploit a central position to prevent dispersed enemy forces from concentrating by fighting a series of separated battles. Or it may call for an extended period of defensive action to reduce the enemy's numerical strength or contain his initial impetus. As an example, Allied defensive operations in the Bulge consisted of a single concept of operations implemented in several phases. Initially, the Twelfth Army Group fought to stabilize the situation by denying key road intersections necessary to the German attack. In the next phase, the allies concentrated on holding the shoulders of the Bulge and generating operational reserves. Finally, Field Marshal Montgomery and General Bradley counter-attacked into the salient formed by the enemy advance to defeat the attacking forces and establish positions from which to resume the offensive.

Whatever its overall concept, the first phase of a defensive campaign plan must control the enemy's attack while preserving the defending force. In particular, the attacker's operational reserves must be contained or defeated. The commander may disrupt its progress in the enemy's rear, contain it as part of the defensive battle or fight it in a separate battle using his own operational reserve.

If he is to succeed, the operational level commander must also take risks. This commonly means that he must economize in areas of low immediate danger to concentrate forces against the more dangerous threats. He will also have to risk offensive actions when the enemy presents him with opportunities to defeat isolated forces.

In assessing risks, the commander should take the long view to determine whether the risk is justified. In some cases, the defender benefits more from delaying offensive actions until his strength has improved; just as often, however, the defender reaches a point at which he must act or lose the opportunity to take the initiative for an extended period or even permanently. In the latter case, he may face a choice between a slim chance for immediate success at great risk or a prolonged defense with no prospect of winning.

TACTICAL DEFENSE

Tactical defenses will occur in both offensive and defensive campaigns. Subordinate units of a defending force may be ordered to attack, delay, withdraw, screen, or defend in execution of the overall commander's plan. The purpose of the force's operations, however, will remain to stop or to defeat the attacker.

Defensive doctrine is not prescriptive. It describes two general forms of defense at tactical levels—area and mobile—but it leaves the commander great freedom in formulating and conducting his defense. He may elect to defend well forward by striking the enemy as he approaches. He may opt to fight the decisive battle within the main battle area. Or, if he does not have to hold a specified area or position, he may draw the enemy deep into the area of operations and then strike his flanks and rear. He may even choose to preempt the enemy with spoiling attacks if conditions favor such tactics. In the past, all four methods have proven effective.

Brigades and divisions perform major defensive tasks for their superior headquarters. They are normally responsible for substantial sectors of a defense or serve as reserves. Brigades, like cavalry regiments, may also serve as covering forces or security elements forward or to the rear of the MBA. Maneuver battalions defend as part of a larger force. They perform a single task as part of their brigade's mission. They defend, delay, attack, or screen. While battalions provide for their own security and support in any operation and may retain reserves, their main role is to cooperate with other battalions in the brigade's defense.

A simple concept of operations, flexible enough to meet the enemy wherever he chooses to attack, is essential to success. The commander tailors his defensive concept to his specific situation, paying particular attention to operations against the enemy in depth and to the wise use of available time.

PLANNING FOR DEFENSE

Planning for defense begins when a commander receives a mission to defend or perceives a need to do so. The commander then formulates a plan for defense which meets the requirements of the mission. He is guided in the design of his plan by the factors of mission, enemy, terrain, troops, and time available (METT-T) and by the considerations he develops in his estimate of the situation.

Mission. The first consideration in planning the defense is the mission. It defines the area to be defended or the force to be defeated, and it must be analyzed in terms of the higher commander's overall scheme.

Defending broad frontages forces the commander to accept gaps. Defending shallow sectors or positions reduces flexibility and requires the commander to fight well forward. Narrow frontages and deep sectors increase the elasticity of the defense and the number of options available. In planning his defense, the commander also considers possible subsequent missions.

Enemy. The enemy's doctrine, habits, equipment, and probable courses of action must also be considered in planning the defense. Defending commanders must look at themselves and their sectors through the enemy commander's eyes. They must look for vulnerabilities that the enemy may exploit and must act to counter them. They should also identify probable enemy objectives and approaches to them. In a defense against an echeloned enemy, they must know how soon follow-on forces can join the attack. If enemy follow-on forces can be delayed, the attack may be defeated in detail—one echelon at a time. If the defender can force the enemy to commit follow-on echelons sooner than planned, the attacker's timetable can be upset, creating exploitable gaps between the committed and subsequent echelons.

Terrain (and weather). The defending force must exploit any aspect of the terrain that impairs enemy momentum or makes it difficult for him to mass or to maneuver. Defenders must engage the attacker at points where the terrain puts him at the greatest disadvantage. Controlling key terrain is vital to a successful defense. Some terrain may be so significant to the defense that its loss would prove decisive. When terrain is a decisive factor in a division or corps defense, the commander must make it a focal point of his defensive plan. Weather and visibility affect how defenders organize the ground; commanders at all levels must take its effects into account as they analyze terrain. The defending commander should use man-made obstacles to improve the natural structure of terrain, to slow or canalize enemy movement, and to protect friendly positions and maneuver.

Troops. The commander must also consider the nature of his force. The mobility, protection, morale, and training of his troops determine to some extent how he will defend. Armor and mechanized forces can move on the battlefield even under artillery fire, while infantry cannot. Light infantry can fight effectively in close terrain and urban areas which limit mounted units. Differences in mobility, training and leadership make some units more suitable for some missions than for others. Relative strengths such as skill in night combat, infiltration, long-range fires or air assault which give the defender an advantage over the attacker should be exploited in designing the defense.

Time Available. The amount of time to prepare is a crucial factor in organizing a defense. When time is available for reconnaissance and occupation of positions, for fortifying the ground, for fire planning, for installing obstacles, and for coordination of maneuver, fires, and logistic support, the defense will be far more effective. To gain time for organization of the main battle area (MBA), the commander may order a delay by a covering force. Lack of time may cause a commander to maintain a larger-than-normal reserve force or to accept greater risks than usual. Time is a critical element for the defender and cannot be wasted. Small units must be capable of defense with minimal preparation, but commanders must recognize that strong defenses take time to organize and prepare.

Based on his analysis, the commander completes his estimate of the situation and formulates a concept of defense. He decides how to defeat the enemy, where to concentrate his effort, and where to take risks. He then assigns missions, allocates forces, and apportions combat support and combat service support resources to tasks within the framework of the overall defense.

A defensive plan is based on locating, containing, and defeating the attacker's main and supporting efforts. The commander must make use of every resource available to him to offset the attacker's numerical advantage, to identify dangerous threats, and to mass combat power against the vulnerabilities of the enemy force. In particular, planners should anticipate the enemy's use of indirect approaches and his ability to project combat power into the rear area by long-range fires, infiltration, air mobility and unconventional warfare.

Defensive planning should accentuate the natural strengths of the defending force and the terrain. Mechanized forces should use their mobility, protection, and long-range fires to fight fluid defenses that avoid the enemy's strongest forces and strike at those least prepared to fight. Light forces should capitalize on their ability to hold ground and mass fire, seeking to stop the enemy in restrictive terrain and destroy him while he is bogged down. Mixed forces should combine the advantages of light and heavy units, using infantry in static positions to break the tempo of the attack and mechanized forces and aviation units to strike at vulnerable spots. Air assault forces can be inserted between enemy units. Artillery and air fires can magnify the effects of direct fires or isolate segments of the attacking force.

The terrain of the sector influences the design of the defense by its natural obstacles and its potential for cover, concealment, and movement. The natural obstacles of a sector must be reinforced with man-made obstacles to enhance the strength of defensive positions and to protect the defender's maneuver. The effects of terrain in the deep battle and the rear battle are equal in importance to its effects in the covering force area (CFA) and MBA and must not be overlooked.

The commander implements his concept of operations by assigning missions to subordinate units. In divisions and brigades, these missions generally require subordinates to perform a single function important to the defense such as delaying the enemy, stopping him forward of a stated feature, or counterattacking him in one of several specified areas.

Commanders task organize based on the missions they have assigned their subordinates. Corps and division commanders divide their sectors into a security area, MBA, and rear area, beginning their deep operations well forward of the security area. They assign sectors within the security area and MBA to their maneuver units. Obstacles are planned throughout the sector to support the concept of operation.

Brigades and battalions commonly use sectors and battle positions to control their maneuver units in defense. Divisions and corps rely chiefly on sectors and phase lines to control their operations though they may designate battle positions or strongpoints in vital places. Reserve positions are designated at all levels and counterattack or blocking options with necessary control measures and fire support plans are developed for maneuver and aviation units held in reserve.

Fire support planning in defense must be flexible enough to permit the massing of fires on any approach in the sector. Usually, the unit making the main effort has the priority of fires initially, but fire planners make provisions to shift that priority to other sectors or to the rear area if necessary.

The commander plans deep operations to support his specific concept of defense in all its phases. Because the enemy will exercise the initiative in the first stages of battle, plans for deep operations must be flexible enough to support a defense in any sector.

Whatever technique of defense the commander chooses, his overall scheme should maximize the use of maneuver and offensive tactics. The full advantage of awaiting the attack has been realized once the enemy has committed his forces. The defender's chief advantage then becomes his ability to seize the initiative and to counterattack over familiar ground protected by his own defensive positions, artillery, obstacles, and ADA.

Because the effective use of time is so important in defense, commanders must use warning orders. They must also consider current task organizations, unit locations, and the natural obstacles available in their sectors as they plan the defense. Unnecessary changes in organization and time-consuming movements should be avoided. Subordinates must receive orders as quickly as possible if they are to gain the full benefit of time.

Finally, defending commanders must mask their preparations from the enemy. They should mount active deception and counterreconnaissance operations as they prepare. Commanders must assume that the enemy will have sophisticated reconnaissance, surveillance, and target acquisition means, and should therefore deploy their units in ways that conceal the design of the defense.

PREPARING THE DEFENSE

Commanders and staff officers must take advantage of all the time available in preparing the defense. Preparations should begin as early as possible and go on continuously until the battle begins.

Preparations are made simultaneously at all levels of command. Among the most important activities are reconnaissance of the sector; preparation of routes, positions, and obstacles; and coordination of maneuver with direct and indirect fire support. Maintenance and supply activities are accelerated to prepare the force for combat. Troops are briefed, trained, and rehearsed for their specific tasks. Liaison takes place between adjacent units and with supporting organizations including the Air Force.

Commanders should wargame their plans and remain flexible enough to amend plans based on these analyses. They should also take advantage of remaining preparation time to develop alternate routes and positions, to time movements between positions and along routes, and to rehearse counterattacks. They should personally inspect the preparations of their troops in all areas. Operations officers should use available time to develop plans for any contingencies which might arise during the defense.

Preparation for defense also entails the stocking of forward supply points, liaison with civilian officials, adjustment of air defense coverage, and arranging for security of installations in the rear area. Alternate sites for command posts, artillery firing positions, and CSS facilities can be prepared if time allows.

The intelligence collection effort must be intensified during preparation for the defense. Early identification of enemy units gives the commander a better idea of when the attack will begin and is vital to executing deep operations.

DEEP OPERATIONS

Whatever type of defense is selected, deep operations are essential to its effectiveness. The commander uses them to create windows of opportunity for decisive action against leading enemy echelons. Deep operations are the commander's means of ensuring the success of his decisive engagements and counterattacks by limiting the enemy's options, disrupting his coordination, and affecting the closure times of his follow-on elements.

Areas of operations and interest must extend far enough forward of the FLOT to give the commander time to react to approaching enemy forces, to assess his options, and to execute operations accordingly. Deep operations begin before the enemy closes with the maneuver forces. They continue against follow-on or uncommitted forces to isolate combat in the security area and MBA, to guard against interference with the commitment of reserves, and to shape the conditions of the next set of defensive engagements.

In conducting deep operations, the commander maintains a current intelligence picture of the enemy throughout his area of interest. At the same time, he focuses his collection effort on areas and units of particular concern. To conduct successful deep operations, the G3, G2, and fire support coordinator (FSCOORD) must cooperate to assure that actions in depth support the central concept of the defense. They must especially ensure that resources employed in deep operations do not divert resources necessary to win key close engagements.

As enemy formations approach the FLOT, the commander monitors their movement, determines which elements of the enemy force are most threatening to his plans, seeks and attacks high value targets, and disrupts and delays selected enemy reserves to facilitate specific actions within his overall defense. For example, a division commander might act to isolate an enemy regiment by interdicting forces that could reinforce or support it during a division counterattack.

Tactical airpower, field artillery fires, Army Aviation, and unconventional warfare forces are the chief means of conducting deep operations. Because they are usually limited in number and effect, commanders must synchronize their use carefully with the overall effort. Generally, more sensors and weapons become available as the enemy nears the FLOT. Effective employment of maneuver units in deep operations requires careful planning and intelligence preparation of the battlefield (IPB) before commitment and responsive surveillance once operations are underway.

SECURITY OPERATIONS

In any defense, a covering force or screening force serves as the forward security echelon in close operations. The security force occupies a sector far enough forward of the forward edge of the battle area (FEBA) to protect MBA units from surprise, to give MBA commanders time to reposition forces to meet the enemy attack, and to prevent enemy medium range artillery from firing on the FEBA. A screening force will be unable to do more than that. A covering force gains and maintains contact with attacking enemy forces, and can also develop the situation, and delay or defeat the enemy's leading units.

Screening Forces. Screening forces may be preferable to covering forces in some defenses. Screening forces repel enemy reconnaissance and keep enemy artillery from firing on the FEBA. They give the commander warning of the enemy's approach and expose the enemy to indirect fire, but they cannot delay the attacker significantly. Some reinforcement of screening forces is usually necessary. Aviation, radar, engineer, and field artillery (FA) units all add to the effectiveness of a screen.

Covering Forces. Corps and division commanders may establish a covering force as the first echelon of a two-echelon defense. When this is done, the covering force fights a major action to destroy leading enemy formations, to cause the commitment of follow-on battalions or regiments, and to force the enemy to disclose his main effort. Covering forces also furnish information which allow MBA commanders to shift forces before the enemy's arrival at the FEBA. The stronger the covering force, the more time it can provide for corps or division commanders to establish their defenses in the MBA.

The size and composition of a covering force depends on the mission, enemy, terrain and weather, forces available, and time. Normally a covering force is organized around tank-heavy task forces and regimental cavalry. Ideally, a corps will employ one or more armored cavalry regiments because they are specially organized, trained, and equipped for security missions. Corps may use divisions or separate brigades instead of cavalry or in addition to it. A light corps may use air cavalry, light armor, or air assault infantry in its covering force area. In any case,

a covering force requires appropriate additional artillery, engineer, military intelligence (MI), air defense artillery (ADA), and Army aviation units to perform its mission.

Either corps or its divisions control the covering force. Covering forces should not be controlled by brigades except where the terrain makes other solutions impractical. Whether corps or divisions control depends on the overall plan for defense, the size of the CFA, the number of battalion-sized units to be employed, and the time that MBA units have for preparing.

Corps and division operations officers monitor covering force operations and ensure their synchronization with deep operations. Above all, covering force operations must be an integral part of the overall defensive plan.

Battalions and squadrons of the covering force make maximum use of the terrain and the force's long-range fires. Carefully planned indirect fires and obstacles augment the firepower of the covering force and assist it in avoiding decisive engagement. A covering force operation based solely on delay, however, will rarely provide the degree of protection the larger force requires. Normally, the covering force will defend, delay, and attack with its maneuver units.

The entire covering force should not be withdrawn automatically just because portions of it have been forced back to the FEBA. It should adjust to the enemy advance and, where possible, continue to fight or screen far forward. Retaining such advanced positions allows surveillance and targeting forward of the MBA, upsets the enemy's coordination by resisting his supporting attacks and reconnaissance effort, and assists the MBA commander to fight one opponent at a time. Finally, retention of advanced positions by elements of the covering force can facilitate counterattack forward of the FEBA by providing observation of and access to the flanks of penetrating forces. In some cases, covering force elements themselves can attack first echelon forces from the rear or drive between echelons to isolate leading enemy units.

Handover. Handover of the battle from the security force to MBA forces requires close coordination. The security force commander must retain freedom to maneuver until he begins rearward passage of lines. Commanders of MBA forces must establish contact points, passage points, passage lanes, and routes through the MBA. Normally battalion-sized units of a covering force hand the battle over to the brigades through which they pass. Screening forces will be much smaller; they will not be able to affect the enemy's movement significantly, but must be able to warn MBA commanders of the enemy's approach. These actions must be completed quickly and efficiently to minimize the vulnerability of both the main battle area and the covering forces.

After passage, elements of the security force normally move to designated areas in the rear area or MBA to prepare for subsequent operations. Those areas must be rearward enough to ensure the withdrawn units do not interfere with MBA operations.

Control of indirect fires passes to MBA units as the security force hands off the battle. This usually occurs in one sector at a time until the security force has been completely withdrawn.

MAIN BATTLE AREA

Whatever the concept of operation, the decisive defensive battle is fought by forces of the MBA. The commander positions forces in the MBA to control or repel enemy penetrations. He employs his reserves there to halt the attack, to destroy penetrating enemy formations, and to regain the initiative.

Division and corps commanders establish MBA sectors as means of implementing their plans. These are assigned to subordinate units based on their capabilities and missions. Each sector usually coincides with a major avenue of approach. The force responsible for the most dangerous sector in the MBA normally receives priority in the initial allocation of artillery, engineer, and close air support. It is usually the initial main effort. The commander can strengthen his defense of the most dangerous approach by narrowing the sector of the unit astride it. He may use armored cavalry units or other maneuver forces to economize in restrictive terrain and to concentrate the major units on the most dangerous approaches, but he must do so without splitting secondary avenues of approach.

A significant obstacle along the FEBA, such as a river, built-up area, swamp, or escarpment, favors an area defense, oriented on the retention of terrain. Such an obstacle adds to the relative combat power of the defender. An area defense may also be structured with elements deployed in depth throughout the MBA.

Open terrain or a wide sector favors mobile defenses which orient on the enemy. The primary function of committed units in such defenses is to control the penetration until it can be eliminated by the counterattack of a large reserve. Obstacles must be used even in open terrain to support static elements of the defense and to slow or canalize the enemy in vital areas.

Corps and division commanders monitor the development of MBA operations and support critical engagements with additional firepower. They may also adjust sectors, control movement of committed forces, or reinforce MBA units with fresh maneuver forces. Corps and division commanders intervene at decisive junctures in the battle with reserves and with close air support.

As MBA operations progress, corps and division commanders continue to conduct deep operations. They monitor events beyond the forward line of own troops

(FLOT) and strike follow-on enemy forces to prevent them from outflanking defensive positions or overwhelming committed forces.

Brigades and divisions fight combined arms actions and are usually responsible for defense of sectors. In mobile defenses, brigade and division commanders bear responsibility for major tasks which must be closely synchronized with the activities of other units. In an area defense, they function more independently and operate with fewer restrictions.

Commanders of brigades and divisions employ units of all arms and services. They coordinate and support the actions of maneuver units to locate, contain, and strike attacking units throughout the defense. They use fires, obstacles, and electronic warfare (EW) to strengthen defended positions and to support maneuver.

Battalions usually perform a single task in a defense directed by a brigade. They defend positions or strongpoints, delay, or attack to defeat enemy units or to regain important positions. Battalions may hold companies in reserve to provide depth and flexibility in their operations.

Mobile enemy forces are likely to penetrate sections of the MBA during the defense. Such penetration and separation of adjacent units is especially likely if nuclear or chemical weapons are used by the enemy. Nonetheless, MBA forces continue to fight while protecting their own flanks, striking at the enemy's, and driving across penetrations to restore continuity to the defense when possible. Division or corps reserves can defeat some penetrations but others may pass into the rear area.

RESERVE OPERATIONS

The primary purpose of reserves in the defense is to preserve the commander's flexibility. He may use reserves to counterattack to exploit enemy vulnerabilities, such as exposed flanks or support units,

unprotected forces in depth, and congestion. He may also use them to reinforce forward defensive operations, to block penetrating enemy forces or to react to a rear area threat. If the reserve is intended to be used decisively, however, the commander must withhold it for major counterattacks and refuse to dissipate it, dealing with local emergencies.

Commanders should decide the mission, composition, and size of the reserve based on their estimate of the situation. It is impossible to generalize about the relative importance of counterattacking, blocking penetrations, reinforcing defending units, or reacting to rear area threats. Each situation is unique. The primary mission of the reserve derives directly from the concept of the defense. Defenses at the dynamic end of the continuum such as mobile defenses rely upon reserves to strike the decisive blow. They demand large mobile combined arms reserves. When conditions favoring counterattack occur, the main effort shifts to the reserve, which then strikes with overwhelming combat power. Defenses at the static end of the spectrum are more likely to use reserves to block and reinforce at lower tactical levels, leaving major counterattacks to divisions, corps, and higher echelons. However, even area defenses at brigade and battalion level may benefit from the use of mobile reserve to strike a decisive blow when such a force is available and the enemy uncovers his flanks.

Commanders of brigades and larger units normally retain about one third of their maneuver strength in reserve, though the actual size of the reserve depends on the commander's concept of operation. Reserves may also be retained at battalion level, but, just as frequently, battalion commanders counterattack with their least committed elements or with elements positioned in depth.

Timing is critical to counterattacks. The commander must anticipate the circumstances calling for the commitment of reserves. When he commits his reserve, he must make his decision promptly with an accurate understanding of movement and deployment times. Committed too soon, reserves may not have the desired effect or may not be available later for a more dangerous contingency. Committed too late, they may be ineffectual. Once he has committed his reserve, the commander should immediately begin reconstituting another reserve from uncommitted forces or from forces in less threatened sectors.

In planning a counterattack, the commander must carefully consider the enemy's options and the likely locations of his follow-on echelons. Then he must determine where to position his reserve, what routes and avenues of approach to use, what fire support will be necessary, and what interdiction or deep attack will be necessary to isolate the enemy's committed forces. Counterattacks like any attack should seek to avoid enemy strength. Brigade and battalion counterattacks seize strong positions from which to fire on the enemy's flanks and rear. Division or corps counterattacks will either strike isolated enemy maneuver units or will pass around the enemy's committed forces to strike directly at his reserves, artillery, and other supporting forces.

Reserves may be air or ground maneuver units. Divisions, brigades, and battalions may be held in reserve as part of their superior commander's defense. When counterattacking, their actions amount to hasty or deliberate attacks.

Reserved air assault forces can respond rapidly. In suitable terrain, they can reinforce positions to the front or on a flank. In a threatened sector, they may be positioned in depth. Air assault forces are also suitable for swift attack against enemy airborne units landing in the rear area. Once committed, however, they have limited mobility.

Because of their speed, mobility and range, attack helicopter units may be held in depth initially and still respond promptly when needed. The mobility and firepower of attack helicopters often make them the quickest and most effective means of reinforcing defenses against armored attacks and of destroying enemy tanks which have broken through. Since weather and the air defense environment limit their use, they should never be the only reserves.

In addition to designating reserves, commanders may choose to shift uncommitted subordinate elements to reconstitute a reserve or to concentrate forces elsewhere. The most easily shifted forces are the reserves of subordinate units. Commanders should shift committed MBA forces laterally only as a last resort because of the risks and difficulties inherent in such lateral movement close to the line of contact.

REAR OPERATIONS

During battle, protection of rear areas will be necessary to assure the defender's freedom of maneuver and continuity of operations. Because fighting in the rear area can divert combat power from the main effort, commanders must carefully weigh the need for such diversion against the consequences, and be prepared to take calculated risks in rear areas. To make such decisions, commanders require accurate information, both to avoid late or inadequate responses and to guard against overreacting to exaggerated reports. They also require clear heads and strong nerves.

To minimize the vulnerability of rear operations, command and control and support facilities in the rear area must be dispersed, redundant and as distant from high speed avenues into the rear as mission peformance will allow. Air defense should be located to protect especially sensitive areas and facilities in the rear. Reserves must be prepared to respond rapidly to rear area threats, and should be prepared to move to any of their objectives by multiple routes. Air assault forces, attack helicopter and air cavalry units, close air support missions, and mechanized forces will be of special value in the rear area.

Threats to the rear area will arise throughout the battle and may require the repositioning of forces and facilities. When possible, the defending commander should contain and avoid enemy forces in his rear area rather than attacking them with forces needed in the MBA. Unless such enemy units pose a serious immediate threat, he should defer attacking them until after the battle is stabilized or won.

For a detailed discussion of rear operations, see FM 90-14.

CONDUCTING THE DEFENSE

As the attack begins, the defender's first concerns will be to identify the enemy's committed units, determine his direction of attack, and gain time to react. Security forces, intelligence units, special operations forces, and air elements conducting deep operations will be the first sources of this information. Information about the form and location of the enemy's attack should be distributed throughout the force during the battle as a basis for subordinate commander's actions.

The commander must slow the enemy's movement in some areas or separate his formations to deny the enemy the ability to mass or to establish a tempo that will make defense impossible. The defending commander will normally have to economize in some parts of his sector to concentrate forces and fires in the areas of greatest danger. He should employ his long-range surveillance means to assist in monitoring economy of force sectors.

Covering forces and ground or air maneuver units can delay in less threatened areas to gain time for actions against committed enemy units. Air and ground

attacks in depth and long-range fires can separate attacking echelons for destruction in detail by defending forces.

In an area defense, committed brigades should begin their local counterattacks as soon as possible. Brigade commanders use their reserves in cooperation with static elements of their defenses—battle positions and strongpoints—to break the enemy's momentum and reduce his numerical advantage. As the attack develops and the enemy's dispositions are revealed, brigade and division commanders should use their reserves and fires to strike at objectives in depth to break up the coordination of the attack.

Mobile defenses anticipate enemy penetration into the defended area and use obstacles and defended positions to shape and control such penetrations. They may also use local counterattacks either to influence the enemy to enter the penetration area or to deceive him as to the nature of the defense. As in area defenses, static elements of a mobile defense must contain the enemy in a designated area. In a mobile defense, the counterattack is decisive; it must be strong, well-timed, and well-supported. Counterattacking forces are preferably committed against the enemy's flanks and rear rather than frontally against deployed attacking units.

During the defense, commanders will have to shift their main effort to contain the enemy's attack until they can take the initiative themselves. This will require the adjustment of sectors, the repeated commitment and reconstitution of reserves, and, usually, modification of the original plan.

To deny the enemy passage through a vital area, a commander may order a force to remain in a strong position on key terrain. He might also leave a unit in position behind the enemy or give it a mission that entails a high risk of being entrapped. It is also possible for defending units to be unintentionally cut off from friendly forces.

Whenever an unintentional encirclement occurs, the encircled commander must understand the mission and the higher commander's intent and concept of operation clearly so that he can continue to contribute.

An encircled force must act rapidly to preserve itself. The senior commander must assume control of all encircled elements and assess the all-around defensive posture of the force. He must determine or judge whether the next higher commander wants the force to break out or to defend the position. He must reorganize and consolidate expeditiously. If the force is free to break out, it should do so before the enemy has time to block escape routes. If it cannot break out, the senior commander must continue to defend while planning for and assisting in linkup with a relieving force.

Nuclear and chemical weapons present the defender with great opportunities and risks. When authorized for use by the defender, they can be employed to isolate or defeat the attack by destroying or disrupting critical enemy units. Used against him, such weapons can create gaps, destroy or disable units, and obstruct his movement. The defensive plan must anticipate the effects of such weapons by providing dispersed positions for forces in depth, last minute concentration of units on positions, multiple routes of approach and withdrawal, and appropriate protective measures in all occupied areas.

Such measures also mitigate the effects of conventional fires. Commanders should consider using them even when nuclear and chemical operations are unlikely whenever the attacker has a substantial advantage in artillery and air support.

CHAPTER 10

Retrograde Operations

Aretrograde operation is a movement to the rear or away from the enemy. Such an operation may be forced or voluntary, but in either case, the higher commander must approve it. Retrograde operations gain time, preserve forces, avoid combat under undesirable conditions, or draw the enemy into an unfavorable position. Commanders use them to harass, to exhaust, to resist, to delay, and to damage an enemy. Retrograde operations are also used in operational maneuver to reposition forces, to shorten lines of communications, or to permit the withdrawal of another force for use elsewhere.

All retrograde operations are difficult, and delays and withdrawals are inherently risky. To succeed, they must be well-organized and well-executed. A disorganized retrograde operation in the presence of a stronger enemy invites disaster.

TYPES OF RETROGRADE OPERATIONS

The three types of retrograde operations are *delays, withdrawals,* and *retirements.* In delays, units give ground to gain time. Delaying units inflict the greatest possible damage on the enemy while preserving their freedom of action. In withdrawals, all or part of a committed force disengages from the enemy voluntarily to preserve the force or free it for a new mission. In retirements, a force not in active combat with the enemy conducts a movement to the rear, normally as a tactical road march.

In a corps or a division operation, the commander usually combines these forms of retrograde operations in simultaneous or sequential actions. For instance, a withdrawal usually precedes a retirement and the retirement of one unit may be covered by the delaying action of another.

The underlying reasons for all retrograde operations are to improve an operational or tactical situation or prevent a worse one from occurring. To accomplish either purpose, retrograde operations must be accompanied by efforts to reduce the enemy's strength, to bring up additional forces, to concentrate forces elsewhere for an attack, to prepare stronger defenses to the rear, or to maneuver the enemy into areas where he can be counterattacked.

As in other operations, depth is important in retrograde operations. Commanders conducting such operations must concern themselves with impeding the enemy's movement in depth and with the security of their own rear areas. Therefore, intelligence on enemy movements in the area of interest will be vital in any form of a retrograde operation. Skillful air support and long-range fires can add appreciably to the effectiveness of delay and may be critical to the security of a withdrawal. Firm control of friendly movement to the rear is essential to retaining control of any retrograde operation.

DELAYS

Delays are conducted when forces are insufficient to attack or to defend or when the defensive plan calls for drawing the attacker into an area for counterattack. Delays gain time for friendly forces to—

- Reestablish the defense.

- Cover a defending or withdrawing unit.

- Protect a friendly unit's flank.

- Participate in an economy of force effort.

CONSIDERATIONS

Commanders preparing to conduct delays should consider the factors of mission, enemy, terrain and weather, troops, time (METT-T) as they make their initial estimate of the situation.

The *mission* of the force states the higher commander's requirements for the delay, develops the concept of the operation for the force as a whole, and specifies the duration and terrain limitations that apply to the operation. If the commander intends to employ the delaying force in his subsequent operations, he must specify the degree of damage or risk to the force he is willing to accept. In this case, the commander *must make clear* which parameter will govern— duration and terrain, or friendly loss.

The strength, location, tactics, mobility, and capabilities of the *enemy* also have a large bearing on how the commander organizes his delay. Among the most important considerations for the delaying commander are patterns of enemy operations and the enemy's vulnerability to counterattack, interdiction, electronic warfare, air attack, and canalization by obstacles. The commander must also examine the enemy's capability to conduct air

attacks on the delaying force, to insert forces behind friendly units, and to employ nuclear and chemical weapons.

The *terrain* over which delays must be conducted limits the commander's options. Open, unobstructed terrain makes delays more difficult to achieve. Such terrain favors the use of armored, mechanized, and aviation units by the delaying force and will require great engineer effort. Close or broken terrain will generally slow the enemy's movement but also makes maintaining contact with him more difficult. In wooded, swampy, or rugged terrain, infantry forces are better suited for the delay and obstacles are easier to construct. Weather's chief effects on the delay are to promote or retard cross-country movement, the use of aviation and air support, and the construction of obstacles. Commanders of brigades and smaller units must pay particular attention to the effects of reduced visibility. Limited visibility requires greater numbers of troop units to cover a given sector and affects the way they maneuver and fight. Early detection of the enemy is more difficult and long-range fires are less effective; decisive engagement is therefore harder to avoid.

The *troops available* to the delaying commander determine his actions to a large extent. As a general rule, a delaying force should be as mobile or more mobile than its enemy. Because the delaying commander usually attempts to avoid decisive combat, his forces should also be capable of delivering accurate, long-range fires and of constructing significant obstacles. Armored, mechanized, and aviation units are generally best suited to delay. Cavalry units are specially organized and trained to conduct security missions and should be used to delay whenever they are available. Infantry units can be employed to delay in close terrain or to occupy positions as part of the delay. When infantry units can be moved by air to positions in depth, they provide great flexibility to a delaying unit although their limited mobility makes them hard to disengage. Delaying forces rely heavily on artillery and engineer support and require substantial numbers of these units if they are to delay for any length of time. Military intelligence units are valuable to a delaying commander by assisting him in maintaining contact with the enemy and in slowing the enemy's movement by interrupting his communications. Air defense around critical points, such as river crossings and passage points, is also important in delays. When nuclear or chemical weapons are authorized for tactical employment, commanders can use them to delay the enemy by destroying critical enemy units, creating obstacles, and slowing the tempo of the attack by requiring masking, decontamination, and dispersed movement.

Time to prepare and the period of the delay are the final preliminary considerations for the commander. He must use available time effectively to prepare for his operation, as well as provide his subordinates with the most time possible to plan and prepare for their own operation. The length of time he is required to delay the enemy will determine the tactics he uses and the risks he will have to accept.

CONDUCTING DELAYS

In the delay, commanders usually deploy most of their forces forward. Because of the width of most delay sectors, combat support units and combat service support (CSS) units will be widely dispersed and must often be attached to the maneuver units they support. Artillery fires should be provided to all committed battalions or squadrons and control of such fires must generally be decentralized. Commanders retain reserves when possible and employ them to assist in disengaging committed units and to slow the enemy by striking his exposed forces. Intelligence officers

actively pursue collection operations to provide information on the enemy's movements in depth, to assist in maintaining contact, and to observe gaps in friendly dispositions.

Delays will occasionally involve entire corps or divisions. Corps may conduct them as part of an operational withdrawal. Divisions may perform them as part of a corps defense or in accomplishing their missions as advance, flank, or rear guard forces for a corps. Such delays are normally organized with subordinate maneuver elements fighting abreast of each other and air and ground reserves held in depth.

Brigades, regiments, battalions, and squadrons are more likely to conduct delays and can perform them in several ways. They may fight from a single set of positions if the delay is a short one, or they may delay using alternate or successive positions. Usually brigade and battalion commanders organize their delays in parallel sectors of considerable depth using a combination of techniques. Attack, defense, and delay from alternate or successive positions may all be combined in such operations. The commander may elect, for example, to delay initially from alternate positions along his most dangerous approach, to delay from successive positions in less threatened areas, and to establish a defensive position in depth to slow the enemy in a particularly critical area. During his delay, he may shift from one technique to another as the operation develops.

Commanders conducting a delay should take the initiative whenever possible. Striking back at the enemy throws him off stride, disorganizes his forces, and prolongs the delay. Contesting the initiative also helps the delaying force avoid a pattern of passivity that favors the attacker. Ambushes, counterattacks, spoiling attacks, CAS and BAI are all means of striking the attacker.

DELAY FROM SUCCESSIVE POSITIONS

STEP 1 Elements of the delaying force disengage and move to the rear to organize the next position.

STEP 2 Elements remaining in contact fight to the rear while maintaining continuous contact.

STEP 3 Elements rejoin parent organizations at the next delay position and continue the delay.

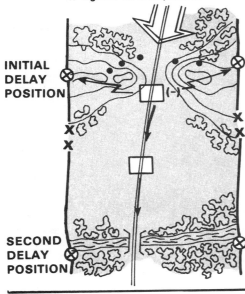
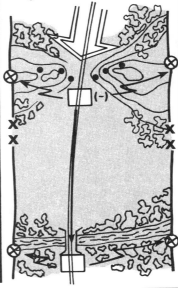
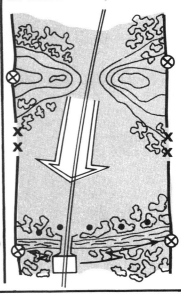

INITIAL DELAY POSITION

SECOND DELAY POSITION

DELAY FROM ALTERNATE POSITIONS

STEP 1 Elements of the brigade organize the initial and second delay positions.

STEP 2 Elements from the initial position delay back through the second position to the third delay position.

STEP 3 Elements at the second position pick up the delay. The third delay position is occupied.

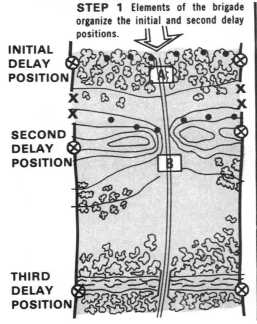
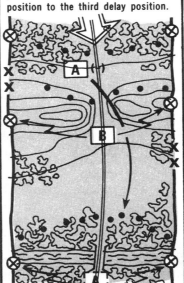
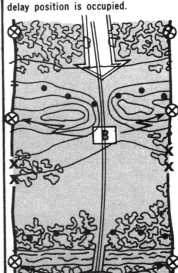

INITIAL DELAY POSITION

SECOND DELAY POSITION

THIRD DELAY POSITION

Usually delaying commanders avoid decisive engagement. They plan and prepare positions in depth to block all avenues of approach through their sectors. Obstacles and indirect fires are of great importance in organizing delay positions because they offset the usually pronounced numerical advantage of the attacking force.

Commanders at all levels should integrate natural obstacles into their delay plans and should enhance such obstacles with scatterable mines, chemical obstacles, or manually installed obstacles and minefields. Most engineer effort in a delay centers on countermobility and continues throughout the operation. As the enemy's attack develops, the delaying commander should shift his engineer effort to the areas of greatest threat.

Engineer units can also improve the mobility of the delaying force and strengthen some of its most critical forces by constructing protected positions. Commanders establish priorities for their supporting engineers based on their concept for each specific operation.

Because of the width of most delay sectors, indirect and air-delivered fires are the commander's fastest means of massing combat power during a delay. All committed maneuver forces must have access to fast, effective fire support to assist them in slowing the enemy's movement and in disengaging. When fighting a powerful, mobile enemy, each committed maneuver battalion should be directly supported by an artillery battalion. The force commander for the delay should also retain some ability to mass fires across battalion or brigade boundaries.

As in other defensive operations, indirect fires should protect defensive positions, cover obstacles, and provide smoke and illumination for maneuver forces. Delaying commanders should also plan to use scatterable mines and, when authorized, chemical, and nuclear weapons to support their maneuver plans.

Aviation units are particularly valuable because of their great speed and mobility. Air cavalry units can screen, delay, and reconnoiter as part of the delay. Attack helicopter units are usually held in reserve initially. They can assist in the delaying actions of ground maneuver units or help ground units to disengage by attacking enemy vehicles and attack helicopters. They can also attack independently to damage and delay the enemy. Commanders can employ combat support aviation units to position infantry units, to move engineers to critical points, and to move supplies during the delay.

The delay is concluded when enemy forces have halted their attack or when the delaying force has completed its mission and has passed through another force. If the enemy force has halted because of attrition or lack of sustainment, the commander of the delaying force can either maintain contact or withdraw for another mission. In the latter case, the delaying commander must assist in the passage of lines and provide information about the enemy and the terrain to the relieving force.

More commonly, a force ends its delay by withdrawing through a friendly defending force. When it does so, it must conduct a rearward passage of lines and handover the battle to the defending unit. Smooth transfer of control requires the commanders involved to coordinate passage points, establish recognition signals, work out supporting fires, and agree on routes through the defended position. When possible, handoff should occur just forward of the new defense to conceal the transition and the location and organization of the defense.

In many instances, it will be preferable to pass delaying units to the rear in sectors not under direct attack. Commanders may do so by maneuvering delay forces away from the enemy's front just before reaching the main defense.

WITHDRAWALS

Commanders conduct withdrawals to remove subordinate units from combat, adjust defensive positions, or relocate their entire force. Whether withdrawing locally or as part of a general withdrawal, committed forces voluntarily disengage from the enemy and move to the rear. Withdrawals may be conducted under or free of enemy pressure and with or without the assistance of friendly units. Whatever the case, withdrawals will always begin under the threat of enemy interference.

Battalions and brigades can adjust their positions over short distances by delaying or by withdrawing their main forces under the protection of detachments left in contact. Larger forces and deeper withdrawals require the commander to organize a covering force and a main body. Whatever their size, withdrawing forces must prepare as thoroughly as time allows and be ready to defend themselves if the enemy interferes with the operation.

CONSIDERATIONS

Withdrawals are inherently dangerous, since they involve moving units to the rear away from what is usually a stronger enemy force. An active enemy can prevent or delay a unit's withdrawal unless the withdrawing force is well-trained and well-organized for the operation. In all withdrawals, the commander should attempt to conceal from the enemy his intention to withdraw.

In a general withdrawal, the commander of a brigade or larger force organizes a covering force and a main body. The covering force prevents effective pursuit or interference with the main body's withdrawal. The main body forms behind the covering force and moves to the rear protected by advance, flank, and rear guards and prepared to defend itself.

The withdrawal plan should include a deception plan, provisions for the covering force and main body to defend or delay if necessary, and measures to assure speed in execution. Such measures include multiple routes, additional transportation, route improvement, and coordinated traffic control and movement planning.

Air and ground reserves should be made available to support a general withdrawal. Indirect fires and deceptive measures should be planned to mask movement of friendly forces, and obstacles and fires should be used to retard pursuit by the enemy. Since withdrawing forces are extremely vulnerable to detection and interdiction by enemy air forces, strong air defenses and air superiority in the area of the operation are highly desirable. Demonstrations may be conducted in other areas to distract the enemy in support of a general withdrawal.

Whenever it is possible, withdrawals should take place at night or in adverse weather to delay detection by the enemy. Smoke can also obscure friendly movement. Commanders anticipating withdrawals should avoid signaling their intentions by the obvious relocation of combat support and CSS facilities or by premature installation of obstacles or destruction of routes. Jamming of enemy command nets can slow the enemy's reaction to a withdrawal once it is under way.

Plans and orders for a withdrawal are based on a concept of operations that fully describes the commander's intent and provides for maneuver, fire support, obstacles, deception, and security. The plan also prescribes organization for combat, primary and alternate routes of withdrawal, and the schedule for movement of withdrawing units. Finally, the plan assigns the new positions to be occupied following the withdrawal and alerts each unit to its new mission.

CONDUCTING WITHDRAWALS

Commanders should anticipate enemy interference by fires, direct pressure, and attempts to envelop. When withdrawing under enemy pressure, the covering force will fight a delay to permit the withdrawal of the main body. Main body units will reinforce the covering force as necessary and will themselves delay or defend if the covering force fails to slow the enemy.

All available fires, electronic warfare (EW) assets, and obstacles support the withdrawal of closely engaged friendly forces. Commanders must tightly control rearward movement and maintain synchronization throughout the force. Deep operations may be useful in relieving pressure on units in contact with the enemy.

If the withdrawal begins without enemy pressure, the covering force may remain in position to prolong the deception. If the enemy does not attack during the withdrawal, covering forces and rear guards remain between the enemy and the main body, and the main body moves to the rear as rapidly as possible. When the main body has withdrawn a safe distance, the covering force may be withdrawn to intermediate or final positions.

Every element of the withdrawing force must be capable of defending itself at least temporarily against ground attack, and any contact with the enemy in the rear area must be reported as a matter of great urgency. Should the enemy block movement in the rear, the commander must be able either to shift to alternate routes which bypass the interdicted area or to reduce the roadblock.

When simultaneous withdrawal of all forces is not practical, the commander determines an order of withdrawal. If he withdraws first the most heavily engaged units from the area of greatest actual or potential pressure, the enemy may encircle or destroy remaining elements of the command. If he withdraws the least heavily engaged units first, he may find himself unable to withdraw those most heavily engaged or most dangerously threatened. Commanders must decide which action best preserves the force while accomplishing the mission.

When corps or divisions withdraw, their reserves remain well forward to assist other units by fire or by conducting ground attacks. While units are withdrawing under pressure, reserves can launch spoiling attacks to disorganize and delay the enemy. Reserves may also extricate encircled or heavily engaged forces. Aviation units help forward units maintain contact, secure flanks, delay enemy armor, react to enemy air assaults, assist in command and control, and transport troops and material.

Withdrawing units may be assisted by other units which have established defenses behind the withdrawing force. Such defending forces may be able to provide fire support, EW support, air defense, and logistical assistance to a withdrawing unit. Most important, they assume responsibility for the sector once the withdrawing force has passed through them.

When such a force is in position, the withdrawing unit coordinates for support as early as possible. The withdrawal is conducted in the usual way until the withdrawing force passes behind the assisting force. Once in the defended area, the withdrawing force either joins the defense or continues to the rear in a retirement.

RETIREMENTS

Retirements are rearward movements away from the enemy by a force not in contact. They are normally covered by the security forces of another unit to their rear and conducted as a tactical road movement. Retiring units must be organized to fight, but they do so only in self-defense. A retiring unit may be attacked by guerrillas, air strikes, air assaults, or long-range fires. Its commander must have plans for dealing with such contingencies.

Security and speed are the most important considerations in conducting a retirement. Retiring units move at night when possible. They should move in daylight only if their mission requires it or if the enemy is incapable of interfering with them. When the enemy controls the air or can otherwise interdict friendly movement in depth, a retiring force may have to move by infiltration during daylight. Commanders conducting retirements emphasize the maximum use of operational security measures during their movement.

CSS IN RETROGRADE OPERATIONS

Planning for CSS must reflect the nature of the operation. To ensure uninterrupted support in any retrograde operation, CSS installations should be located well to the rear. To reduce congestion and interference with combat units and losses, commanders should have CSS units displace early and, when possible, at night.

Because retrograde operations move rapidly, commanders often attach supporting elements to the maneuver force. Because delaying actions consume large amounts of fuel and ammunition, CSS units may carry ammunition forward to fighting positions and locate the necessary fuel and ammunition stocks forward during the delay. In withdrawals and retirements, fuel and ammunition must be available for emergency issue and positioned in depth.

To solve the complex maintenance and recovery problems associated with retrograde operations, CSS unit commanders should furnish contact teams to committed units. They should also consider augmenting these teams with additional personnel.

To avoid destroying or evacuating supplies unnecessarily in any retrograde action, commanders must control the flow of supplies into forward areas. When commanders contemplate a delay, withdrawal, or retirement, they should plan for early removal of excess supplies and early displacement of logistic facilities. By positioning supplies along routes of withdrawal, CSS commanders can simplify support and can reduce the enemy's ability to interfere with logistic operations.

PART IV

JOINT, COMBINED, AND CONTINGENCY OPERATIONS

CHAPTER 11
Joint and Combined Operations

AirLand Battle doctrine as set forth in Parts I, II, III of this manual provides guidance for operational and tactical level employment of US Army units worldwide. National policies and strategies; alliance and bilateral international agreements; US joint military policies and doctrine; and specific theater military policies, strategies, and doctrine provide the framework for application of AirLand Battle doctrine in NATO Europe, Northeast Asia, Southwest Asia, and other theaters to be established in case of war. AirLand Battle doctrine is predicated on the assumption of routine cooperation of Army units with other services in joint operations. In most cases, Army forces will cooperate with the military forces and civilian agencies of other nations as well. This chapter summarizes standing arrangements for joint operations and presents general considerations for combined operations.

National strategy and theater strategy will dictate the ends and means of major operations and the purposes and conditions of tactical battles and engagements. Cooperation with the US Air Force will be vital always as will cooperation with US Navy and Marine forces in many cases. It would also be difficult to conceive of future US Army deployments in mid- to high-intensity

CONTENTS

theaters without some level of allied cooperation. In cases such as Europe and Korea, with allied command structures in place, close cooperation with allied forces will be routine.

JOINT OPERATIONS

ORGANIZATION AND COMMAND AND CONTROL

Command and control of joint forces will conform to the provisions of the Joint Chiefs of Staff (JCS) Publication 2. Each service's doctrine and applicable joint doctrine will guide employment. Joint forces include unified and specified commands and joint task forces (JTFs). Each military service is responsible for providing its contingent (composed of various types of units) to unified and specified commands. These contingents are called service components but may have other titles, such as theater

TYPES OF JOINT FORCE ORGANIZATIONS

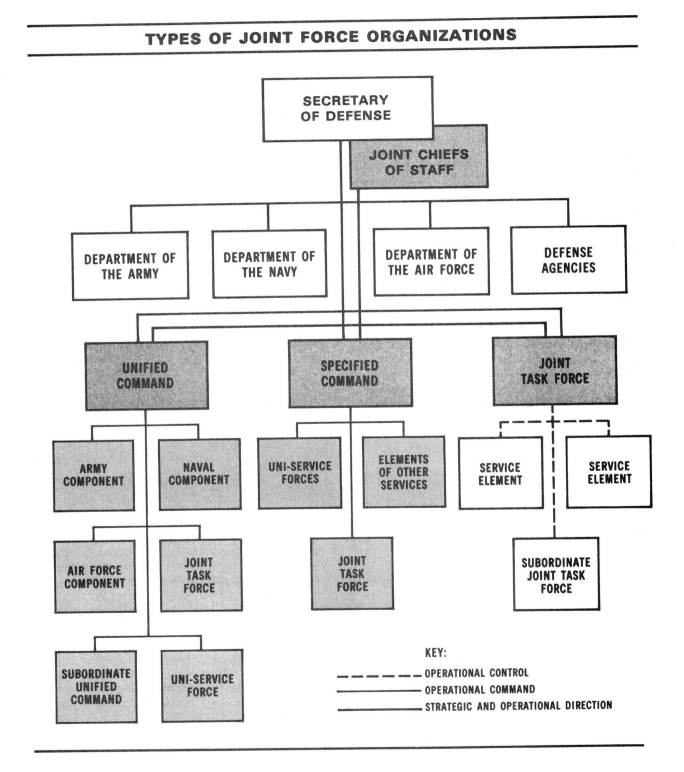

army, naval fleet, fleet marine force, or theater air force. JTF normally draw units from the components. For command and control, normally forces are *assigned* to unified and specified commands, but are *attached* to a JTF.

Joint forces operate within two distinct chains of command—one for operations, another for administrative and logistical matters. For operations, orders to commanders of unified and specified commands are issued by the President or the Secretary of Defense through the JCS. The JCS prepare plans and provide strategic direction for the armed forces, including operations by commanders of unified and specified commands. These commanders are, however, responsible to the President and Secretary of Defense for accomplishing their assigned tasks.

The administrative and logistical chain of command encompasses those functions of the military services not included in strategic direction. The military departments are responsible for administrative and logistical support of their forces wherever employed. Forces assigned to unified and specified commands deal directly with their respective departments and services on matters which are the responsibility of the departments or services.

Joint commanders are granted the authority necessary to accomplish their missions. Operational command and operational control are terms used to describe the authority exercised by joint commanders over subordinate components. These terms are synonymous. *Operational command* describes the authority granted commanders of unified and specified commands by the National Security Act of 1947. *Operational control* describes operational command when applied to other than unified and specified commanders. Both operational command and operational control empower joint commanders to—

- Establish the composition of subordinate forces.
- Assign tasks.

- Designate objectives.
- Direct actions necessary to accomplish the mission.

The critical factors that determine the structure of a joint organization are—

- Responsibilities, missions, and tasks assigned to the commander.
- Nature and scope of the operation.
- Forces available.
- Duration of the operation.

The organization should provide for centralized direction, decentralized execution, and common doctrine based on the characteristics and service identity of forces available to the command.

UNIFIED COMMANDS

A unified command is established by direction of the President to perform a broad, continuing mission. It is composed of forces assigned by two or more services, operating under the operational command of a single unified Commander in Chief (CINC). The CINC is responsible to the Secretary of Defense for accomplishing his mission and operates under the strategic direction of the JCS. He normally exercises operational command through component commanders and the Special Operations Command. When he deems it necessary, he may establish a subordinate unified command or JTF to conduct specific missions. Under emergency conditions, the CINC has the authority to use all facilities and supplies of assigned forces to accomplish his mission.

The CINC of the unified command develops operation plans (OPLAN), operation plans in concept format (CONPLAN), and operation orders (OPORDs). He is responsible for a specific geographical area.

SPECIFIED COMMANDS

Like the unified command, a specified command is established by direction of the President to accomplish a broad, continuing mission. Unlike a unified command, however, a specified command is primarily a single service command, though it may have elements of other services assigned. Like a unified command, a specified command receives strategic direction from the JCS.

JOINT TASK FORCES

A (JTF) may be constituted by the Secretary of Defense or by the commander of a unified command, specified command, or an existing JTF. It is composed of elements of two or more services operating under a single JTF commander. Normally it performs missions having specific, limited objectives or missions of short duration. It dissolves when it has achieved its purpose. The JTF commander is responsible to the JTF establishing authority. He has operational control over the entire force. He will usually augment his own staff with representatives from the other services. He

exercises logistical coordination or control only as necessary to meet his subordinate commanders' logistical needs.

COMPONENT COMMANDS

Each component commander is responsible for the proper employment of his forces and for accomplishing operational tasks assigned by the joint commander. He is also responsible for—

- Internal administration and discipline.
- Training in his own service doctrine, techniques, and tactics.
- Designation of specific units to meet joint requirements.
- Logistics functions normal to the component.
- Tactical employment of service component forces.
- Service intelligence matters.

COMBINED OPERATIONS

In addition to operating as part of a joint force, the Army must be prepared for combined operations with land, air, and naval forces of allied governments. Army forces in the North Atlantic Treaty Organization (NATO) area will operate under one of NATO's Major Commands (Allied Command Europe, Allied Command Atlantic, or Allied Command Channel). Those in the Republic of Korea will fight as part of the United States-Republic of Korea (US-ROK) Combined Forces Command (CFC). In these theaters, doctrine, procedures, and principles have been developed and practiced to minimize the problems of inter-allied coordination.

Elsewhere, agreements on doctrine, principles, and operating techniques are only partially developed or do not exist at all. In such theaters, US and allied forces will have to work out procedures for combined operations under the pressure of imminent conflict or even while operations are under way.

Campaign planning in combined theaters of operations imposes special considerations not present in unilateral theaters. In combined theaters, the allies share a compelling need to maintain the political cohesion of the coalition as a prerequisite for maintaining the military effectiveness and cohesion of the allied military organization. Accommodation of differences in political-military objectives is therefore of the highest importance. Similarly, accommodation of differences in capabilities among the allies' military forces requires careful planning and tailored coordination and liaison between the forces. Logistical support, while normally a national responsibility, must be coordinated in a combined effort to permit proper synchronized employment of the various allies combat formations. Campaign planning in all of its facets is inherently a combined activity in coalition warfare.

AirLand Battle doctrine must be adapted to each conflict. The following section describes the chief considerations for Army units in combined operations. Specific arrangements for existing alliances are contained in standardization agreements and allied tactical publications (ATPs). Appendix A contains a partial listing of these documents. Upon ratification, the provisions of these standardization agreements are incorporated into appropriate field manuals, technical manuals, and training manuals.

CONSIDERATIONS

The US Army has fought alongside allied forces in a wide variety of operational situations. In high- and mid-intensity conflicts, allied officers have commanded US formations as large as field armies. Likewise, US commanders have both employed and cooperated with armies, corps, and divisions of other nations. In low-intensity conflicts, cooperation between smaller forces have been just as common. Maneuver, fire support, air operations, combat support, combat service support (CSS), and naval support have all been effectively synchronized between allies in support of combined operations.

AirLand Battle doctrine as a broad approach to war is entirely consistent with the demands of combined operations. Its emphasis on actively seeking the initiative, operational and tactical agility, campaigns and battles in depth, and synchronization of all efforts retain their validity in combined operations. AirLand Battle doctrine accommodates, but is not dependent on, highly sophisticated equipment. It can equally well accommodate the employment of weapons and units different from those in US forces.

Special efforts have always been necessary to coordinate the operations of a multi-national force. Such efforts will continue to be required in future combined operations. The chief considerations in planning and conducting such operations are—

• Command and control.

• Intelligence.

• Operational procedures.

• Combat service support.

Interoperability between US Army and allied forces is an essential condition for efficient combat operations in combined or coalition warfare. In established alliances, specialized agencies and procedures exist to facilitate common or compatible development of doctrine, tactics, techniques, procedures, training methods and exercises, professional education, organizational design, and materiel developments. The ultimate objective of these efforts is to ensure the synchronized employment of US Army and allied combat capabilities to achieve the military objectives in a theater of operations.

COMMAND AND CONTROL

Unity of command is essential in all operations. In combined operations, it proceeds from the political and strategic leadership of the alliance. It is exercised in the theater of war by a supreme allied commander or commander in chief appointed by the leaders of the alliance.

National contingents usually retain command of their own forces, relinquishing operational command or operational control of the forces they commit to combined operations. This will be the usual arrangement for Army forces participating in combined operations. Army commanders will fight at the direction of the allied commander, but some administrative functions of command will usually be retained by a US Army officer who may be a theater army commander or the commander of a subordinate force.

Special communication and liaison arrangements are required when command relationships are established between US units and superior, subordinate, or adjacent allied headquarters. This is true at the highest levels where US field armies or corps may operate at the direction of an allied headquarters alongside field armies or corps of other nationalities. It is also true within corps containing divisions of different armies and within the areas of operations of smaller units who must cooperate with local self-defense forces or civil authorities.

Personalities and sensitivities of allied military leaders are unavoidably a consideration in combined operations. In fact, General Jacob Devers, Commander of the Sixth Army Group in World War II, considered the problem of personal relationships to be the greatest challenge of combined command. As an example, cooperation of US and Vietnamese forces was frequently impeded by misunderstandings rooted in cultural differences.

Commanders and staff officers in combined operations must therefore take personal and national characteristics into account in all their actions. In some cases, such considerations will largely dictate the disposition of forces and the assignment of missions. Tact, appreciation of national differences and capabilities, and an understanding of allied national goals and interests are essential to commanders, staff officers, and troops involved in combined operations.

Multi-national staffing can help coordinate operations within large forces. In any case, deliberate and detailed planning is necessary to assure coordination within a combined force. The exchange of liaison parties with reliable communications is usually required when an operation depends on close cooperation between allied units.

Specialist liaison officers—such as aviation staff officers, fire support officers, engineers, or intelligence specialists—may be exchanged when allied or US forces employ units or equipment with which they are unfamiliar. Whenever possible, such liaison officers should be familiar with the staff and operational organizations, doctrine and procedures of the force with which they will work. They should either speak the language of that force or be accompanied by interpreters.

Civil affairs officers and staff officers can assist in the control of operations that require the cooperation of host nation civilian authorities.

INTELLIGENCE

Allies normally operate separate intelligence systems in support of their own policy and military forces. In war, the products of national collection that affect operations must be shared and early coordination should be made to assure that the intelligence operations of allies are coordinated. Specific provisions for combined intelligence operations and the utilization of national systems must be arranged at the highest levels of the alliance.

For operational and tactical purposes, it is essential that arrangements be made for the rapid dissemination of military intelligence and for the use of available intelligence assets by all partners in the operation. This will usually require the formation of a combined intelligence staff at theater level, the establishment of an intelligence network with dedicated communications and liaison officers to link allied headquarters, and the assignment of tactical intelligence units throughout the force in a way that optimizes their use. Technical intelligence collectors such as drones, direction finders, and radars and EW assets of the national contingents will differ. Their capabilities should be considered by the combined intelligence staff and, if it is advantageous, these collection means should be distributed throughout the force to assure that the command's full potential for intelligence collection is realized.

COORDINATING COMBINED OPERATIONS

AirLand Battle doctrine is based on the flexible application of friendly strengths against enemy vulnerabilities and is adaptable to combined operations at the operational and tactical levels in offense or defense. The design of combined operations should make maximum use of the strengths of all participating forces while compensating for their comparative vulnerabilities. In many operational and tactical activities, standing operating procedures will have to be developed to assure effective cooperation between the forces of different nations.

At the operational level, combined forces pursue campaign objectives designed to achieve theater objectives for the alliance. Plans should reflect the special capabilities of each national contingent in the assignment of missions. The mobility, intelligence collection assets, size and sustainability of formations, air defenses, capabilities for long-range fires, special operations forces, training for operations in special environments, and preparation for operations in nuclear and chemical environments are among the significant factors in combined operations at this level. The cooperation of US, British, and Canadian forces in France; United Nations forces in Korea; and German and Italian forces in North Africa exemplify the way in which complementary capabilities can be harmonized in large force operations.

Usually the military forces of each nation are employed together and national contingent commanders are charged with responsibility for their own operations and support. Some functions, however, may be assigned to the forces of a smaller group of allies. Rear area security responsibilities, for instance, may be given to home defense or police forces of the host nation. Likewise, air defense, coastal defense, or some special operations may be entrusted to one ally based on that force's special capabilities.

Tactical cooperation requires more precision since it deals with immediate actions in combat. Among the disparities that adjacent and supporting allied commanders must reconcile are dissimilar tactical control measures, differences in tactical methods and operating procedures, varying organizations and capabilities of units, and differences in equipment. Weapons, radios, maps, and intelligence collection systems usually differ among allied armies.

Liaison, equipment exchanges, and combined training can offset some of these problems. More basically, though, the commander of a combined force must plan and conduct his operations in ways that exploit complementary strengths and minimize problems of coordination. Habitual relationships between units should be established and maintained when one nation's forces will be assigned to another's for an extended period. Detailed planning with emphasis on rehearsals and careful wargaming should precede operations in which allied units will cooperate for the first time.

Specifically, tactical plans should address recognition of allied units, soldiers, and vehicles; fire control measures; air support arrangements; communications; liaison; and movement control. The commander's intent and the concept of the operation should also receive special attention because of differences between allies in doctrine and terminology.

Plans for close operations must reflect the capabilities of all available forces. Allied units in adjacent zones or sectors must understand their neighbors' concepts of operations and maintain contact as necessary just as adjacent forces of the same nationality would. Tactical differences deriving from national doctrine—how flank security is handled, how passages of lines are conducted, when and whether small enemy forces will be bypassed or permitted to penetrate a defense, how much ground will be given up—must be clearly understood.

Deep operations plans of a US force containing allied units must also provide for the intelligence and long-range fire support needs of such forces. When allied artillery, air, electronic warfare (EW), or special operating forces (SOF) can contribute to deep operations or improve the overall capability of the force, their capabilities must be understood and their efforts coordinated with the overall tactical plan. US units operating under allied command should use their own capabilities for deep operations to accomplish their missions in consonance with the allied commander's concept of operations.

Rear operations must also be coordinated between allied units. This should be done by assigning responsibility for all areas in the rear. When reserves or supporting forces must pass through or fly over a unit's rear area, careful coordination must be made in advance. Similarly, the movements of enemy forces in the rear area must be reported promptly when such forces pass from one ally's area into another's. Territorial forces or home defense units, police organizations, and civil authorities with rear operations responsibilities in the rear area of a US force must be included in rear operations planning, kept informed, and kept in communications with the headquarters they support.

COMBAT SERVICE SUPPORT

The logistical support of military forces is normally a national responsibility. Nonetheless, allied commanders will have to coordinate the use of facilities such as highways, rail lines, ports, and airfields. They will also have to seek and usually regulate within the force, the support available in the theater of operations or from the host nations. For these reasons, combined commanders should form a combined logistics staff section as early as possible.

Movement control, operation of ports and airfields, theater communications, some supply functions, and airspace command and control are significant matters that may have to be coordinated above the level of national contingents. To assure coordination and to prevent duplication, commanders of combined forces must establish clear responsibilities for such functions. Lower level commanders and staff officers responsible for operating in

the theater will have to resolve the problems of liaison, language, and compatibility of equipment inherent in multi-national military operations.

Transportation, construction services, medical support, and some classes of supply will often be available in the theater. Host nation support may be used to supplement or substitute for US services, supplies, and facilities. Water, food, and construction materials may also be available and may have to be obtained by a central allied agency and shared equitably between national contingents. The civil military operations (CMO) officers can identify and coordinate US requirements for local resources, facilities, and support.

In many instances, the US has supplied allied forces with material and has received combat support or combat service support from the military or civilian authorities of other alliance partners in exchange. Such arrangements can lead to significant economies of force and effort and support agreements between allies should be sought early in a combined operation.

When allies use the same equipment, provisions should be made for resupply, maintenance, or other support operations across national lines, routinely if that is feasible and in case of tactical emergency in any event. Petroleum, oil, and lubricants (POL), medical supplies, barrier materials, mines, and some tools and vehicles can usually be used by all members of an alliance. In the interests of simplicity of operations and economy of effort, these may be obtained and distributed through a single combined supply agency in some cases.

CHAPTER 12
Contingency Operations

The National Command Authorities (NCA) may direct contingency operations of US forces overseas in support of national policy. Contingency operations are military actions requiring rapid deployment to perform military tasks in support of national policy. Such operations are normally undertaken when vital national interests are at stake and direct or indirect diplomacy and other forms of influence have been exhausted or need to be supplemented by either a show of force or direct military action. Contingency operations involving Army forces may provide a rapid show of force in support of a threatened ally to deter aggression by a hostile neighbor, react to the invasion of a friendly government, protect property of US nationals, rescue hostages or perform other tasks directed as by the NCA. Contingency operations are always joint undertakings conducted within the framework of the Unified Command System. The size of a contingency force, its mission, and its area of operations will vary. Once deployed, Army units operate

in accordance with the principles described in Parts I, II, and III of this manual. This chapter describes the unique factors affecting the organization, deployment, and use of Army elements as part of a contingency force.

CONSIDERATIONS

The Joint Chiefs of Staff (JCS) and unified and specified commands provide for the most effective use of forces committed to a contingency. These military planners seek to—

- Provide best available intelligence information, including political, social, and economic considerations as well as information on terrain, climate, and friendly/enemy forces.

- Provide multiple options to the NCA in support of national objectives, and explain the capabilities and limitations of the military forces in each option.

- Use the most current and authoritative guidance available. They should know before hostilities occur what US political

authorities are prepared to do in responding to threats to national interests.

- Inform civilian authorities of the risks associated with proposed plans.

- Judge what additional resources would effectively reduce those risks.

The overall national policy aims must always be clear when military contingencies are planned. Rules for limitations on use of force must be observed. At this level, military planners harmonize plans with diplomatic efforts to deter hostile actions, facilitate military actions, and provide a framework of policies to govern military action.

JCS and unified and specified command planners consider nine factors involving total force readiness, availability, and appropriateness in their plans. The considerations include:

- *Mission.* The mission analysis determines the tasks. A large force may have to deter or defeat enemy forces that attempt subversion or invasion. A small force may be deployed to perform any of a number of specialized missions.

- *Adequacy.* A trained force adequate to the task should be available.

- *Deployability.* The means should be available to deploy the necessary force in the required time.

- *Supportability.* The means should be available to support and sustain the force long enough to accomplish the mission.

- *Affordability.* The forces and other resources for one mission must be weighed against vital missions elsewhere.

- *Availability of forces.* Light forces can be deployed quickly and are easiest to support. When adequate to the threat, they are the preferred Army force. Before an impending crisis develops into open hostilities which may increase risks to US interests, early deployment of light forces may deter an opponent and thus prevent a costly subsequent engagement. Light forces would not be appropriate, however, to face tank-heavy forces or to operate over great distances. Heavy forces take longer to deploy and are more difficult to support, but they may be necessary to defeat the enemy. Planners weigh the considerations in each case to arrive at a proper combination of forces.

- *Use of indigenous forces.* An indigenous force may be available to accomplish all or a part of the mission and to assist in supporting US units. The capabilities and limitations of indigenous forces enter into contingency planning. Combined with a small US combat force or appropriate US logistic and fire support, an indigenous force may be sufficient. Given these circumstances, US forces can operate under either a US national command or a combined command.

COMMAND AND CONTROL

The command and control needs in contingency operations might lead to forming a joint task force (JTF) from assets within the unified command responsible for the contingency area. A JTF could also be organized and deployed from forces of a supporting Commander in Chief (CINC) and transferred to control of the supported CINC just before employment. The gaining unified command could be responsible for employing the JTF or the NCA might retain control of the JTF through the JCS.

STRATEGIC DEPLOYMENT

The commander of the United States Army Forces Command (FORSCOM) is also Commander in Chief of the United States Army Forces, Readiness Command (CINC-USARRED). He supports USREDCOM. Readiness Command forces may fill Army requirements in a deploying JTF or may augment Army components of unified commands overseas. Army forces normally deploy on receipt of a JCS deployment order, but they may also receive some movement instructions from JCS warning or alert orders. Transportation by sea or air is under supervision of supporting or supported unified commanders and monitored by the Joint Deployment Agency (JDA).

During deployment planning, the gaining Army component commander ensures the arrival of Army units into the operational area according to the CINC concept of operations. The Army component commander develops an operational scheme for employment of Army forces and determines the forces required to accomplish the missions assigned to the CINC. After coordinating with the other services, the Army component commander develops his deployment plan. The location, nature, and intensity of the conflict will determine the composition of units needed and how they will be phased during deployment.

EMPLOYMENT

The scope and nature of the contingency influences both force organization and operations. Economy of force, mobility, surprise, and bold, aggressive actions should be emphasized to achieve decisive results. In keeping with the AirLand Battle doctrine, operations should be characterized by flexibility, imaginative leadership, thorough planning, and skillful, decentralized execution. Support from the other services is essential to the success of the Army mission in joint operations.

Commanders at appropriate levels maintain contingency plans for rapid force deployment. At the time of deployment and under guidance from the NCA, they modify these plans to fit existing conditions. The Army component for a contingency operation may consist of any size Army force—a small specialized element, a battalion or a brigade, a corps, or a multiple-corps force.

In planning to function as part of a joint force in a contingency operation, the Army component commander considers the operational environment and support requirements.

Operational considerations involve—

- The joint force mission and the land component's tasks.
- Assumptions under which the planning was conducted.
- The joint commander's concept of the operation.

- The probable or actual composition and size of land, air, and naval forces of the joint force and any allied force.
- Command relationships within the joint force.
- Specific operational aspects including fire support (all services), communications, nuclear and chemical warfare guidance, intelligence, psychological operations, and unconventional warfare.
- Enemy capability for ground, air, naval, electronic, and nuclear, biological, and chemical operations.
- Enemy capability for unconventional and psychological operations.
- Geography, weather, and terrain.
- The political situation and civil-military responsibilities.
- Language requirements.
- In-country facilities.

Support operations involve—

- Maximizing use of local resources.
- Limiting supplies to essentials.
- Formulating a maintenance policy.
- Formulating a medical evacuation policy.
- Maintaining and securing necessary stockage levels.
- Phasing in additional combat service support (CSS) capabilities with follow-up elements as required.

Force planners normally seek to maximize combat capability and to reduce support to the essentials. A contingency force relies heavily on strategic airlift for rapid deployment and resupply from Continental United States (CONUS). Early air superiority, continuous tactical air support, logistic resupply by air, and maintenance of air lines of communications are essential for such an operation to be successful. Sealift of outsized equipment, armored units, and bulk supplies may be necessary. Additionally, the Army component of a joint force will have to provide certain CSS commodities, services, and facilities to other service components in the area of operations.

A lack of adequate communications and intelligence may hamper the initial phase of contingency force operations. Limited knowledge of the enemy may dictate that initial combat actions consist of a movement to contact or a reconnaissance in force. Long-range communication should be established early to ensure an effective flow of information for decision making.

Contingency planning requires an all-source intelligence system organized to meet the needs of the commander of the deploying force prior to deployment. The intelligence planning process should be continuous and aggressively managed. It should develop, maintain, and update a data base that is keyed on worldwide contingency requirements. This data base incorporates intelligence preparation of the battlefield (IPB). On alert notification, the intelligence officer focuses his effort on the specific objective area. He should rapidly provide the commander *only that information* that is critical to the combat operation.

Maintaining the intelligence data base permits commanders to identify intelligence gaps. These gaps become immediate collection requirements in a crisis. Updating the data base and satisfying intelligence gaps requires active coordination between the contingency force and national intelligence systems. National intelligence systems support for early deployed units play a key role in fulfilling the commander's intelligence needs. After deployment, these systems can supplement the contingency force's organic collection assets in the objective area.

Army forces in contingency operations should be more mobile than their potential enemy. To achieve superior mobility, they may need to include mechanized, armored, and aviation units. Although it is costly, mobility improves the commander's ability to fight.

Principles Of War

The US Army published its first discussion of the principles of war in a 1921 Army training regulation. These principles were taken from the work of British Major General J. F. C. Fuller, who developed a set of principles of war during World War I to serve as guides for his own army. In the ensuing years, the original principles of war adopted by our Army have been slightly revised, but they have essentially stood the tests of analysis, experimentation, and practice. Today's Army recognizes the principles of—

- Objective.
- Offensive.
- Mass.
- Economy of force.
- Maneuver.
- Unity of command.
- Security.
- Surprise.
- Simplicity.

OBJECTIVE

Direct every military operation towards a clearly defined, decisive, and attainable objective.

The strategic military objective of a nation at war must be to apply whatever degree of force is necessary to attain the political purpose for which the war is being fought. When the political purpose is the total defeat of the adversary, then the strategic military objective will most likely be the defeat of the enemy's armed forces and the destruction of his will to resist. Strategic, operational, and tactical objectives cannot be clearly identified and developed, however, until the political purpose has been determined and defined by the President and Congress. Once developed, these objectives must be constantly analyzed and reviewed to ensure that they accurately reflect not only the ultimate political purpose but also any political constraints imposed on the application of military force.

Operational efforts must also be directed toward clearly defined, decisive, and attainable objectives that will achieve the strategic aims. And tactical objectives must achieve operational aims. Similarly, intermediate operational and tactical objectives must quickly and economically contribute, directly or indirectly, to the purpose of the ultimate operational or tactical objective. The selection of objectives is based on the overall mission of the command, the commander's assigned mission, the means available, the characteristics of the enemy, and the military characteristics of the operational area. Every commander must understand the overall mission of the higher command, his own mission, and the tasks he must perform. He must communicate clearly the intent of the operation to his subordinate commanders.

OFFENSIVE

Seize, retain, and exploit the initiative.

The principle of offensive suggests that offensive action, or maintenance of the initiative, is the most effective and decisive way to pursue and to attain a clearly defined, common goal. This is fundamentally true in the strategic, the operational, and the tactical senses. While it may sometimes be necessary to adopt a defensive posture, this should be only a temporary condition until the necessary means are available to resume offensive operations. An offensive spirit must be inherent in the conduct of all defensive operations—the defense must be an active, not a passive one. This is so because offensive action, whatever form it takes, is the means by which the nation or a military force captures and holds the

initiative, maintains freedom of action and achieves results. It permits the political leader or the military commander to capitalize on the initiative, impose his will on the enemy, set the terms and select the place of confrontation or battle, exploit vulnerabilities and react to rapidly changing situations and unexpected developments. No matter what the level, the side that retains the initiative through offensive action forces the foe to react rather than to act.

MASS

Concentrate combat power at the decisive place and time.

In the strategic context, this principle suggests that the nation should commit, or be prepared to commit, a predominance of national power to those regions or areas of the world where the threat to vital security interests is greatest. For nations such as the United States, which have global security interests in terms of politico-military alliances and commitments and resource dependencies, the accurate and timely determination of where the threat to vital national interests is greatest is becoming increasingly more difficult. In today's volatile world, the nature and source of threat often change in dramatic fashion.

It is therefore incumbent upon military strategists to anticipate the most likely areas of concern and to develop suitable contingency plans. Since every possible contingency or trouble spot cannot be anticipated, much less planned for, it is absolutely essential for Army planners and Army forces to retain flexibility of thought and action.

In the operational and tactical dimensions, this principle suggests that superior combat power must be concentrated at the decisive place and time in order to achieve decisive results. This superiority results from the proper combination of the elements of combat power at a place and a time and in a manner of the commander's choosing in order to retain the initiative. The massing of forces, together with the proper application of other principles of war, may enable numerically inferior forces to achieve decisive campaign and battle outcomes.

ECONOMY OF FORCE

Allocate minimum essential combat power to secondary efforts.

As a reciprocal of the principle of mass, economy of force in the strategic dimension suggests that, in the absence of unlimited

resources, a nation may have to accept some risks in areas where vital national interests are not immediately at stake. This means that, if the nation must focus predominant power toward a clearly defined primary threat, it cannot allow attainment of that objective to be compromised by necessary diversions to areas of lower priority. This involves risk, requires astute strategic planning and judgment by political and military leaders, and again places a premium on the need for flexibility of thought and action.

At the operational and tactical levels, the principle of economy of force requires that minimum means be employed in areas other than where the main effort is intended to be employed. It requires, as at the strategic level, the acceptance of prudent risks in selected areas in order to achieve superiority in the area where decision is sought. Economy-of-force missions may require the forces employed to attack, to defend, to delay, or to conduct deception operations.

MANEUVER

Place the enemy in a position of disadvantage through the flexible application of combat power.

In the strategic sense, this principle has three interrelated dimensions: flexibility, mobility, and maneuverability. The first of these involves the need for flexibility in thought, plans, and operations. Such flexibility enhances the ability to react rapidly to unforeseen circumstances. Given the global nature of US interests and the dynamic character of the international scene, such flexibility is crucial. The second dimension involves strategic mobility, which is especially critical for an insular power·such as the United States. In order to react promptly and to concentrate and to project power on the primary objective, strategic airlift and sealift are essential. The final strategic dimension involves maneuverability within the theater of operations so as to focus maximum strength against the enemy's weakest point and thereby gain the strategic advantage.

Tactically and operationally, maneuver is an essential element of combat power. It contributes significantly to sustaining the initiative, to exploiting success, to preserving freedom of action, and to reducing vulnerability. The object of maneuver is to concentrate or to disperse forces in a manner designed to place the enemy at a disadvantage, thus achieving results that would otherwise be more costly in men and materiel. At all levels, successful application of this principle requires not only fire and movement, but also flexibility of thought, plans, and operations, and the considered application of the principles of mass and economy of force. At the operational level, maneuver is the means by which the commander sets the terms of battle, declines battle, or acts to take advantage of tactical actions.

UNITY OF COMMAND

For every objective, ensure unity of effort under one responsible commander.

This principle ensures that all efforts are focused on a common goal. At the strategic level, this common goal equates to the political purpose of the United States and the broad strategic objectives which flow therefrom. It is the common goal which, at the national level, determines the military forces necessary for its achievement. The coordination of these forces requires unity of effort. At the national level, the Constitution provides for unity of command by appointing the President as the Commander in Chief of the Armed forces. The President is assisted in this role by the national security organization, which includes the

Secretary of Defense and the Joint Chiefs of Staff at the highest level, and the unified and specified commands and joint task forces at the operational levels.

In both the operational and tactical dimensions, it is axiomatic that the employment of military forces in a manner that develops their full combat power requires unity of command. Unity of command means directing and coordinating the action of all forces toward a common goal or objective. Coordination may be achieved by cooperation; it is, however, best achieved by vesting a single commander with the requisite authority to direct and to coordinate all forces employed in pursuit of a common goal.

SECURITY

Never permit the enemy to acquire an unexpected advantage.

Security enhances freedom of action by reducing friendly vulnerability to hostile acts, influence, or surprise. At the strategic level, security requires that active and passive measures be taken to protect the United States and its Armed Forces against espionage, subversion, and strategic intelligence collection. However, implementation of such security measures must be balanced against the need to prevent them from severing the link between the American public and its Army.

Security is also necessary in planning and conducting campaigns. Security measures, however, should not be allowed to interfere with flexibility of thought and action, since rigidity and dogmatism increase vulnerability to enemy surprise. In this regard, thorough knowledge and understanding of enemy strategy, tactics, and doctrine, and detailed staff planning can improve security and reduce vulnerability to surprise.

At the tactical level, security is essential to the protection and husbanding of combat power. Security results from the measures taken by a command to protect itself from surprise, observation, detection, interference, espionage, sabotage, or annoyance. Security may be achieved through the establishment and maintenance of protective measures against hostile acts or influence; or it may be assured by deception operations designed to confuse and dissipate enemy attempts to interfere with the force being secured. Risk is an inherent condition in war; application of the principle of security does not suggest overcautiousness or the avoidance of calculated risk.

SURPRISE

Strike the enemy at a time or place, or in a manner, for which he is unprepared.

To a large degree, the principle of surprise is the reciprocal of the principle of security. Concealing one's own capabilities and intentions creates the opportunity to strike the enemy unaware or unprepared. However, strategic surprise is difficult to achieve. Rapid advances in strategic surveillance technology make it increasingly more difficult to mask or to cloak the large scale marshaling or movement of manpower and equipment. This problem is compounded in an open society such as the United States, where freedom of press and information are highly valued. However, the

United States can achieve a degree of psychological surprise due to its strategic deployment capability. The rapid deployment of US combat forces into a crisis area can forestall or upset the plans and preparations of an enemy. This capability can give the United States the advantage in both a physical and psychological sense by denying the enemy the initiative.

Surprise is important at the operational and tactical levels for it can decisively affect the outcome of battles. With surprise, success out of proportion to the effort expended may be obtained. Surprise results from going against an enemy at a time and/or place or in a manner for which he is unprepared. It is not essential that the enemy be taken unaware, but only that he become aware too late to react effectively. Factors contributing to surprise include speed and alacrity, employment of unexpected factors, effective intelligence, deception operations of all kinds, variations of tactics and methods of operation, and operations security.

SIMPLICITY

Prepare clear, uncomplicated plans and clear, concise orders to ensure thorough understanding.

In the strategic, operational, and tactical dimensions, guidance, plans, and orders should be as simple and direct as the attainment of the objective will allow. The strategic importance of the principle of simplicity goes well beyond its more traditional military application. It is an important element in the development and enhancement of public support. If the American people are to commit their lives and resources to a military operation, they must understand the purpose which is to be achieved. Political and military objectives and operations must therefore be presented in clear, concise, understandable terms: simple and direct plans and orders cannot compensate for ambiguous and cloudy objectives. In its military application, this principle promotes strategic flexibility by encouraging broad strategic guidance rather than detailed and involved instruction.

At the operational and tactical levels, simplicity of plans and instructions contributes to successful operations. Direct, simple plans, and clear, concise orders are essential to reduce the chances for misunderstanding and confusion. Other factors being equal, a simple plan executed promptly is to be preferred over a complex plan executed later.

APPENDIX B

Key Concepts of Operational Design

This appendix discusses three concepts central to the design and conduct of campaigns and major operations: the center of gravity, the line of operations, and the culminating point. While not new to the US Army in application, they have not been dealt with in doctrinal literature for some time, and their terminology may therefore be unfamiliar to many American soldiers. In view of the increased emphasis of current doctrine on operational art, some further explanation of these concepts may be useful. Readers desiring additional elaboration should consult the extensive published literature on classical and contemporary operational theory.

THE CENTER OF GRAVITY

The concept of centers of gravity is key to all operational design. It derives from the fact that an armed combatant, whether a warring nation or alliance, an army in the field, or one of its subordinate formations, is a complex organism whose effective operation depends not merely on the performance of each of its component parts, but also on the smoothness with which these components interact and the reliability with which they implement the will of the commander. As with any complex organism, some components are more vital than others to the smooth and reliable operation of the whole. If these are damaged or destroyed, their loss unbalances the entire structure, producing a cascading deterioration in cohesion and effectiveness which may result in complete failure, and which will invariably leave the force vulnerable to further damage.

The center of gravity of an armed force refers to those sources of strength or balance. It is that characteristic, capability, or locality from which the force derives its freedom of action, physical strength, or will to fight. Clausewitz defined it as "the hub of all power and movement, on which everything depends." Its attack is—or should be—the focus of all operations.

Tactical formations can and frequently will have centers of gravity—a key command post, for example, or a key piece of terrain on which the unit's operations are anchored. But the concept is more usually and usefully applied to larger forces at the operational level, where the very size of the enemy force and the scale of its operations make difficult the decision where and how best to attack it.

Even at this level, the center of gravity may well be a component of the field force—the mass of the enemy force, the boundary between two of its major combat formations, a vital command and control center, or perhaps its logistical base or lines of communication. During the Battle of the Bulge in 1944, St. Vith became a center of gravity for defending American forces, failure to retain which might have resulted in the complete collapse of the Allied center, with potentially disastrous strategic consequences. But an operational center of gravity may also be more abstract—the cohesion among allied forces, for example, or the mental and psychological balance of a key commander.

Finally, at the strategic level, the center of gravity may be a key economic resource or locality, the strategic transport capabilities by which a nation maintains its armies in the field, or a vital part of the homeland itself. But it may also be a wholly intangible thing. At Verdun in 1916, for example, German and French armies sacrificed over a million men contesting a piece of real estate of little intrinsic tactical or operational value, but whose *moral* importance to both sides made its uncontested surrender unthinkable. Similarly neither Dien Bien Phu nor TET seriously threatened the operational capacity of French and American forces respectively. But both attacks struck directly at their strategic centers of gravity—popular and political support of the war.

At any level, identifying the enemy's center of gravity requires extensive knowledge of his organizational make-up, operational patterns, and physical and psychological strengths and weaknesses. Moreover, centers of gravity can change. A major shift in operational direction, the replacement of a key enemy commander, the fielding of new units or weaponry—any of these events can shift the center of gravity significantly, just as adding new

weights to a scale alters its point of balance. The commander seeking to strike his enemy's center of gravity must be alert to such shifts, recognize them when they occur, and adjust his own operations accordingly.

Finally, it should be remembered that while attacking the center of gravity may be the surest and swiftest road to victory, it will rarely be the easiest road. More often than not, the enemy recognizing his center of gravity will take steps to protect it, and indirect means will be required to force him to expose it to attack. In the process, the enemy will do his best to uncover and attack our own.

Identification of the enemy's center of gravity and the design of actions which will ultimately expose it to attack and destruction while protecting our own, are the essence of the operational art.

LINES OF OPERATION

Lines of operation define the directional orientation of a force in relation to the enemy. Lines of operation connect the force with its base or bases of operation on the one hand and its operational objective on the other. Normally, a campaign or major operation will have a single line of operation, although multiple lines of operation in a single campaign are not uncommon. Often, such situations produce difficulties, as in the Allied campaign in northern France and the low countries, where Montgomery and Patton competed for resources which might better have been concentrated in support of one or the other commander.

As that example suggests, the decision whether to operate on one or several lines of operation will depend heavily on the availability of resources. Given adequate resources, operations on multiple lines have the advantage of forcing the enemy to disperse his efforts. They have the disadvantage of being difficult to synchronize

and of making several forces vulnerable to interposition by the enemy and piecemeal defeat. Napoleon nearly destroyed the Allied armies in Belgium in 1815 by just such a maneuver and then was himself defeated at Waterloo after dividing his own army. Overall, the historical evidence suggests that multiple lines of operation are most likely to produce success when the enemy is weak, irresolute, or lacks freedom of maneuver.

Finally, classical theory makes special note of the relationship between opposing lines of operations. A force is said to be operating on interior lines when its operations diverge from a central point and when it is therefore closer to separate enemy forces than the latter are to each other. Interior lines benefit a weaker force by allowing it to shift the main effort laterally more rapidly than the enemy. Germany's decisive victory at Tannenberg was a classic example of the use of interior lines.

A force is said to be operating on exterior lines when its operations converge on the enemy. Successful operations on exterior lines require a stronger force, but in return offer the opportunity to encircle and annihilate a weaker opponent. The partial encirclement and destruction of German armies in the Argentan pocket following the allied breakout in Normandy resulted from effective operations on exterior lines.

While lines of operation are important considerations in the design of campaigns and major operations, their importance should not be overdrawn. History is replete with examples of armies which overcame positional disadvantages by audacity, agility, and sheer tenacity. The operational commander should choose his line of operation carefully, but he must not hesitate to alter it when presented with an unanticipated opportunity.

CULMINATING POINTS

Unless it is strategically decisive, every offensive operation will sooner or later reach a point where the strength of the attacker no longer significantly exceeds that of the defender, and beyond which continued offensive operations therefore risk overextension, counterattack, and defeat. In operational theory, this point is called the culminating point. The art of attack at all levels is to achieve decisive objectives *before* the culminating point is reached. Conversely, the art of defense is to hasten the culmination of the attack, recognize its advent, and be prepared to go over to the offense when it arrives.

Strategic and operational offensives reach a culminating point for several reasons. The forward movement of supplies may be insufficiently organized or may lack needed transport, or available stocks may be exhausted. The need to protect lines of communications from partisans or regular forces operating on the flanks or in the rear may have sapped the strength of forward forces to the point that the attacker no longer has the needed quantitative advantage. The attacking force may have suffered sufficient combat losses to tip the balance of forces. The attacker may have entered terrain which is more easily defended. The soldiers of the attacking army may become physically exhausted and morally less committed as the attack progresses. The defending force may have become more determined as large portions of territory are lost. The defender may

have been joined by new allies who now also feel threatened. All of these causes, and combinations of them, have resulted in offensive culminating points. Today another can be added. If the defender possesses nuclear weapons, he may at some point be pressed into using them in spite of the risk of retaliation.

Tactical attacks can also reach culminating points for similar, but scaled down, reasons. Usually tactical attacks lose momentum when they encounter heavily defended areas which cannot be bypassed. They also reach a culminating point when the supply of fuel and ammunition fails to keep up, the attacking troops become physically exhausted, casualties and equipment losses mount, and repair and replacement don't keep pace. But tactical attacks also stall when reserves are not available to continue the attack, the defender is reinforced, or he counterattacks with fresh troops. Several of these causes may combine to halt an attack.

There are numerous historical examples of strategic, operational, and tactical offensives which reached culminating points before reaching their objectives. Often this was because planners were not able to adequately forecast the drain on resources of extended fighting at great depths.

At the strategic level, classic examples in this century of armies arriving at culminating points before a decision was reached include the German attack into

France in 1914, the German invasion of Russia in 1941, and the Japanese offensive into the South Pacific and Southeast Asia in 1941-42. In each case, commanders and planners failed to concentrate their efforts in key areas and appreciate the resource drain of extended operations over great distances.

Classic operational examples of the same phenomenon just in WWII were Rommel's drive into Egypt which culminated at El Alamein, the Japanese drive from Burma into India which culminated at Imphal-Kohima, Patton's rapid advance across France which bogged down for lack of supplies in Lorraine, the December 1944 German counteroffensive through the Ardennes which resulted in the Battle of the Bulge, the advance of General Paulus' 6th German Army to Stalingrad, and the combined penetration of the Russian 6th Army and Popov's Tank Corps Group into the Ukraine which precipitated the third battle of Kharkov.

Examples of tactical attacks reaching culminating points are equally numerous in military history but are rarely recorded. In most instances, they resulted from over-ambitious objectives or from violations of principles of offensive operations (concentration, surprise, speed, flexibility, and audacity) and less often because of logistic insufficiency.

In some cases momentum can be regained, as in the Patton example above, but always after difficult fighting and a period of operational stasis. In many cases, as in the other examples given, a turning point battle is fought and won by the defender.

Fighting a defensive battle after reaching a culminating point is extremely difficult for several reasons. Defensive preparations are hasty and forces are not adequately disposed for defense. Reorganization for defense requires more time than the enemy allows. Usually the attacking forces are dispersed, extended in depth, and weakened in condition. Moreover, the shift to defense requires a psychological adjustment. Soldiers who have become accustomed to advancing, and thus "winning," now must halt deep in enemy territory and fight defensively (sometimes desperately) on new and often unfavorable terms. Finally, attacks rarely culminate on ground ideally suited for defense. If a decision is made to conduct retrograde operations to more defensible ground, the psychological adjustment of soldiers is compounded.

From the foregoing discussion, it should be clear that culminating points are equally important to the attacker and the defender. From a planning perspective, the attacker must seek to secure operationally decisive objectives before the force reaches its culminating point. If this cannot be anticipated, the attacker must plan a pause to replenish his combat power, and phase his operation accordingly.

For his part, the defender must seek to bring the enemy attack to or past its culminating point before it reaches an operationally decisive objective. To do so, he must operate not only on the enemy force itself, but also on its sustainment system. The more readily the defender can trade space for time without unacceptable operational or strategic loss, the easier this will be.

Once operations begin, the attacking commander must sense when he has reached or is about to reach his culminating point, whether intended or not, and revert to the defense at a time and place of his own choosing. For his part, the defender must be alert to recognize when his opponent has become overextended and be prepared to pass over to the counteroffensive before the attacker is able to recover his strength.

APPENDIX C
Echelons of Command

Different levels of command perform different tactical and operational functions. These vary with the type of unit and, particularly at echelons above corps, with the organization of the theater, the nature of the conflict, and the number of friendly forces committed to the effort. This appendix describes the general operational functions of Army units from company to theater army level.

COMPANIES/BATTERIES/TROOPS

Company-sized units consist of two or more platoons usually of the same type with a headquarters and, in some cases, a limited capacity for self-support. Companies are the basic elements of all battalions. They are also assigned as separate units of brigades and larger organizations.

All close combat companies can fight massed or by separate platoons. In infantry, armor, and attack helicopter battalions, companies normally fight as integral units. Cavalry troops and attack helicopter companies more frequently fight with their platoons in separate zones, sectors, or areas.

Company-sized close combat units are capable of fighting without additional reinforcements. Ordinarily, however, companies or troops are augmented for operations with SHORAD units and ground surveillance radar teams. They may also be reinforced with maneuver platoons of the same or different types and with engineer squads or platoons to form teams. Company teams are formed to tailor forces for a particular mission. Such tailoring matches forces to missions with greater precision but often disrupts teamwork within the company. Company teams should, therefore, be formed only after careful consideration and should train together before they are committed whenever possible.

Field artillery (FA) batteries are the basic firing units of FA battalions. They are organized with a firing battery, a headquarters, and limited support sections. They may fire and displace together or by platoons. Normally, batteries fight as part of their parent battalion. Occasionally, they are attached to other batteries or FA battalions and, in some cases, they respond directly to a maneuver battalion or company. Multiple Launch Rocket, Lance, and Pershing batteries will more often operate independently. Armored cavalry squadrons have organic howitzer batteries.

Air defense artillery (ADA) batteries operate as the fighting elements of ADA battalions or, if they are short-range in air defense (SHORAD) batteries, in direct support of maneuver brigades or battalions. Separate SHORAD batteries exist in separate brigade-sized organizations.

Combat engineer companies control three or four engineer platoons. They may be employed by their own battalion in a variety of tasks or they may support maneuver brigades or battalions. Separate brigades and regiments usually have an assigned combat engineer company.

Most other combat support and combat service support (CSS) units are formed as companies. Such companies vary widely in size, employment, and assignment.

BATTALIONS/SQUADRONS

Battalions and cavalry squadrons consist of two or more company-sized units and a headquarters. Most battalions are organized by branch, arm, or service and, in addition to their operational companies, contain a headquarters company that gives them the ability to perform some administrative and logistic services. Typically, battalions have three to five companies in addition to their headquarters.

Combat arms battalions are designed to perform single tactical missions as part of a brigade's tactical operations. Battalions attack, defend, delay, or move to assume new missions. Air and ground cavalry squadrons also perform reconnaissances and security missions. FA battalions fire in support of any of these missions.

Maneuver battalions can be reinforced with other combat and combat support companies to form task forces for special missions. FA battalions can be reinforced with batteries of any kind to form artillery task forces.

Engineer, ADA, and signal battalions assigned to or supporting divisions routinely operate throughout the division area of operations. Their commanders also perform the additional duties of division special staff officers.

Combat support and CSS battalions vary widely in type and organization. They may be separate divisional or non-divisional battalions, but, in any case, they normally perform functional services for a larger supported unit within that unit's area of operations. All battalions are capable of at least limited, short-term self defense.

BRIGADES/REGIMENTS/GROUPS

Brigade-sized units control two or more battalions. Their capabilities for self support and independent action vary considerably with the type of brigade.

Maneuver brigades are the major combat units of all types of divisions. They can also be organized as separate units. They can employ any combination of maneuver battalions and they are normally supported by FA battalions, aviation units, and by smaller combat, combat support, and CSS units. While separate brigades and armored cavalry regiments have a fixed organization, division commanders establish the organization of their brigades and change their organizations as frequently as necessary.

Brigades combine the efforts of their battalions and companies to fight engagements and to perform major tactical tasks in division battles. Their chief tactical responsibility is synchronizing the plans and actions of their subordinate units to accomplish a single task for the division or corps.

Separate brigades of infantry, armor, FA, ADA, engineer or aviation, and armored cavalry regiments can be used to reinforce corps or divisions and can be shifted from unit to unit to tailor forces for combat. Separate brigades and regiments are usually employed as units when attached to corps or divisions.

Other combat, combat support, and CSS brigades and groups are organized to control non-divisional units for corps and larger units. Engineer, ADA, signal, aviation, MP, and transportation brigades are typical of such units. They may also be the building blocks of large unit support structures such as corps and theater army support commands and of combat support commands such as engineer commands. Divisions are supported by an organic brigade-sized support command of mixed CSS battalions and companies.

DIVISIONS

Divisions are fixed combined arms organizations of 8 to 11 maneuver battalions, 3 to 4 FA battalions, and other combat, combat support and CSS units. Capable of performing any tactical mission and designed to be largely self-sustaining, divisions are the basic units of maneuver at the tactical level. Infantry, armored, mechanized infantry, airborne, air assault, and motorized infantry divisions are all presently in the force.

Divisions possess great flexibility. They tailor their own brigades and attached forces for specific combat missions. Their combat support and CSS battalions and

separate companies may be attached to or placed in support of brigades for the performance of a particular mission.

Divisions perform major tactical operations for the corps and can conduct sustained battles and engagements. They almost never direct actions at the operational level (campaigns or major operations), but they may be used by corps or field armies to perform tasks of operational importance. These may include exploiting tactical advantages to seize objectives in depth, moving to gain contact with enemy forces, or moving by air to seize positions behind an enemy force.

CORPS

Corps are the Army's largest tactical units, the instruments with which higher echelons of command conduct maneuver at the operational level. Corps are tailored for the theater and mission for which they are deployed. Once tailored, however, they contain all the organic combat, combat support, and combat service support capabilities required to sustain operations for a considerable period.

Corps plan and conduct major operations and battles. They synchronize tactical activities including the maneuver of their divisions, the fires of their artillery units and supporting aerial forces, and the actions of their combat support and CSS units. While corps normally fight as part of a larger land force—a field army or army group—they may also be employed alone, either as an independent ground force or as the land component of a joint task force. When employed alone, they

may exercise operational as well as tactical responsibilities.

Corps may be assigned divisions of any type required by the theater and the mission. They possess organic support commands and are assigned combat and combat support organizations based on their needs for a specific operation. Armored cavalry regiments, FA brigades, engineer brigades, ADA brigades, and aviation brigades are the non-divisional units commonly available to the corps to weight its main effort and to perform special combat functions. Separate infantry or armor brigades may also be assigned to corps. Signal brigades, MI groups, and MP groups are the usual combat support organizations present in a corps. Other units such as psychological operations (PSYOP) battalions, special operating forces (SOF), and civil affairs units may be assigned to corps when required.

FIELD ARMY

Field armies may be formed by theater Army commanders in coordination with the CINCs of unified command to control and direct the operations of assigned corps.

They will normally be constituted from existing army assets and structured to meet specific operational requirements. In joint and combined operations, the subordinate units of field armies may include units of other services or of allied forces. When the field army is the largest land formation in a theater of war, its commander may serve as the land component commander (LCC), and he may design and direct the land campaign for the entire theater.

Field armies exercise major operational responsibilities. When subordinated to an army group, field armies become the primary units of operational maneuver, conducting the decisive operations of the land campaign. When operating independently or as the land component of a joint force, field armies may be charged with planning and conducting the land campaign in a theater of war or a theater of operations.

In either case, field army commanders employ subordinate corps to concentrate combat power, to accept or decline battle, and to exploit the outcome of tactical actions.

Field armies and equivalent organizations are primarily operational headquarters. They may establish priorities for CSS among their subordinate forces, but CSS is normally provided by a theater army, service component command, or national support organization. In contingency operations, the field army may assume responsibility for the logistic support of army forces in the field. In such an operation, the field army would require the assignment of support organizations from the theater army or unified command.

ARMY GROUP

In a mature theater of war where a large number of forces are employed, theater army commanders, in coordination with the CINCs of unified or combined commands, may form army groups to control the operations of two to five field armies. Army groups have not been employed by the US Army since World War II, but, in a large conflict, they might be necessary again. As in the past, their main function would be to design and direct campaigns in a theater. In some cases, an army group commander might be designated the LCC.

Army group commanders perform major missions for which they usually receive broad operational guidance. They control a variable number of field armies depending on their mission and should also control separate units necessary for their operations. SOF units, PSYOP units, civil affairs organizations, other support forces including engineer, aviation, MI, MP, signal, and CSS units are commonly needed to support the operations of army groups. Army groups also require the full range of air support for their operations.

Like field armies, army groups will be activated from existing army units. They will often be multinational forces and their headquarters will then be staffed by officers of participating allied forces.

THEATER ARMY

Theater army is normally the Army service component command in a unified command. Third US Army, Eighth US Army, and US Army, Europe (USAREUR) are current examples of theater armies. The theater army as the service component

has both operational and support responsibilities. Its exact tasks are assigned by the theater CINC and may be exclusively operational missions, solely logistic tasks, or a combination of both types of responsibility.

Theater army commanders are responsible to the unified commander in a theater for recommending how US Army forces assigned to them should be allocated and employed. Their support responsibilities include the requirements to organize, equip, train, and maintain Army forces in the theater.

The organization of theater armies is not standard. It varies between theaters according to the size of the US Army component in a force and with the factors of mission, enemy, terrain, troops, and time available (METT-T). Other levels of command can also perform theater army functions. For example, a corps staff could perform the theater army function if only a single corps were committed to a contingency area. Or a larger separate staff may be necessary to handle the administrative, legal, logistical, personnel, intelligence, operations, and communications tasks of a large force deployed overseas. Liaison between a theater army and another headquarters employing its forces must be performed whenever theater armies release operational command of their units.

Glossary

ACC — Army Component Commander

ADA — air defense artillery

AI — air interdiction

ALOC — air lines of communication

A2C2 — Army Airspace Command and Control

ATP — allied tactical publication

BAI — battlefield air interdiction

CAS — close air support

CEOI — communications-electronics operations instructions

CEWI — combat electronic warfare intelligence

CFA — covering force area

CFC — Combined Forces Command

CINC — Commander in Chief

CINCUSARRED — Commander in Chief of the United States Army Forces, Readiness Command

CMO — civil-military operations

COMMZ — communications zone

CONPLAN — operation plans in concept format

CONUS — Continental United States

CRC — control and reporting center

CSR — controlled supply rate

CSS — combat services support

DCA — defensive counter air

E&E — evasion & escape

EMCON — emission control

EMP — electromagnetic pulse

EW — electronic warfare

EWSE — electronic warfare support element

FA — field artillery

FEBA — forward edge of battle area

FLOT — forward line of own troops

FORSCOM — United States Army Forces Command

FSCOORD — fire support coordinator

HIMAD — high- to medium-altitude air defense

HNS — host nation support

ICD — imitative communication deception

IPB — intelligence preparation of the battlefield

IR — information requirements

JCS — Joint Chiefs of Staff

JDA — Joint Deployment Agency

J-SEAD — joint suppression of enemy air defenses

JTF — joint task force

LCC — land component commander

LIC — low intensity conflict

LOC — lines of communication

MBA — main battle area

MED — manipulative electronic deception

METT-T — mission, enemy, terrain, troops, and time available

MI — military intelligence

MOPP — mission-oriented protective posture

MP — military police

NAI — named areas of interest

NATO — North Atlantic Treaty Organization

NBC — nuclear, biological, chemical

NCA — National Command Authority

NCO — noncommissioned officer

OCA — offensive counter air

OPLAN — operation plan

OPORD — operation order

PIR — priority intelligence requirements

POD — ports of debarkation

POL — petroleum, oil, and lubricants

PSYOP — psychological operations

ROK — Republic of Korea

RPV — remotely piloted vehicle

RSR — required supply rate

SEAD — suppression of enemy air defenses

SHORAD — short-range air defense

SLOC — sea lines of communication

SOF — special operating forces

SOP — standing operating procedure

UW — unconventional warfare

USAREUR — US Army, Europe

References

REQUIRED PUBLICATIONS

Required publications are sources that users must read in order to understand or to comply with this publication.

Field Manuals (FM)

100-1	The Army
101-5-1	Operational Terms and Graphics

RELATED PUBLICATIONS

Related publications are sources of additional information. They are not required in order to understand this publication.

Army Regulations (AR)

105-86	Performing Electronic Countermeasures in the United States and Canada

Field Manuals (FM)

3-100	NBC Operations
3-101	Chemical Units
5-100	Engineer Combat Operations
5-101	Mobility
5-102	Countermobility
5-103	Survivability
6-20	Fire Support in Combined Arms Operations
7-7	The Mechanized Infantry Platoon/Squad
7-8	The Infantry Platoon/Squad (Infantry, Airborne, Air Assault)
7-10	The Infantry Rifle Company (Infantry, Airborne, Air Assault Ranger)
7-20	The Infantry Battalion (Infantry, Airborne, Air Assault)
7-30	Infantry, Airborne, and Air Assault Brigade Operations
8-10	Health Service Support in a Theater of Operations
11-50	Combat Communications Within the Division
11-92	Combat Communications Within the Corps
1-111	Combat Aviation Brigade
1-112	Attack Helicopter Battalion
17-95	Armored Cavalry Regiment
19-1	Military Police Combat Support for the AirLand Battle
22-100	Military Leadership
24-1	Combat Communications
31-22	Command, Control, and Support of Special Forces Operations
31-71	Northern Operations (to be revised as FM 90-11)
33-1	Psychological Operations: US Army Doctrine
34-1	Intelligence and Electronic Warfare Operations
34-10	Military Intelligence Battalion (CEWI) (Division)
34-20	Military Intelligence Group (CEWI) (Corps)
34-30	Military Intelligence Company (CEWI) (Armored Cavalry Regiment/Separate Brigade)
34-81J	Weather Support for Army Tactical Operations (AFM 105-4)
41-10	Civil Affairs Operations
44-1	US Army Air Defense Artillery Employment
44-3	Air Defense Artillery Employment: Chaparral/Vulcan/Stinger
44-23	Air Defense Artillery Employment: Redeye
44-90	Air Defense Artillery Employment: Hawk

63-1	Combat Service Support Operations, Separate Brigade
63-2	Combat Service Support Operations, Division
63-3J	Combat Service Support Operations, Corps
63-4	Combat Service Support Operations, Theater Army Area Command
71-1	The Tank and Mechanized Infantry Company Team
71-2	The Tank and Mechanized Infantry Battalion Task Force
71-3	Armored and Mechanized Brigade Operations
71-100	Armored and Mechanized Division, and Brigade Operations
71-101	Infantry, Airborne, and Air Assault Division and Brigade Operations
90-2	Tactical Deception
90-3	Desert Operations
90-4	Airmobile Operations
90-5	Jungle Operations
90-6	Mountain Operations
90-8	Counterguerrilla Operations
90-10	Military Operations on Urbanized Terrain (MOUT)
90-13	River Crossing Operations
90-14	Rear Battle
100-2-1	Soviet Army Operations and Tactics
100-2-2	Soviet Army Specialized Warfare and Rear Area Support
100-2-3	Soviet Army Organization and Equipment
100-10	Combat Service Support
100-15	Corps Operations

100-16	Echelons Above Corps (Revision will be entitled "Theater Army, Army Group, and Field Army Operations")
100-20	Low Intensity Conflict
100-26	Air-Ground Operations
100-27	USA/AF Doctrine for Tactical Airlift Operations
101-5	Staff Officers' Field Manual: Staff Organization and Procedure (will be revised as "Staff Organization and Operations")
101-10-1	Staff Officers' Field Manual: Organizational, Technical, and Logistical Data

Standardization Agreements (STANAGs)

2003	Patrol Reports
2008	Bombing, Shelling, Mortaring, and Location Reports
2014	Operation Orders, Annexes to Operation Orders, Administrative and Logistics Orders
2017	Orders to the Demolition Guard Commander and Demolition Firing Party Commander
2019	Military Symbols
2020	Operational Situation Reports
2022	Intelligence Reports
2036	Land Minefield Laying, Marking, Recording, and Reporting
2041	Operation Orders, Tables and Graphs for Road Movement
2047	Emergency Alarms of Hazard or Attack (NBC and Air Attack Only)
2067	Straggler Control
2070	Emergency War Burial Procedures
2077	Order of Battle (Non-NATO Troops)

2079	Rear Area Security and Rear Area Damage Control	3465	Safety, Emergency, and Signaling Procedures for Military Air Movement Fixed-Wing Aircraft
2082	Relief of Combat Troops		
2083	Commanders Guide on Nuclear Radiation Exposure of Groups	3466	Responsibilities of Air Transport Units and User Units in the Loading and Unloading of Transport Aircraft in Tactical Air Transport Operations
2088	Battlefield Illumination		
2091	Population Movement Control		
2096	Reporting Engineer Information in the Field		
2099	Fire Coordination in Support of Land Forces	3570	Drop Zones and Extraction Zones—Criteria and Marking
2101	Principles and Procedures for Establishing Liaison	3700	NATO Tactical Air Doctrine - ATP-33
2103	Reporting Nuclear Detonations, Radio-Active Fallout, and Biological and Chemical Attacks and Predicting Associated Hazards	3736	Offensive Air Support Operations - ATP-27
		3805	Doctrine and Procedures for Airspace Control in the Combat Zone - ATP-40
2104	Friendly Nuclear Strike Warning to Armed Forces Operating on Land	5048	The Miminum Scale of Communications for the NATO Land Forces - Requirements, Principles, and Procedures.
2113	Destruction of Military Technical Equipment		
2129	Recognition and Identification of Forces on the Battlefield		

PROJECTED RELATED PUBLICATIONS

Projected publications are sources of additional information that are scheduled for printing but are not yet available. Upon print, they will be distributed automatically via pinpoint distribution. They may not be obtained from the USA AG Publications Center until indexed in DA pamphlet 310-1.

2868	Land Force Tactical Doctrine - ATP-35	
2356	Comparative Formation/Unit Designations	
2889	Marking of Hazardous Areas and Routes Through Them	

Field Manuals (FM)

2904	Airmobile Operations - ATP-41	
3204	Aeromedical Evacuation	17-50-3	Joint Air Attack Tactical (JAAT) Operations
3345	Data/Forms for Planning Air Movements	22-999	Senior Military Leadership
3463	Planning Procedures for Tactical Air Transport Operations for Fixed-Wing Aircraft	90-11	Winter Operations (to supersede FM 31-71)
		100-37	Terrorism Counteraction

OTHER PUBLICATIONS

JCS 1   Dictionary of Military and Associated Terms

JCS 2   Unified Action Armed Forces (UNAAF)

JCS 8   Doctrine for Air Defense from Overseas Land Areas

AFM 1-1   Basic Aerospace Doctrine for the United States Air Force

COMMAND

Command publications cannot be obtained through Armywide resupply channels. Determine availability by contacting the address shown. Field circulars expire three years from the date of publication unless rescinded.

Field Circulars (FC)

101-55   Corps and Division Command and Control. February 1985. Commandant, US Army Command and General Staff College, ATTN: ATZL-SWA-DL, Fort Leavenworth, Kansas 66027-6900

TRADOC Pam

525-45   General Operating Procedures for Joint Attack of the Second Echelon (J-SAK). Commander, TRADOC, ATTN: ATDO-C, Fort Monroe, Virginia 23651-5000.

Index